THE INDIAN TIPI

ITS HISTORY, CONSTRUCTION, AND USE

Second Edition

THE INDIAN TIPI

ITS HISTORY, CONSTRUCTION, AND USE
Second Edition

BY REGINALD AND GLADYS LAUBIN
(Tatanka Wanjila na Wíyaka Wastewín)

With a History of the Tipi
BY STANLEY VESTAL

NORMAN : UNIVERSITY OF OKLAHOMA PRESS

By Reginald and Gladys Laubin

The Indian Tipi: Its History, Construction, and Use (1957, 1977)
Indian Dances of North America: Their Importance to Indian Life
  (1977)

Library of Congress Cataloging in Publication Data

Laubin, Reginald.
    The Indian tipi.

    1. Indians of North America—Dwellings.
I. Laubin, Gladys, joint author. II. Vestal,
Stanley, 1887–1957. The history of the tipi.
1977. III. Title.
E98.D9L3 1977   301.5'4   77-23039
ISBN 0–8061–1433–9

Dedicated to
the Plains Indians in the hope that their young people will recapture
a pride of race, a love of color and beauty, and an appreciation of the
good things in their own great heritage—today the heritage of all
Americans.

FOREWORD

THIS BOOK will show you how to make, use, and enjoy the best of all movable shelters, the Indian tipi or tepee. No other book I know can do that.

The American Indian was a strictly practical man. But he was also a born artist. As a result, his inventions are commonly as beautiful as they are serviceable. Sometimes we can make these of more durable materials, but we can never improve on the design. Among his notable contributions to civilization are his canoe, his snowshoe, his moccasin, and his tipi. And of these, the last is by no means the least admirable. The Sioux word *tipi* is formed of *ti*, meaning to dwell or live, and *pi* meaning used for; thus, *tipi* means used to *live* in. It is well named.

Other tents are hard to pitch, hot in summer, cold in winter, badly lighted, unventilated, easily blown down, and ugly to boot. The conical tent of the Plains Indians has none of these faults. It can be pitched, if necessary, by a single person. It is roomy, well ventilated at all times, cool in summer, well lighted, proof against high winds and heavy downpours, and, with its cheerful inside fire, snug in the severest winter weather.

Imitation is the sincerest flattery. Our soldiers, campaigning on the frozen Plains, so envied the Indian his snug tipi that they invented the Sibley tent, attempting (not very successfully) to rival it.

Moreover, its tilted cone, trim smoke flaps, and crown of branching poles, presenting a different silhouette from every angle, forms a shapely, stately dwelling even without decoration. Properly made, pitched, and furnished in the true Indian way, it offers all the requirements of a good home, safety, comfort, privacy—even luxury. In short, other tents are made to sell. The tipi was made to live in.

And what a wealth of history, legend, folklore, ceremony, tradition, song, and story haunts the Indian tent. What fateful councils have been held in it, involving such events as Custer's death and

Sitting Bull's surrender—the wars and treaties of the centuries. And many a famous white man made the tipi his home—men such as Kit Carson, Buffalo Bill, Jim Bridger, Joe Meek, William Bent, General John Charles Frémont, besides many another frontier scout, soldier, trapper, missionary, trader, writer, and artist.

Other tents are just contrivances of stakes and ropes and canvas; the tipi preserves the memory of great men, heroes, orators, and warriors, of wild freedom, lavish hospitality, and intimate family life.

Under modern conditions the tipi suffered one great disadvantage, the difficulty of transporting the poles which form its framework. But now the authors of this book have solved that problem and have cruised all over the country in their coupe, carrying their tipi, poles and all, along. So now there is no reason why anyone should not travel with his tipi.

Everyone who has had occasion to live in a tipi has approved it, and not a few have attempted to tell us how to make and manage this unrivaled tent. But so far nobody has succeeded. And certainly the commercial tipis offered for sale nowadays fall sadly short of Indian standards. Every outdoor man, every nature lover, everyone who likes things handsome about him and enjoys the association of heroic history should rejoice at the publication of this book.

The authors are highly qualified to remedy this lack, and preserve this great American invention for our benefit. They are internationally known for their sympathetic, accurate, and artistic interpretations of old Indian ceremonies and dances. But their love for Indian ways never stopped at the footlights. In fact, they spent their honeymoon in a tipi, and for many years have camped with the Indians, or by themselves, at all seasons, and in every sort of weather—in hot summers on the windy plains, and amid deep snows in the Rockies with the temperature at twenty-three degrees below zero.

So perfectly have they followed the old trail that I have seen Indians crowd into their tent to see what an old-time Indian lodge was like. The reader may rest assured of the truth of my claims for this book and the tipi. Like Mr. Laubin, I acquired my first tipi as a boy, and from that time have seldom been without one— usually one of Indian make. Growing up among the Cheyennes in Oklahoma, and often camping with them, I had ample opportunity to observe and learn the tipi, a subject which I have pursued in research among other tribes up to the present time. Some thirty years ago, I myself planned to write a book on the tipi, but I never found the time. So now to see such a book so well done is the happy realization of a lifelong dream.

Here is your tipi.

STANLEY VESTAL

Norman, Oklahoma

ACKNOWLEDGMENTS

WE WISH to express our sincere appreciation to Stanley Vestal, whose love for the tipi was as great as our own. Without his generous help and encouragement this book would not have been written. For it was through him we were first introduced at Standing Rock, where we met Chief One Bull.

Also, we owe much to Judge Frank Zahn, or Flying Cloud, who served often as interpreter and furnished us with valuable information; to Chief One Bull and his wife, Scarlet Whirlwind, who adopted us into their family, and to our many Indian friends on the Standing Rock, Pine Ridge, Crow, Tongue River, Shoshoni, and Blackfoot reservations who have added to our knowledge of tipi life and the old ways.

Unless otherwise credited, the photographs illustrating this volume were made by us, and the drawings are ours. Occasionally it has seemed necessary to use the first person instead of the usual "we." When this is done, it should be understood that "I" means Reginald Laubin.

The inclusion of two of the color plates in this book was made possible through the generosity of Mr. and Mrs. Irl C. Martin, in memory of their son, Charles Woodward Martin—"Chuckie"—the little boy who so enjoyed our tipi that he made it his home during his last summer at the foot of the snowy Tetons in Jackson Hole.

REGINALD AND GLADYS LAUBIN

Moose, Wyoming

CONTENTS

ILLUSTRATIONS

COLOR ILLUSTRATIONS

BLACK AND WHITE ILLUSTRATIONS

FIGURES

THE INDIAN TIPI
ITS HISTORY, CONSTRUCTION, AND USE
Second Edition

There is only beauty behind me,
Only beauty is before me!
                              Cree Song

1. THE HISTORY OF THE TIPI

CONICAL SHELTERS have no doubt been used for hundreds, perhaps thousands, of years, wherever the climate demanded shelter from the weather, if straight poles, bark, grass, sod, materials for making mats, or the skins of large animals were available.

Sedentary people may be content with heavy mats or bark for covering the framework of their permanent dwellings, but migratory hunters, fishermen and pastoral people, who have to keep moving or make seasonal journeys to find game, fish, or forage for their domestic animals, require light, movable dwellings which can be easily transported. A conical tent of skins meets that need.

In fact, within historic times, we find people living in conical skin tents all around the Arctic Circle—the Lapps in Europe, the Americanoid Yukaghir in Siberia, Indians throughout the entire Mackenzie Area of Canada, among the Caribou Eskimo west of Hudson Bay, and in Labrador. In all these tents we have the inside central fire, the smoke hole centering around the crossing of the poles at the top, the eastern entrance, the place of honor within opposite the door, just as in the tipis of the Plains Indians. Indeed, because of these fundamental similarities, such shelters have sometimes been inaccurately described as "tipis."

But, in fact, they are not true tipis, for they all lack two essentials of the tipi as known to the buffalo hunters on our Great Plains. For the true tipi is not a symmetrical cone like these, but is always a tilted cone, steeper at the back, with the smoke hole extending some distance down the more gently sloping side, or front of the tent, and with two flaps—called smoke flaps, ears, or wings—flanking the smoke hole and supported by movable outside poles to regulate the draft, ventilate the tent, and carry off the smoke. Compared with the true Plains Indian tipi, those primitive conical skin tents are only miserable, smoky dens.

This being so, we may wonder who added these features to the ancient skin tent and so invented the true tipi, and when and where this happened.

3

It has been plausibly suggested that the smoke flaps on our tipi grew out of an attempt to improve the ventilation of the primitive skin tent by tying a skin between the tops of two outside poles leaned against the structure. The smoke flaps on the true tipi are supported and managed by outside poles opposite each other, and it would seem a simple step to attach the hide to the tent proper, and so make a handier arrangement. But this, of course, is only supposition.

The earliest mention in European records of skin tents in use on our Great Plains will be found in the reports on the expedition of Francisco Vásquez de Coronado, 1540–42. He encountered buffalo hunters living in skin tents whom he called *"Qerechos,"* because they spent their winters with Pueblo Indians of the Keres group. Most historians have assumed that these Indians were Apaches.

Both Coronado and Jaramillo comment on the Indian tents: "They fasten . . . poles at the top and spread them apart at the bases," covering the frame with buffalo hides. Their dogs were "larger" than those of Mexico.

"They load the dogs like beasts of burden and make light pack-saddles for them like ours, cinching them with leather straps. . . . The dogs go about with sores on their backs like pack animals. . . . When they move—for they have no permanent residence anywhere, since they follow the cattle [buffalo] to obtain food—these dogs transport their houses for them. In addition to what they carry on their backs, they transport the poles for the tents, dragging them fastened to their saddles. A load may be from 30 to 50 pounds, depending on the dog."[1]

These tents are described as "tall" and "beautiful." Nothing is recorded of smoke flaps or tilted cones, but the passage in which these tents are mentioned is acknowledged to be the classic description of Plains Indian culture, never to be superseded. Inasmuch as this description exactly fits the Plains tribes in every other respect, it is no unreasonable assumption that their tents were true tipis.

However, Don Juan de Oñate gives a fuller account in his report on the expedition of 1599: "There were 50 tents made of tanned hides, very bright red and white in color and bell-shaped, with flaps and openings, and built as skillfully as those of Italy, and so large that in the most ordinary ones four different mattresses

[1]See H. E. Bolton, *Coronado, Knight of Pueblos and Plains.*

and beds were easily accommodated.[2] The tanning is so fine that although it should rain bucketfuls, it will not pass through nor stiffen the hide, but rather upon drying it remains as soft and pliable as before. . . . the *Sargento Mayor* bartered for a tent and brought it to this camp, and although it was so very large, it did not weigh over two *arrobas* [50 pounds]."[3]

"Openings" here obviously refers to doorway and smoke hole. If "flaps" mean smoke flaps, then the tipi as we know it was already in general use before 1600.

It is possible, however, that the tipi as we know it is much older, for the literature and photographs, as well as the testimony of living Indians, inform us that where loose stones were available on camp sites, the skirts of tipis were weighted down with them whenever a severe windstorm threatened, or when in winter it was impossible to drive pegs into the frozen ground, or simply to keep out small animals, insects, and cold drafts. This was also sometimes done in pitching burial tipis. On many, many sites on the plains and along the Rocky Mountains from Edmonton, Canada, into New Mexico, we find clusters of circles of small stones known as "tipi rings."[4]

Professor Carling Malouf of Montana State University, who has been extremely helpful in our research on tipi rings, has mapped over two hundred such ring clusters. His findings follow:

These rings vary from four to eighty feet in diameter, and those twenty feet across or more seem to be primarily ceremonial in origin, such as the famous Medicine Wheel in northern Wyoming and those on the Smith River and Sun River in Montana. These contain lines of stone radiating from the center, like spokes in a wheel. Smaller rings, sometimes as many as 130 in one cluster, are actually walled structures ten feet in diameter, probably used by shamans seeking *mana*. On the average we find fifteen rings in a group.

In nearly all cases the smaller rings are near water, fuel, and other resources, and appear to be the remains of dwellings. Some-

---

[2]Assuming beds 2x6 feet each, this would require a tent with a diameter of at least 12 feet.

[3]See H. E. Bolton, ed., *Spanish Exploration in the Southwest*, 223ff.

[4]Sister M. I. Hilger, "Arapaho Child Life and Its Cultural Background," Bureau of American Ethnology, *Bulletin 148*, 93. Also see George Bird Grinnell, *The Cheyenne Indians, Their History and Ways of Life*, I, 51.

times in mountain areas these rings are on or near the ridges, where people might avoid the deep snowdrifts in the side draws. On the plains, rings are generally clustered near or along drainages. However, in early spring, when water was found everywhere on the prairie, this was not necessary, and tipi rings were then made higher up and some distance from the streams. Sometimes artifacts, chips, and stone scrapers, knives and points—usually the corner-notch type—are found. But though central rings of stone occur, fire hearths and storage pits are rarely found. Such circles abound in Utah, eastern and western Colorado, Montana, and Wyoming.

True, by no means all these rings are actually tipi rings. Some on high points were obviously used as lookouts. Some were apparently defensive, and many appear to have been ceremonial.

An archaeological survey of the High Western Plains[5] exploring 1,436 sites found 858 old camps and several hundreds of probable remnants of camp sites partly obliterated or blown out. The fact that these sites were used over and over again is shown by the varying depths of the stones and circles and the fact that they touch each other, or overlap, or cross over one another. In some sites more than one hundred rings can still be counted. The fact that no post or post holes are found in these rings may indicate that the shelters were tents, not permanent dwellings.

The average width of these tipi rings is from twelve and one-half to seventeen and one-half feet. Allowing for the fact that the stones must have been displaced and probably more widely separated when the tent was moved and the skin cover pulled out from under the stones, it would appear that many of these tents were quite small, which may indicate that the rings were made before horses replaced dogs as draft animals.[6]

The Spanish explorers were not only impressed by the tents of the Indians, but also by their use of dogs.

Oñate goes on to say, "The Indians . . . are as well sheltered in their tents as they could be in any house."

Oñate also reports that these Indians had "great trains" of dogs to carry their goods, "traveling, the ends of the poles dragging

[5]E. B. Renaud, *Archaeology of the High Western Plains.*
[6]See G. L. Wilson, "The Horse and the Dog in Hidatsa Culture," *Anthropological Papers of the American Museum of Natural History*, XV, 225, and Figure 56 on p. 226.

on the ground," and Fray Alonso de Benavides reports "five hundred dogs in one train, following one another."[7] With enough big dogs, light poles up to twenty feet in length might be so transported. Tribes on the Southern Plains in historic times preferred poles of red cedar, much lighter than those of lodge-pole pine. Fir, where available, was even lighter.

It is noteworthy that in these early Spanish accounts, there is no mention of the two-pole-and-basket dog-drawn vehicle known as the travois.

Clark Wissler believed that the travois antedated the tipi because the tips of its dragging poles were pointed to make it slip easily over the ground. It seems just as probable that, since tipi poles must be pointed to hold their place on the ground when the tent is pitched, tipi poles antedated the travois. It is hardly likely that an Indian would put a dog's comfort ahead of his own convenience.

The first account of a tipi describing the smoke flap and its use will be found in the *Report of An Expedition from Pittsburg to the Rocky Mountains performed in the years 1819 and '20 by order of the Hon. J. C. Calhoun, Sec'y of War; under the command of Major Stephen H. Long, From the Notes of Major Long, Mr. T. Say and other gentlemen of the exploring party, compiled by Edwin James Botanist and Geologist for the Expedition in Two Vols. with an Atlas. Philadelphia, 1823.*[8]

The tents described are those of the Kaskaias, usually identified today as Kiowa-Apaches, or Bad Hearts. The description is accompanied by an illustration showing three lodges with smoke pouring from their tops entitled "Movable Skin Lodges of the Kaskaias." The description runs as follows: "When pitched, the skin lodge is of a high conic form; they are comfortable, effectually excluding the rain, and in cold weather a fire is kindled in the centre, the smoke of which passes off through the aperture in the top; on one side of this aperture is a small triangular wing of skin, which serves for cover in rainy weather, and during the rigors of winter to regulate the ascent of the smoke."

The drawing by T. R. Peale, however, clearly shows a second flap hanging loose on the side nearest the reader, while the far flap is erected against the wind. Of course, it is not unusual for the

[7]*Memorial* (1630), 74.
[8]See I, 206.

leeward flap to be left hanging idle when it can be of no use. Here, then, we have our first description and portrayal of the true tipi with smoke flaps. The report goes on to say, "The doorway is a mere opening in the skin, and closed when necessary, by the same material."

As is usual in these early pictures of the tipi, no attempt was made by the artist to show the arrangement of the poles in the smoke hole, and Peale here shows the ends of only seven poles protruding from the top of the tent, though his drawing plainly indicates seven poles showing like ribs through the tipi cover on the visible side. Just what supported the other side of the tent is not clear! Like most painters who have sketched or painted Indian tipis, Peale reproduced the painted designs on the tent more accurately than the tent itself. For it is reported here: "They are often fancifully ornamented on the exterior, with figures, in blue and red paint, rudely executed, though sometimes depicted with no small degree of taste."

In another passage we learn that "These skin lodges are the only habitation of the wandering savages during all seasons of the year. Those of the Kaskaias differ in no respect from those already described, as used by the Otos and others of the Missouri Indians."[9] Thus, it appears that smoke flaps were in common use on the tipis of other tribes Major Long visited.

"The poles, which are six or eight to each lodge, are from 20 to 30 feet in length and are dragged constantly about in all their movements. . . . When they halt to encamp, the women immediately set up these poles, four of them being tied together by the smaller ends;[10] the larger ends, resting on the ground, are placed so far apart as to include as much space as the covering will surround. The remaining poles are added to strengthen the work and give it a circular form.

"The covering is then made fast by one corner to the end of the last pole, which is to be raised, by which means it is spread upon the frame with little difficulty. The structure, when completed, is in the form of a sharp cone. At the summit is a small opening, etc., out of which the lodge poles project some distance, crossing each

[9]See II, 105.

[10]Photographs taken in the late nineteenth century show Kiowa-Apache tipis using three instead of four poles for the foundation. This may have come about through intermarriage with the Kiowas. The Otoes also were three-pole people in recent times.

other at the point where the four shortest are tied together. . . .
The poles, necessary for the construction of these movable dwellings, are not to be found in any part of the country of the Kaskaias, but are purchased from the Indians of Missouri, or others inhabiting countries more plentifully supplied with timber. We are informed by Bijeau, that five of these poles are, among the Bad-hearts, equal in value to a horse."

In 1832 the painter, George Catlin, set out up the Missouri, inspired with an enthusiastic determination to produce a "literal and graphic delineation of the living manners, customs, and characteristics" of Indians—a pursuit in which he spent several years.[11] He painted many pictures of tipis of the Sioux, Crows, and other tribes, pictures which plainly show the smoke flap, smoke hole and other features common to the tipi. He declares, "The Crows, of all the tribes in this region, or on the Continent, make the most beautiful lodge." After telling how the Crows "beautifully garnish" their tipis "with porcupine quills, and paint and ornament them in such a variety of ways as renders them exceedingly picturesque and agreeable to the eye," Catlin describes his own Crow tent in his usual glowing style as "highly ornamented, and fringed with scalp-locks . . . with the Great or Good Spirit painted on one side, and the Evil Spirit on the other."

However, his sketch (Plate 20) is not convincing and does not correspond to his description. The painted figure (Good or Evil Spirit?) carries a gun, and in other respects the tent does not differ from those represented by this artist as of other tribes. In one detail the sketch is certainly false, namely, in representing a rope about the crossing of the poles above, a device which is entirely impracticable in a four-pole tipi. Catlin also omits the characteristic streamers on the tips of Crow poles mentioned by Maximilian.

The smoke flap, as represented by Catlin, is not Crow in design and he must have exaggerated in saying that his poles were "about thirty in number." And his tipis are *not* tilted cones. Catlin gives us our first picture of a travois (Plate 21).

Karl Bodmer, the artist accompanying Prince Alexander Philip P. Maximilian von Wied-Neu-Wied, painted four Blackfoot tipis in his picture of the fight which took place outside Fort McKenzie on August 28, 1833 (Plate 75). Though rather more taper than

[11]George Catlin, *Letters and Notes.* . . .

Blackfoot tents today, they do have the high smoke hole and the oval door.

Like Peale, Bodmer shows, protruding from the tops of his tipis, only a few crooked sticks. Smoke flaps are shown more ragged in outline than the trim flaps in Peale's drawing.[12]

Bodmer's picture (Plate 16 in the *Atlas*), "Tent of an Assiniboin Chief," shows the smoke hole and flaps, the lacing pins and pegs, and the door flap. The smoke hole is high and the threshold of the doorway is some inches above the ground. All this is accurate. Even a travois is included.

Yet, like Peale, Bodmer shows protruding from the top only as many poles as are indicated on the near side of the tent. The paintings on the tent, however, are carefully reproduced. Apparently the smoke flap is supported through a slit, instead of a pocket as was usual later in tents of this tribe.

Alfred Jacob Miller accompanied Captain William Drummond Stewart into the Rocky Mountains in 1837 and painted many water colors of the Indians and their encampments. These have been reproduced.[13] But Miller's tipis of whatever tribe are all alike, tall and beautiful, with the poles tied together with a rope at the apex, streamers from the ends of the poles and pockets on the flaps. His smoke holes are invariably high, so high, in fact, that the back of the cover shows sometimes higher than the crossing of the poles—a sheer impossibility. And the top of the tent cover is falsely represented as loose and falling into folds around the smoke hole.

Rudolph Friederich Kurz, who went up the Missouri in 1846, though he made no close studies of the tipi, was somewhat more accurate in his sketches.[14]

It was not until photography became common that more accurate representations of the tipi were painted. Yet, even William Henry Jackson paints tipis with sagging poles, resembling inverted morning-glory blossoms.[15] To make a cover that would fit such a sagging framework would tax the best skill of a London tailor.

E. S. Paxson, in one of his oils in the Missoula (Montana) courthouse, entitled "Father Ravalli and the Indians," paints Flat-

[12]Maximilian, Prince of Wied, *Travels in the Interior of North America*, Vol. XXV (Atlas) of *Early Western Travels*, ed. by Reuben Gold Thwaites.
[13]See A. J. Miller, *The West of Alfred Jacob Miller* (1837).
[14]See *Journal of Rudolph Friederich Kurz*, Plates 39 and 45, "Omaha Village."
[15]See H. R. Driggs, *The Old West Speaks*, Plates 2, 3, 5, 8, 27.

head tipis with smoke flaps, each supported by *two* poles and raised far above any point where they could be useful, looking like wings on a windmill!

Charles Russell, Charles Schreyvogel, and Frederic Remington also fall short of the accuracy of Henry Farny.

But our point is that these paintings, however inaccurate in detail, show that the tipi as we know it was in general use by 1840 all over the Plains, both in this country and in Canada.

Our best early written account of the manufacture and use of the (Sioux) tipi is that of Lieutenant J. Henry Carleton.[16]

Most of the tribes which used tipis are known to have migrated to the Great Plains within historic times, some pushed westward by enemies stronger or better armed by white traders, some moving in to share in the buffalo bonanza, a movement greatly accelerated after the Indians obtained horses. With horses, buffalo hunters could kill enough meat in one day to feed their families for weeks or months ahead.

The Mandans appear to have settled on the Plains long before the rest, and were already established there when La Verendrye reached their village in 1738. Most of the other tribes seem to have begun their migrations in the seventeenth or eighteenth century. The Plains Crees moved from their home far north of the Great Lakes in 1650 and were well established on the Plains by 1820. The Blackfeet, with their cognate tribes, Bloods and Piegans, leaving the present Plains Cree country, moved southwest into their historic location about the same time. The Assiniboines shifted from their country northwest of Lake Superior in Minnesota in the late 1600's, swinging north through Canada about 1775, then west and southwest to straddle the boundary between North Dakota and Canada by 1820. The Atsinas or Gros Ventres of the Prairie moved about the same time and were found in 1750 in eastern North Dakota and Minnesota, from which they arrived in northeastern Montana in 1820. The Crows, leaving their Hidatsa relatives on the Missouri in North Dakota, arrived in southern Montana and northern Wyoming about the middle of the eighteenth century.

The Sioux, found in the late eighteenth century near Duluth, moved southwest into Minnesota and then on west into the Plains in the 1700's. Some of them reached the Black Hills in 1775. The

---

[16]J. H. Carleton, *The Prairie Logbooks*, 268-71.

Arapahoes in Minnesota moved to eastern North Dakota in 1670, where they parted with their kin, the Gros Ventres of the Prairie (Atsinas), afterward angling southwest across the northwest corner of South Dakota and eastern Wyoming, arriving in Colorado about 1800. Their allies, the Cheyennes, reaching central Minnesota in the mid-seventeenth century, moved through southern North Dakota in 1720 to 1780 and through southwestern South Dakota to south central Colorado in 1820. The Kiowas and Kiowa-Apaches moved from western Montana to southeastern Wyoming about 1805, and on to Oklahoma and the Texas Panhandle about 1830. The Comanches in 1700 shifted from southeastern Wyoming, across eastern Colorado about 1750, settling in the Texas Panhandle and below in 1800.

From these known migrations, it is obvious that there were many contacts between these tribes in the course of their wanderings, so that it is difficult to determine or even guess intelligently as to who taught whom to make and use the tipi. The known variations of detail in tipi structure and furnishings are so many and so diverse that even those tribes whose tipis are most similar are not always allied or cognate tribes or of the same linguistic stock.

It is now too late to learn much of the structure of the conical bark lodges used by these tribes in the woodlands from which they came, and to find out whether they had a three-pole or four-pole foundation and so used it in building their tents, or whether they may have taken over a new method from the first tipi-dwellers they met. It should not be forgotten that sedentary tribes like the Mandans may have used tipis on seasonal hunts into the plains long before there were any tribes living on the plains in skin tents.

Also, the first tipis used by newcomers to the plains may have been obtained through purchase, through capture, or as gifts. Or they may have learned from some captive woman of a tipi-dwelling tribe.

Moreover, where we find tipis of two tribes almost identical in structure and decoration (as with the Cheyennes and Arapahoes), this may be due merely to long association, even though originally each tribe learned its craft from some other.

George Bird Grinnell believed, although he gives no reasons for his faith, that the widespread use of the tipi did not long precede the coming of the horse to the plains, since in fact even as late as 1850 not half the Cheyennes were using tipis.

Horses were brought from Mexico, and thence about 1650 were stolen or purchased and moved along the mountains northward through the related Comanches, Utes, and Shoshonis, reaching Colorado and Wyoming in 1720 and passing on to Montana and Canada by 1750. As early as 1650, another route was east from Santa Fé to near Clovis, New Mexico, from which horses were driven east to Oklahoma and southeast into Texas by 1720.

Horses had also moved from eastern Colorado and western Nebraska and South Dakota by 1750, and by the same date reached Iowa and Minnesota.

Once horses were plentiful on the Plains and in the adjacent mountain regions, the tipi spread to the Dakotas east of the Missouri River and west to the Utes, Flatheads, Nez Percés, Cayuses, Umatillas, and Kootenais. We know that the Nez Percés obtained their tipis from the Crows. In like manner, the tipi spread north to the Stoneys and the Crees. There it came so late that the Indians never used the travois, preferring a cart.

Thus, it appears that the tipi became larger after horses were available to transport it, and that it spread rapidly among the marginal tribes who wished to share in the prosperity of the buffalo hunters.

With the destruction of the buffalo and the substitution of canvas for hides, the tipi remained much the same. But, since canvas will not hold when stakes are driven through it and will ravel out if cut into fringes, peg loops were introduced, and the pattern of the smoke flaps became trimmer and more standardized. Also, the light weight of canvas, as compared with tanned hides, encouraged Indians to make larger tents—twenty, twenty-five, or even thirty feet in diameter.

The tipi went out of common use on the Plains during the first decades of the present century. But today Indians, encouraged by popular interest, pitch and occupy tipis every summer wherever they gather sociably together for sports, ceremonies and dances or just for old times' sake.

Reginald Laubin, "mother" Scarlet Whirlwind, Gladys Laubin, and "father" Chief One Bull in the Laubin Tipi. Credit: The Laubin Collection.

2. UTILITY AND BEAUTY

NO DWELLING in all the world stirs the imagination like the tipi of the Plains Indian. It is without doubt one of the most picturesque of all shelters and one of the most practical movable dwellings ever invented. Comfortable, roomy, and well ventilated, it was ideal for the roving life these people led in following the buffalo herds up and down the country. It also proved to be just as ideal in a more permanent camp during the long winters on the prairies.

One need not be an artist to appreciate its beauty of form and line, and no camper who has ever used a tipi would credit any other tent with such comfort and utility. Warm in winter, cool in summer, easy to pitch, and, because of its conical shape, able to withstand terrific winds or driving rain, the tipi is a shelter that should appeal to every outdoorsman. It is not only an all-weather tent but a home as well.

Often the tipi is confused with the wigwam. Actually both words mean the same thing—a dwelling—but "tipi" is a Sioux word, referring to the conical skin tent common to the prairie tribes, and "wigwam" is a word from a tribe far to the East, in Massachusetts, and refers to the dome-shaped round or oval shelter, thatched with bark or reed mats, used by the people of the Woodland area. Consequently, we prefer to use the term "tipi" to designate the Plains type of shelter and "wigwam" to designate the bark- or mat-covered Woodland dwelling even though both types are now covered with canvas. Indians, wherever they lived, made their dwellings of the best material at hand and to suit their conditions of life.

The word "tipi" has often been spelled "tepee" or "teepee," but since learning to write in their own language, the Sioux themselves spell it "tipi," which is simple and is accepted by students everywhere.

To one familiar with the charm and comfort of a real Indian tipi, it is little wonder that Kit Carson refused to accompany Lieutenant John Charles Frémont on his first expedition of exploration unless a tipi was taken along. The famous scout did not mind roughing it

15

when necessary, but when the time came for rest and relaxation, he wanted the most comfort a traveling existence could afford. Now Kit had lived for years in tipis pitched by his Indian wives, but there were no women in Frémont's party, and Kit did not know how to erect his tipi. Fortunately a trader happened along with his Indian wife. She taught Kit how to do it. He found it quite a simple trick after all.

For all that, very few white men ever acquired the skill; and today hardly any Indians remember or understand the technique.

Differences in the outward appearance of various tribal styles of tipis are due primarily to the arrangement of the poles, since this determines the cut of the hide or canvas cover. Generally speaking, all the tribes about whom we have reliable information used tipis employing one of two possible types of pole arrangement. One of these types has a foundation of three poles, a tripod; the other has a foundation of four poles. This structural difference determines certain features that distinguish the two types.

The open fire in the center of the tipi is its principal attribute, and, of course, the smoke vent should be above this central fire. If the tipi were a true cone, this vent or smoke hole would center around the crossing of the poles at the apex. Such a vent, to be practical, would have to be so large that it could never be closed in wet weather. The Indians solved this problem by tilting the cone and extending the smoke hole down the long side, the front of the tent. The crossing of the poles is thus at the top end of the smoke hole instead of in the middle, so that it is possible to close the hole entirely by means of the projecting flaps or ears. But this also means that the poles must be arranged neatly and compactly. A haphazard arrangement would result in such a bulky mass of poles that they would choke the smoke hole and make it impossible to fit the cover smoothly or close the hole.

In a small tipi, using few poles, this is a minor problem, but in a large one it is of the utmost importance. Indians solved the difficulty by developing a definite pattern or order of placing the poles, that order depending upon the type of tipi.

A number of observers have reported the placement of the poles upon the ground, but have neglected to mention the far more essential information of how they are placed in the crotches of the foundation poles. The order of placement in the four-pole type is practically the reverse of that in the three-pole type, but the solution of the problem is the same in both. The majority of the poles

are grouped in the front crotch of the foundation—in the smoke hole
and away from the cover at the back of the tipi—making it possible
to fit the cover tightly and smoothly instead of bunching it around
an ungainly and bulky mass of poles.

Actually, the three-pole foundation provides the better solution, for it is possible to group more poles in the front crotch, and
obviously it is more efficient to place the remainder in two crotches
than in three. Consequently, the cover fits better, making it easier
to close the smoke hole during a storm.

The three-pole tipi is also stronger than the four-pole, for two
reasons. It usually has more poles and they are bound together at
the top, which is not done in the four-pole type. The four-pole tipi
has from one to four outside guys, whereas the three-pole tipi seldom uses even one. Also, a tripod is a more rigid foundation than
(to coin a word) a quadripod. For service, therefore, the three-pole
type is unequaled.

Tribes using the three-pole tipi included the Sioux, Cheyennes,
Arapahoes, Assiniboines, Kiowa, Gros Ventres of the Prairie, Plains-
Cree, Mandans, Arikaras, Pawnees, and Omahas.

The Teton Sioux, or Lakota, were located centrally on the
Plains and many traits of Plains Indian culture seem to have been
diffused from them. They were also the largest group on the Plains.
Therefore, we have chosen the Sioux tipi as representative of the
three-pole tents.

Chief One Bull and his wife, Scarlet Whirlwind, who adopted
us into their family because of our interest in the old ways and our
efforts to bring about a better understanding of the Indian people,
showed us how to pitch a Sioux tipi. One Bull was a nephew of the
famous Sitting Bull and lived with his uncle until the latter's death
in 1890. These old people used to win all the tipi-pitching races at
the tribal fairs. Such races were popular until about 1915, but
since that time there have been few tipis on the Sioux reservations.
For the race a tipi and poles were carried on a wagon. The wagons
of the various contestants lined up at a starting line, and at a signal
all raced to another line, where everything was unloaded and the
tipis pitched. The family that succeeded in erecting its tipi first
did not necessarily win unless it had also pitched the best tipi, so
the actual winners were truly experts.

As the tipis wore out, they were replaced with wall tents. At
one time the government issued new canvas for tipis, but a policy
of discouraging everything Indian was inaugurated and ended this

practice. The tipi represented savagery, whereas the wall tent was the white man's, consequently civilized.

Poles were also hard to get. The nearest place was the Black Hills, more than three hundred miles from Standing Rock, and in those days Indians had to get a pass from the agent to leave the reservation. Such permission was not granted for any such heathen mission as gathering new tipi poles.

For many summers we were the only persons actually living in a tipi on the Standing Rock Sioux reservation in North and South Dakota and on the Crow reservation in Montana. The Indians tell us they have not seen a lodge like ours, furnished and arranged as in buffalo days, in more than seventy years. In writing this book, therefore, we hope we can bring to others something of the fun, fascination, and relaxation that tipi life has brought to us.

3. THE SIOUX TIPI

POLES

THE LENGTH of the poles you are able to obtain and the traveling you intend to do will determine the size of your tipi. Indians used small lodges, about 12 feet in diameter, for hunting expeditions when they wished to travel fast and with little equipment. Chief One Bull had one of these small lodges of buffalo skin until 1936, when he sold it to a collector. Such a lodge requires poles only about 15 feet long.

In recent times the average family lodge has been from 18 to 20 feet in diameter, requiring poles 21 to 25 feet long. This is a good size if ease of moving the tipi is not too important and if more room is desired.

For a permanent camp there is much satisfaction in owning a lodge of from 23 to 30 feet in diameter, but such a tipi needs poles 27 to 40 feet long and is impractical for any other kind of use. We have developed a method of transporting a tipi under modern conditions that enables us to carry an 18- to 20-foot tipi, using poles 25 feet long, but we dare not go beyond that length because of traffic regulations.[1]

A tipi cover is cut like a semicircular sleeveless cape with long lapels near the middle of the straight edge. When stretched over the framework of poles and "buttoned" down the front, it forms a cone. The distance from a point between the lapels to the ground at the back will be the radius of the semicircle.

The poles must be several feet longer than the radius of the cover (or diameter of the finished tipi) in order to allow for tying them together and building the frame. In short, the size of the tipi is in direct ratio to the length of the poles.

The poles should be perfectly straight and smooth, peeled of bark, and pointed at the butts so that they will not slip on the ground. They should project well above the finished tipi, 4 to 6

[1]See Chapter 8, "Transportation."

feet if possible. The Crows use such long poles that their tipis have somewhat the appearance of a huge hourglass. In the early days, an Indian woman's reputation as a housekeeper was partially dependent upon the appearance of her tipi poles. Crooked or poorly trimmed poles gave her a bad name.

In the Rocky Mountain region lodge-pole pine was usually available and was prized by the Indians for poles—hence its name. In some sections western yellow pine was more readily obtainable and served very well, but it is heavier than lodge-pole pine. In the north, tribes in Minnesota and Wisconsin used tamarack for poles. It is strong, but quite heavy. Where available, white cedar was particularly prized. It is exceptionally light and strong—the lightest wood in North America. Red cedar also made beautiful, light, and strong poles and was used by tribes on the southern plains. Both cedars, however, are very large at the butt and required a great deal of trimming with a draw knife to bring them down to useful size.

Regardless of the kind of wood to be used for the poles, the best will always come from a thick stand of young trees. In fact, such a location is the only place where suitable timber can be found. Poles for an 18- to 20-foot tipi must be approximately two inches in diameter where they cross and tie, and three to four inches thick at the butts. Fifteen will be needed for the frame and two for the smoke flaps. These latter poles should be smaller and need be no more than two inches thick at the butts.

Poles for other sizes of tipis must be of proportionate size. A larger tipi needs 20 poles, 18 in the frame and 2 for the smoke flaps.

In selecting the young trees, you will find it necessary to choose them slightly larger than you wish the poles to be, for the bark noticeably increases their size, and they shrink as they dry. It takes some little practice to select fine, straight poles. Each pole must be examined on all sides, and you must learn to estimate the size necessary for the tipi you have in mind. After felling the trees, all knots and branches should be trimmed off with an axe. You must remember that this is done by striking "up the tree," not against the grain.

Sometimes, in order to get a good straight pole, it is is necessary to cut one larger at the base and much longer than desired. In this case, always cut off the *lower end* of the pole to bring it to the length really wanted. *Never* cut off the tip, unless you want to cut the pole down to an easier length for carrying on top of the car. But before cutting off tips, locate the place where the pole will be about two inches in diameter *after* it is peeled. A little over two inches is all right for the three main poles and the lifting pole, a little under for the others; then measure from here toward the butt the length you will want to support the cover, or about 18 feet for a tipi the size we have been talking about. This is where you cut off the pole, toward the butt, and it should leave a pole 25 to 28 feet long in total. If you want to cut the poles shorter for later transportation on a car top, you can sacrifice a few feet of the tips, but never cut them less than 22 feet long for this size tipi, as they will appear too short. The farther the poles project above the top of the tipi, the better they look.

We know several people who ruined perfectly beautiful sets of poles by cutting off the tips first to make them 22 or 23 feet long. This left them so thick at the tip ends that even after pointing them with a draw knife they did not look too well, and the poles were left much heavier over all than necessary. This also makes the poles too thick where they cross and tie, resulting in difficulty in setting up the tipi, for it makes too big a bundle of poles in the throat. Such a large bunch of poles in the smoke hole cuts down on the draft, too.

Indians usually gathered poles as early in the spring as it was possible to travel, sometimes even while snow was still on the ground. Since the poles were dragged from camp to camp, they were constantly worn shorter, and it was necessary to replace them, usually every other year, sometimes as often as every year. But nowadays, when poles are no longer dragged in moving, a good set of poles will last for years.

Peeling the poles is essentially simple. First, make a buck of two 6-foot stakes, crossed and driven into the ground at an angle, the butts about 3 feet apart so that they cross at a height of 4½ or 5 feet. Tie the stakes together where they cross. Lay the butt of the pole to be peeled in this crotch. Sometimes you can find a tree with a fork at the proper height, and this can be utilized instead of making a buck. Or the pole can be laid across two saw-bucks or two sawhorses. If sawhorses are used, nail a couple of blocks of wood on one, about four inches apart, to keep the pole from rolling to one side.

With a sharp draw knife it is not difficult to peel the poles if the larger knots have been removed with the axe. Straddle the pole, peel a few feet, beginning at the butt, then shove ahead and peel some more. As you approach the tip of the pole, the heavy end tends to overbalance it, but you will find that your own weight straddling the pole will keep it nicely in position, if it is not crooked. Indians usually left the pole the full length of the tree, but we have found it necessary to cut ours to a standard length in order to travel with them. The Crows were horrified when they saw us cut off the poles, but when we tapered and pointed the small ends again, they were greatly relieved.

Dry the poles in the sun before using them, and let them season for at least three weeks. This is usually done by setting them up as for the finished lodge and letting them stand in the sun and air, turning them occasionally as they dry (see Color Plate II). If the cover is used before the poles are well seasoned, they will become so badly bowed that the cover will not fit well and the lodge will look sloppy. Likewise, if the poles are too limber, the lodge will appear to be caved in on the sides; if rough and full of knots, not only will they tear holes in the cover but rain will drip all over everything inside. Crooked or unpeeled poles definitely will not do. Sometimes, even here in lodgepole pine country, it is easier to find stands of dead poles than live ones. Sound, standing, dead poles can be used satisfactorily. They are much more difficult to peel, but have the advantage of being already seasoned, and when well peeled reveal the nice light color of recently dried poles.

Some Indians dry their poles and store them when not in use by piling them on the ground, keeping them straight and in position with stakes driven about every four feet, staggered on opposite sides of the pile. They are prevented from coming into direct contact with the ground by placing short pieces or blocks of wood of uniform thickness under the poles every three or four feet. The Crows lean their poles in forks of large trees when not using them, as do other tribes when suitable trees are near by.

If it is impossible to get poles from the woods, 2x4's of first quality, without knots, from a lumber yard can be used. Rip them lengthwise, taper them toward one end, and round off the corners with a draw knife, or have them rounded off on a "joiner" or a "dado" machine, and a set of poles will result that will do very well. Such poles should be handled with gloves to avoid splinters.

Do not consider using metal poles or jointed poles with metal ferrules. They would be dangerous in an electrical storm.

It seems ironical that the dwellers on the treeless prairies required the finest products of the forest. The forest dwellers could use almost anything for poles in the frames of their bark wigwams. But the prairie people had to make long excursions periodically to get new tipi poles. They prized them highly and took the best possible care of them. A set of poles, used as they are today, traveling not at all or by car or truck, will last for many years. Treating them with an application of pentachloraphenol will help to preserve them. This is especially good for the butts, since they rest on or in the ground. The pentachloraphenol helps to preserve their original color, too, and a coat of log oil or of floor hardener will also help in this respect. Newly cut and peeled poles, projecting far above the tipi, have a beauty hard to describe, and it should be worth a great deal to preserve this appearance. But varnishing them is useless and a waste of time and money.

MATERIALS

Materials, in addition to 17 poles 25 feet long, and the quantities required for the tipi pattern given in Fig. 1 are listed below. This tipi is nearly 20 feet from rear to door and 17½ feet across. (Since a tipi is a tilted cone, its floor is not truly round, but egg shaped, so that the actual size averages about 18 feet.)

Cloth: Canvas, heavy muslin, or one of the new light-weight fabrics can be used for a tipi. It is not necessary or desirable to use extra-heavy material. The Craighead brothers, in teaching their courses on survival to the United States Air Force, found that a parachute could quickly and easily, with no sewing and little cutting, be made into an emergency tipi which would withstand the most rigorous cold and wind. But a medium-weight canvas or eight- to ten-ounce duck is most usual. We made a tipi of heavy muslin and waterproofed it so that it was impervious to any rain, but it lasted only four years, whereas canvas ones we have owned lasted from six to ten years.

.   *Cover:* 24½ yards of 72-inch material, plus 21 1/3 yards of 36-inch material, or, if 72-inch material is unavailable, a total of 68 yards of 36-inch material is required.

Lining: 17 2/3 yards of 72-inch material or 35 1/3 yards of 36-inch will be needed for the lining, or dew cloth.

Door: 2 yards of 36-inch material is required, or the door can be made by sewing together a couple of large scraps.

Ozan: If an *o'zan* (an inside rain cover) is desired, approximately

3 1/4 yards of 60-inch and an additional 5 yards of 30-inch material will be needed.

[Note: The widths listed above are usually obtainable and make up most easily and economically. But other widths may be used. Many Indian tipis are made of 30-inch, or even 28-inch, material. Naturally, if different widths from the ones listed here are used, the yardage will have to be refigured according to the dimensions specified. A little arithmetic will take care of this.]

Cord: Approximately 158 feet of 3/16-inch cotton cord will be needed for peg loops, tie strings, and for hanging the lining, plus about 53 feet of twill tape 1/2 or 3/4 of an inch wide. More soft cotton cord can be substituted for the twill tape, but the tape is better.

Rope: About 8 feet of 1/4- or 3/8-inch Manila and 45 feet of 1/2-inch Manila rope will be needed for tying the poles and for an anchor, or guy rope.

Pegs: 25 pegs, preferably of chokecherry or ash, but other hardwood will do, about 18 inches long and 3/4 to 1 inch in diameter, are needed, and at least one other larger one (some prefer two) for anchor pegs. An anchor peg should be at least 1 1/2 inches in diameter and 2 1/2 to 3 feet long.

Sharpen these pegs to a point at one end, but leave the bark on the other end for five or six inches to keep the peg loop from slipping. The bark end is often nicely carved with one or two rings. We have been told that the Southern Cheyennes use pegs that have an inverted fork or a knob to prevent slipping, but a set of pegs we bought from a Northern Cheyenne woman were all straight, as just described.

Lacing pins: Eleven or more pointed sticks of chokecherry, ash, or dogwood, 12 to 14 inches long and 3/8 of an inch in diameter, are needed for lacing pins. The large pith in the center of an ash sapling makes it less desirable than chokecherry or dogwood. Peel the pins of bark except for three or four inches on the blunt end. This bark is often carved with rings, as mentioned for the pegs, for added attractiveness. Season the pins and pegs, as you did the poles. Of course, you can use dowel rods to make these lacing pins. They save work and serve just as well, but are not as "Indian," and unless painted with stripes at the ends do not look as well.

Waterproofing: Standard brands of waterproofing compounds usually cover about 100 square feet per gallon, which means that about 6 gallons will be necessary for the cover and 3 gallons for the lining. It is more important to waterproof the lining than the cover. Whenever possible, it is wise to immerse the material in a chemical waterproofing solution instead of applying a wax compound. If the solution is used, allow for shrinkage of perhaps 5 per cent in length and 2 per cent in width. We prefer the chemical treatment because it has been our experience that fabric treated with wax preparations tends to rot more quickly when exposed to the sun for a long time. Whether you have the fabric treated by a professional or apply a waterproofing solution yourself, you will find it very much worthwhile, even though it involves extra cost and takes more time and effort.

A friend informed us that he has a tipi made of only eight ounce duck which he has used for thirty years. He first treated it with a solution of lead acetate and alum, which he said is not only a good preservative but is practically fireproof as well. He did not give the formula for the solution he used, but one is given in Horace Kephart's *Camping and Woodcraft.*

According to Kephart, it is best to use rain water to make the solution, and before treating the tipi it should be first soaked in water. Better yet, treat the canvas before making the tipi. Two big wash tubs are needed. In one dissolve 1/4 pound of alum to each gallon, using hot soft water. In the other, with the same amount of hot water dissolve the same proportion of sugar of lead (lead acetate, *poison*). Let each solution stand until clear; then add the sugar of lead solution to the alum solution. Let stand for about four hours, or until the lead sulphate has precipitated. Pour the clear remaining solution back into the other tub to eliminate the dregs; then thoroughly work the cloth into it until every part is penetrated, and let soak overnight. Next morning rinse, stretch, and dry.

Some fabrics on the market are already waterproofed, but unless they are white or some bright color, like vermilion or yellow, they are not desirable. The browns, olive drabs, blues, and greens make a dark, gloomy tipi, and no one who has ever been in a beautiful, bright tipi would consider them.

COVER

While the tipi made from the pattern in Fig. 1 will not be as large as many of the present-day canvas tipis, it was planned to make the most efficient use of the material. At the same time it is

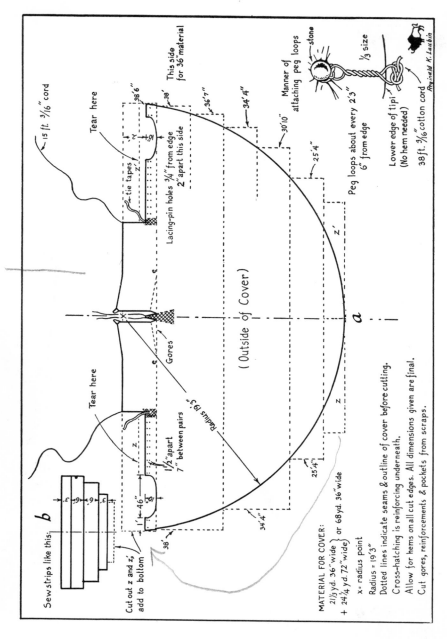

Fig. 1. Pattern for Sioux Tipi (18-foot).

large enough to be roomy and attractive and is easier to handle than larger ones. It is the size of average buffalo hide tipis when horses were used for transportation. This has proved to be a practical size for us to carry around as we visit various reservations. Indeed, it would be impossible to carry a larger one unless we could be satisfied with shorter poles in proportion to the size, and we have come to have the Crow fondness for long poles.

By keeping the proportions shown in the pattern, a tipi of any desired size can be made. We also have a Cheyenne tipi with a 22-foot radius, but it has the same proportions as the smaller one in these plans.

The radius point x, for any tipi as large as the pattern and up to 22 feet in radius, remains constant; that is, it lies 3 feet above seam e-e, but other measurements are in proportion to those on this pattern. For tipis having a radius of less than 19 feet or more than 22 feet the location of point x should be proportional to other changes of measurement.

Fig. 1 shows the most common method employed by the Indians to lay out their canvas tipis. This plan, with detailed specifications, is Sioux. In studying a number of Sioux and Cheyenne tipis, the only differences we have been able to discover are that the Cheyennes use an extra little free curtain or extension at the base of their smoke flaps and the Cheyenne flaps are narrower, giving them the appearance of being longer. These small extensions—9 inches to 15 inches—are shown in Fig. 2 as optional, but they do help in closing the flaps in a storm. The Sioux usually omit these extensions, and it is easier to make the tipi without them. But some Sioux tipis have similar extensions only 4 or 5 inches long, so that they are almost unnoticeable.

We have mentioned that a real Indian tipi is always a tilted cone, steeper up the back than the front. Some tribes tilted their cones more than others. Four-pole tipis generally were less tilted than three-pole ones, but in recent years some Crow tipis have been almost perpendicular in the back. The Crows are fond of extremely tall and slender tipis, as are the Arapahoes. The tipis of some other tribes seem rather broad and squat by comparison.

It has been said that the Sioux formerly tilted the cone of their tipis more than did the Cheyennes, but we have not been able to verify this from the few tipis still to be seen, or even to be sure of it from old photographs. Such a tipi would not be as graceful in appearance as one made from the pattern given here, but if you prefer a more tilted cone, set the radius point farther out from the edge and shorten the gores for the smoke flaps. The construction of smoke flaps will be discussed later.

It takes less time and should not cost very much to have the heavy sewing done by a tent- or awning-maker, but he should be instructed very carefully, else the tipi may turn out to be a sad-looking affair. We know whereof we speak, for we have had the experience. All the commercially made tipis we have seen have looked rather peculiar. Apparently their designers have strange ideas about how a tipi should look. Certainly they could never have paid much attention to the real thing.

We still favor a top grade canvas, as it was the original Indian substitution for hides. The modern synthetics do not interest us, for they have no historic or romantic appeal, are unnatural products, and most of them are too light to stand the beating they take on the poles in a high wind. We have known properly waterproofed canvas tipis to last ten years, in continuous service, in Florida, with its damp climate, which makes us think our preference for canvas is well founded.

Although only one of the many companies now making tipis has consulted us personally, we can see that others have at least followed the book enough to make the most popular size an 18 footer, as we have described. Formerly most commercial tipis were available only in 16 foot diameter, and earlier articles about tipis, like Seton's,[2] pertained to tipis of only 10 or 12 foot diameters.

Flat seams are best. Tentmakers usually double-stitch a seam, the two rows of stitching being made about as wide as the blue line along the selvage. The strips of cloth should be laid like shingles so that the water will run off, instead of under, the seams. Cut each strip to length, find the center and lay it out from the center points. If you do the sewing yourself, make the flat type of seam used in sewing shirts. Perhaps you can also persuade a tentmaker to use this type of seam.

Sometimes the size of a tipi is spoken of as being so many strips—a seven-strip tipi, or an eight-strip tipi, etc. Of course, this is no real indication of its size unless one knows the width of the strips.

After sewing the cover (Fig. 1a), cut out pieces z and z', as indicated. To do this, first spread the cover out flat and locate the

[2]Ernest Thompson Seton, *Two Little Savages.*

center of the upper, or longest, strip. On each side of this center point mark off another point 8 feet, 6 inches away. This is the proper length for the smoke flap for a tipi of this size. Make perpendicular cuts at these points to a depth of 2 feet. (On some old Sioux tipis this cut would be made 2 feet, 3 inches deep, which widens the base of the smoke hole but makes it harder to close in a storm. See Fig. 2a.) On these perpendicular cuts mark off 1 foot, 8 inches, from the outer edge, then rip out sections z and z'. Sew these together into one long strip and add them to the bottom of the tipi cover. They should be adequate in width and more than long enough to complete the cover. In this way there is very little waste of cloth in making a tipi (Fig. 1b).

Notice that the cover, when finished, is not a true half-circle. Set a peg at the radius point (x in Fig. 1), which is the same as the center point we located above, i.e., the center of the edge of the longest strip. Using a piece of rope and a piece of charcoal or chalk, swing the curved outline on a radius of 19 feet, 3 inches. From a point perpendicularly below radius point x, on the first seam, mark the width of the tie flap—the little tongue projecting between the smoke flaps—3 inches on either side, and cut back to radius point x. This leaves a tie flap which is much too long and should be trimmed and hemmed until about 8 or 10 inches in length. To this tie flap attach tie tapes or soft cotton cord 4 or 5 feet long.

The detail page of Making Smoke Flaps (Fig. 2 & 2b) shows how the gores are inserted. Open seams ef and fe from the base of the tie flap for a distance of 39 inches each way, and into these openings insert gores, which, after allowing an inch for the seams, will measure 39x39x7 inches. It is perhaps easier to sew in the gores by hand, after the long strips have been sewed together, as described above, although they can be sewed by machine. These gores, which help a great deal toward making the cover fit the poles, have been completely overlooked by all the popular writers on the subject of tipis.

The smoke flaps, when finished, are two feet wide at their bases. Use the extra four inches we allowed in ripping down the front for a hem before making the holes for the lacing pins. This hem is actually 3 1/2 inches wide, but if you have ever made a hem, or examined one, you know that another 1/2 inch is needed to turn under so as to have no raw edge. This hem makes reinforcement for the front of the tipi.

Space the lacing-pin holes along this hem in pairs extending

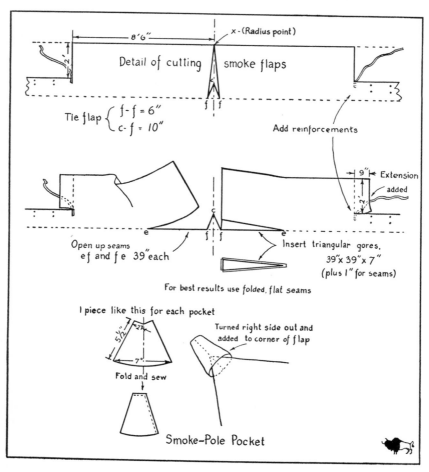

Fig. 2. Making Smoke Flaps.

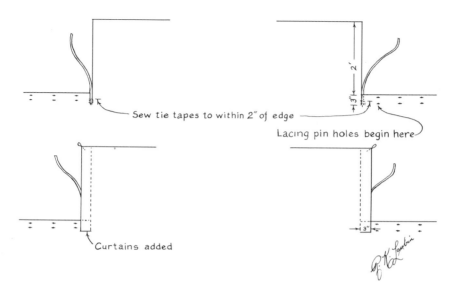

Sew tie tapes to within 2″ of edge

Lacing pin holes begin here

Curtains added

Fig. 2a. Optional Bases for Sioux Smoke Flaps.

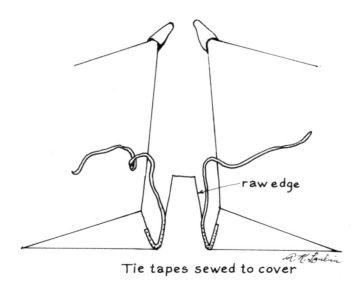

raw edge

Tie tapes sewed to cover

Fig. 2b. Cheyenne Tie Flap.

between the base of the smoke flaps and the doorway. We have seen them spaced from 4 to 7 inches apart. This is a matter of choice. As you observe in the pattern, on the left the centers of each pair of holes are 1 1/2 inches apart, starting 3/4 of an inch from the edge and 3/4 of an inch above the doorway. The right-hand side is the same, except that the centers of each pair are 2 inches apart.

Mark the other pairs, 7 inches between pairs, and continue up the front of the tipi almost to the base of the smoke flap. No lacing-pin holes are needed directly at the base of the smoke flaps because a tie strap or tape goes here. We have chosen a 7-inch space between pairs because it means fewer holes, and when you start buttonhole-stitching every hole, you will be glad to do as few of them as possible. Make lacing-pin holes just below the doorway, either for two more lacing pins, or for one pin and one hole on each side through which to run a peg loop. After marking the lacing-pin holes, cut a little cross in the canvas with the point of a knife, about 1/4 inch each way, and buttonhole-stitch with heavy thread waxed with beeswax. A round hole, a little over 3/8 of an inch in diameter, will result. Or merely cut single slits with the knife, each about 1/2 inch long, parallel with the length of the cloth, and make real button holes of them. This is the way the Cheyennes do it, and we think it may be the best. We prefer unbleached shoemaker's thread, number 10, for the work, although some of the new dacron or nylon thread may do as well. It is not necessary to reinforce these holes with iron rings or grommets, as is done on commercial tents and tipis.

If the little Cheyenne extensions at the base of the smoke flaps are wanted, the details in Figs. 2 and 2a show how they are applied better than can be explained in writing. These extensions can be made from 3 to 15 inches long. Sioux are short, Cheyenne long. Whether they are used or not, the base of the flaps should be reinforced, as indicated by the crosshatching.

Sew tie tapes, about 18 inches long, made of canvas strips 3 inches wide and folded twice (three thicknesses), at the base of each smoke flap, the one on the left to the top side of the hem, the one on the right to the under side of the hem. These simplify the job of pinning the tipi down the front. All reinforcements, as indicated, are necessary, and are easiest to apply by hand. Reinforcements should be made of three or even four thicknesses of material. If using lightweight material, it is a good idea also to reinforce along the top edge of the smoke flaps and around the tie flap with a piece of 1/4 or 3/16-inch cord, sewed over and over with the heavy waxed thread.

Many Indians, especially in the South, do not cut a doorway, but merely hem the tipi all the way down the front. The material between the lacing pin above the entrance and peg loops at the lower corners sags enough to provide a doorway and will stretch into somewhat of an oval with use. If the doorway is cut according to the diagram, a lacing pin is used to hold it together at the bottom and a peg loop is attached to one side of the cover and pulled up through a hole in the other side, just one peg being used in front of the door; or two lacing pins can be used below the doorway and a peg loop attached to the lower one.

The Indian way of attaching peg loops, as illustrated, is not only ingenious but easy and sturdy—far better than either sewn or stamped grommets. Place a pebble about 3/4 of an inch in size on the under side of the canvas, about 6 inches from the edge, gather the canvas around the pebble, and fasten it there with a piece of 3/16 inch cord. The cord should be about 22 inches long. Double it, and, where it bends at the center, tie it around the pebble (over the canvas, of course) in a square knot. You can use a clove hitch but the square knot is easier to untie if it is necessary to do so. Either way make sure the tie is as close and tight as you can make it. Gently pull out as many puckers as possible. The ones that remain help to keep the tipi snug and tight around the bottom. Marbles will do if you cannot find smooth round pebbles. We have even seen little wads of cloth, chips of wood, or pieces of corncob inserted, to which the peg loops were tied. One loop at the doorway, as already mentioned, and twelve on each side of the cover are about right. The bottom of the tipi need not be hemmed since the cloth is cut on the bias and will not ravel. In fact, Indians do not usually hem the bottom—certainly a saving in labor.

Some writers suggest merely adding a little triangular piece of canvas to the corner of the smoke flap for a pole pocket, but most of the real Indian tipis have a separate pocket sewed on. Again, the detail of Making Smoke Flaps (Fig. 2) shows how to do this. It is better if the pockets are made from two thicknesses of material. These elongated Indian pockets look more attractive and it is easier to insert the poles into them. A lock of hair, such as a human hair switch, a horsetail, or a strip of buffalo hide with the hair on, is usually tied to the tip of the pole pocket and makes a pleasing decoration.

In the lower corner of each smoke flap, buttonhole-stitch another hole, or sew a small cloth or tape loop on the corner, and attach about 15 feet of the 3/16-inch cord, as shown in the diagram. The cover is now finished except for waterproofing it or painting designs on it, or both, if desired.

4. PITCHING THE TIPI

IN MOST tribes a man spoke of the tipi as "mine," but actually the women made them, just as they made most of the furnishings. And it was the women who selected the camp site, erected the tipi, and determined the arrangements inside. Certain "medicine" tipis seem to have been owned by men, but with these exceptions we think we can safely say that the women owned the tipis. The women were "bosses" in the home, even in a medicine tipi, except during some of the ceremonies and formal gatherings. In some tribes, to divorce her husband, the woman had merely to throw his possessions out the door. In truth, the Indian woman's tipi was her castle.

Men painted the covers and the war records on the linings, but otherwise had little to do with the tipi. Formerly it was considered beneath the dignity of a warrior to be asked to help with any household chores. Among the Blackfeet, according to McClintock,[1] men took no part in erecting a tipi. But in the years since his time things have changed. I was with the men who helped put up some large tipis at Browning, Montana. Such help would not have been welcome, if offered, not many years ago. But among some tribes older men and boys were expected to help with the heavy work of setting up the poles and hoisting the cover into place. Nowadays Indian women have won their independence, as have their sisters in the white man's world, and in every Indian camp we have visited, any men at hand were expected to help with this work. But the women still bossed the job!

There was keen rivalry among the women concerning who would pitch the first new tipi in the spring and who would have the neatest tent and best tanned robes and skins. The Cheyennes had a housewives' guild which taught all the arts of Cheyenne housekeeping and maintained high standards in decorations and furnishings. All the best families in the camp belonged to it, and

[1] Walter McClintock, *The Old North Trail.*

the women, working together, learned to make furniture, tipi linings, tipis, and parfleches. Women rated highly in the tribe for
their skills in these domestic arts. A woman could have a party
and tell of her honors, which consisted of the number of buffalo
hides she had tanned and decorated in her lifetime, just as her
husband boasted of his war deeds. Grinnell tells of Cheyenne women
who each decorated as many as thirty buffalo robes with porcupine
quills. It was believed that quilling this many robes insured good
fortune and long life.[2]

It is just as important to select a good camp site for a tipi as
for any other type of tent. If possible, choose a place slightly higher
than the surrounding area so that it will drain in wet weather. At
least it should be as level as possible. Stubs, roots, and stones
should be removed. It is best not to camp directly under trees, for
they are dangerous in wind or lightning and will drip on the tent
for hours after a rain is over.

A tipi is the best kind of a tent when there is no shade, for it
is so well ventilated that it can be kept comfortable even in the
broiling sun. But if there are trees near by, a tipi can be pitched
so as to take advantage of their shade and yet eliminate the undesirable conditions mentioned above. The tipi should be pitched
to the northeast of the tree or clump of trees, so that it is in the
shade from late morning until late afternoon. Sun in the morning
is welcome and is one of the reasons why tipis usually faced east.
If camping near a river or stream, make sure the site is high enough
not to be under water in a heavy or prolonged rain or in flash floods
caused by rains higher up the valley. In the old days a good camp
site included the availability of plenty of firewood, water, and grass.
We have heard many old-timers say, "That was a good place to
camp. Good grass and water there, and plenty of firewood."

To pitch the tipi, select the three heaviest poles for a tripod.
Lay aside one other heavy pole for the lifting pole—the one to
which the cover will be tied—and two light poles for the smoke
flaps. Measure the tripod poles for tying according to Fig. 3a, laying
them on top of the outspread cover. It is a good practice to mark
them where they cross so that it is not necessary to measure them
every time the lodge is set up. Some Indians plant the tripod poles
in the ground several inches. If you do this, make allowance for the
depth they are to be planted at this time of measuring.

[2]George Bird Grinnell, *The Cheyenne Indians*, Vol. I, 164–65.

Some instructions for setting up a tipi direct you to tie the poles three or four feet from their upper ends, but this is ridiculous, for it has nothing to do with the actual size of the tipi. We have tried several ways of tying the tripod poles and have decided that the best way is the way our Indian "mother," Scarlet Whirlwind, showed us.

In most parts of the country east of the Rockies, the prevailing winds are westerly, and so tipis usually faced east. Consider then, that we are facing the tipi in that direction as we give the following instructions.

In order to hoist the tripod into proper position, lay it on the ground at the time of tying, with the butts of two poles near the black circle S on the ground plan, Fig. 3c, and the base of the door pole, D, at the position marked by the black circle D. Dotted lines on the drawing show the positions on the ground. Rest the single door pole, D, on top of the other two poles of the tripod.

To tie the poles as Scarlet Whirlwind did, start as in the detailed drawing, with a clove hitch. Leave several feet of rope and wrap it around three or four times and then finish with two half-hitches. This tie rope should be of good-quality half-inch Manila about 45 feet in length. If the rope is new and stiff, it is better first to make the tie just described with about 7 or 8 feet of 1/4- or 3/8-inch rope, ending in a square knot, then repeat with the half-inch Manila, this time ending with two half-hitches, leaving the long end loose.

Get someone to hold the long end of this rope, bracing against it, holding it taut, while you raise the poles, starting near the upper ends and walking up under them as they are raised. When they are nearly erect, spread them by swinging the *outer right-hand pole* of the two back poles, N (Fig. 3b), *toward* you. This locks the tripod so that it will not slip. Its final appearance should be checked with the drawing, for this is one of the most important steps in pitching the tipi. Remember, as you raise the tripod, the front, or door, is to your left, the rear to your right.

Place the tripod poles as nearly in their final position as possible. The first time this is largely a matter of trial and error, although one who has had experience in setting up tipis can judge quite accurately. After once getting them right, the simplest way of insuring that they will be right every time is to set a peg near the center of the tipi and measure from it, with a piece of cord, to the door pole and to each back tripod pole. The distance from the

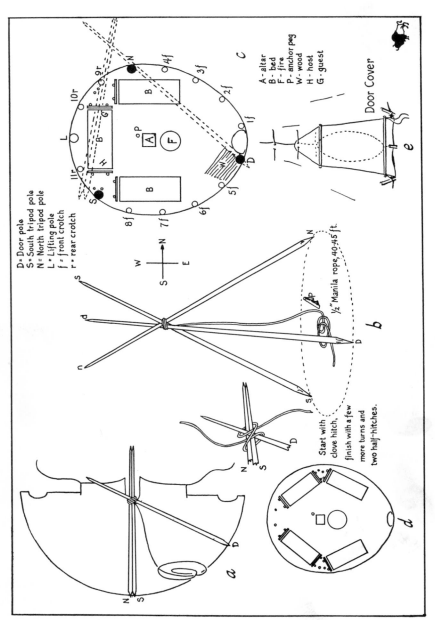

D = Door pole
S = South tripod pole
N = North tripod pole
L = Lifting pole
f = front crotch
r = rear crotch

A - altar
B - bed
F - fire
P - anchor peg
W - wood
H - host
G - guest

Door Cover

Start with clove hitch, finish with a few more turns and two half-hitches.

½" Manila rope, 40-45 ft.

Fig. 3a, b, c, d, and e. Erecting the Sioux Tipi.

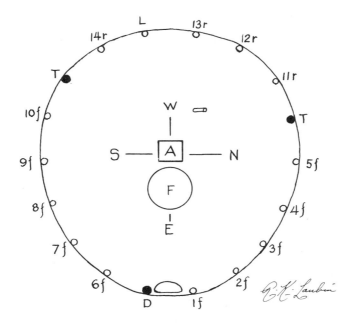

Fig. 3f. 18 Pole Frame Sioux Tipi.

peg to each back tripod pole should be the same, but that to the door pole should be a bit longer. If a loop is tied in the end of the cord, so that it can be swung on the peg as a pivot, and a knot tied at each of the two measurements made, the same cord can be saved and used each time for setting the tripod properly. This is our own idea. We have never seen Indians measure with a string like this.

The cord we use measures 8 feet 4 inches to the first knot and 10 feet 9 inches to the second knot. These measurements should be close enough if you are making a tipi the size of the pattern given here. You can also lay three stakes as markers, with the peg as a center, to point to the tripod poles, so that they indicate the points of an equilateral triangle on the ground.

An old rancher once paid us a visit in our tipi. He had no more than entered when he said, "How did you get this thing up?" When we started to explain about first erecting the tripod, he said, "Yes, I know that, but how do you fasten the tripod? Every fall, when we butcher, we hoist the hog up on three poles like that. Sometimes it works all right, but usually we just get him up and the whole damn thing comes tumbling down!" If the above instructions for locking the tripod are followed, the thing will not come tumbling down.

To put a pole into position, grasp it near the center, lift the tip up, setting the pointed butt on the ground, and walk up under it, just as you did with the tripod. An assistant can help by placing his foot against the butt so that it does not slip. When the pole is straight up, you will find that it balances very nicely and you can carry it in this position to the location where it should rest in the frame. In fact, this is the *only* way one person can handle the long, heavy poles necessary for a large tipi.

Lay the poles in consecutively, according to the numbers on the ground plan (Fig. 3c): 1, 2, 3, and 4 *all* in the front crotch *ns* (Fig. 3b); 5, 6, 7, and 8 *on top* of the first four, in the *same crotch, ns.* This puts two-thirds of the poles in the front crotch and in the smoke hole, so that they make the least possible bulk under the cover. Lay poles 9, 10, and 11 in the rear crotch, skipping one space between 10 and 11, where the lifting pole, L, will go eventually. Even with 20 poles—that is, 18 in the frame instead of 15 (Fig. 3f)— they are still grouped in the same way, two-thirds of them going into the front crotch *ns.*

This arrangement of poles achieves two important objectives: First, a framework which the cover will fit when stretched taut, and second, a smaller opening at the top of the tent.

Set all these loose poles on the ground closer to the center so that they will indicate a circumference smaller than that of the finished lodge. After pole 11 is in place, wrap the rope around all of the poles now standing. This adds to the sturdiness of the tent. Carry the rope outside the framework, starting at pole *S,* and walk to the left, *clockwise,* or as the Indians say, "with the sun." Continue around the framework, whipping or snapping the rope up into place and drawing it tight as you go. This action is very similar to a Maypole dance, and the rope is carried around *four* times. This is the sacred, or lucky, number in Indian figures, but is also practical, as it gives more leverage for drawing the rope tight.

After you have finished wrapping the rope four times, bring it over pole *N,* the north tripod pole, and let it hang free near the center of the floor until you drive a stout peg, about 3 feet long and 1 1/2 inches thick, at an angle at *P* (Fig. 3c) for an anchor. Some prefer to use two crossed pegs instead of a single peg. If only one is used, it should have either a fork from a cut-off branch as a hook

ising the Tripod.

2. First four poles
in place (east).

Laying Poles in Place.

4. Second group, all in the same crotch
(east).

Steps in Erecting the Tipi.
Credit: The Laubin Collection

6. Bracing Lifting Pole with Foot

5. The Finished Frame.

7. Raising Cover into Place.

8. Spreading the Cover Around

9. Tying on the "Ladder."

10. Pinning up the Front.

11. Pinning up the Front,
seen from Inside the Tipi.

12. Placing Smoke-flap Pole into Position.

Steps in erecting the Tipi
Credit: The Laubin Collection

on its upper end, or a section of bark left on so that the rope will not slip. Then tie the loose rope snugly to the anchor peg (or pegs) before raising the canvas into place. Or, if there is no wind, just let the rope hang until the lodge is completely up.

In windy country, we learned the hard way that it is wise to tie the anchor rope down even when the weather seems calm, for a gust can come up in seconds that may topple the whole frame before the canvas is in place. This happened to us once, knocking down the poles and breaking most of them. Two of the main tripod poles were broken at the tie, so had to be discarded and new ones cut. Others were broken off farther out towards the tips. We patched them together again, just for looks, sewing them up in wet rawhide, which shrinks and dries almost as hard as the wood itself. High up in the air as they were, the patches did not show and the poles still looked well.

Stanley Vestal says that in his experience with Cheyenne and Arapaho tipis in Oklahoma, he has seldom seen an anchor peg used, but it has been a part of all the tipis we have seen in the North. However, if there is no wind and none is likely to come up, the rope is merely spiraled down the north tripod pole, N, and fastened with a half-hitch. In the South the rope is sometimes spiraled down the south tripod pole, S.

Now lay the lifting pole, L, upon the cover (which is still spread flat on the ground since measuring the tripod) in the same line in which poles N and S were formerly laid. Mark it where the tip of the tie flap comes, making sure that the cover is pulled taut. The lifting pole could have been measured, of course, at the same time as the tripod poles.

Next, lay the lifting pole to one side again and fold the cover by taking a corner of it near the doorway and bringing it to the center at the back, so that the edge with the lacing-pin holes lies down the line where you just measured the lifting pole. Fold the cover again on itself and repeat until this half of the cover is folded in a long triangle about two feet wide at its base. Repeat the procedure on the other side of the cover, beginning at the opposite corner. Complete by folding these two triangles together, making one long triangular bundle of the canvas cover.

Now bring the lifting pole alongside, butt to the base of the triangle, tie flap to the mark already made, and tie the tapes of the tie flap to the pole. These tapes should be long enough to wrap crisscross (in opposite directions) around the pole, coming back over the flap itself and wrapping around several times to bind it securely to the pole.

Hoist the entire bundle, pole and all, into position, set the butt of the lifting pole according to the ground plan, the upper end, with canvas attached, dropping into the last space in the rear crotch. It is best to have help with this, as you will find the pole and canvas quite heavy. Turn the pole so that the canvas is on top of it as you lift it, have your helper brace his foot against the butt of the pole while you walk up under it from the small end until you can get a hold on it and give the final heave that drops it all into place. As it falls into place, twist the pole so that the cover comes right side up again. Take care that the cover fits snugly up against the crossing of the poles at the back. If it does not, it has been tied improperly to the lifting pole, either too high or too low.

Now it is a simple matter to unroll the cover from each side and carry it around to the front so that the two sides meet between the door pole, *D*, and pole number 1. Modern Indians now use a small ladder, but the old way was to tie a couple of crossbars across these two front poles high enough to enable one to reach the bottom of the smoke flaps when standing on the top bar. We use only one bar—the long stake or pole which will later be set in front of the door and the smoke flaps tied to it—and swing up onto it as one would onto a trapeze. Sometimes pieces of stout rope are tied across instead of crossbars, but the bars are better. Another method the Indians used to reach the top lacing pin was to have a small person stand on another's shoulders, or small boys were given the job of shinnying up the front poles.

First, tie together the tapes at the bottom of the smoke hole (previously described and shown in Figs. 1a, 2, and 2a), thus pulling the cover together and making it easier to insert the top lacing pin. The canvas cover should be slack enough on the frame that it can be pinned easily.

Still assuming that your tipi is to face east, lap the south side of the cover over the north side, left over right, and then from the right, insert the pins you previously made into the matching holes you have prepared. You will remember that the holes on the south side were made half an inch farther apart than those on the north or under side to allow for the pin and prevent the cover from bunching. When the pins can be reached while standing on the ground, remove the ladder or crossbar, for it is no longer needed and will only be in the way.

After the cover is pinned down the front, insert the smoke-flap poles, which will have to be cut to size. These are the only poles that need to be cut off toward the tips. Make sure the tips are rounded so they will not poke holes through the pockets. They should be long enough to stretch the flaps tight and reach a point on the ground close to the edge of the tipi and near the center of the back. The smoke-flap poles for our tipi this size are 21 feet 6 inches long, but you should check your own just to make sure.

On a Sioux tipi the smoke-flap poles are crossed at the back of the tent when the flaps are open wide (for a west wind). On Cheyenne and Crow tipis the poles are set so that they just meet at the back. This is because their flaps are narrow. The object of either method is to stretch the flaps as tight as possible for neatest appearance. We have never seen or heard of a Sioux or Cheyenne lodge, or of lodges of any of the three-pole people, in which the smoke-flap poles were held in place in any way but with the little pockets.

Until the tipi is pegged down to the ground all the way around, the smoke flaps should not be stretched tight—just enough to help even up the cover on the frame. Now, from the inside, push the poles out against the cover to make the tipi floor plan symmetrical, but do not remove all the slack in the cover until after it is pegged to the ground. If the poles are pushed out too far, it will be impossible to peg the cover down properly. Be sure the poles are spaced evenly. If you want to set the tripod poles in the ground and measured them before tying them to allow for this, now is the time to do it. Use a shovel or a crowbar, and be sure the tripod is set in its final position, for you will not be able to move it again without a great deal of difficulty.

In order to have the tipi look its best and to aid in bracing it against wind and storm, a large number of pegs is needed. After inserting a peg in a peg loop, twist the loop by twirling the peg. It can be made very tight and will never slip. Peg the cover down at the door first and then at the back, filling in each side after the front and back are down.

When making camp on extremely hard or stony ground, we have found an iron pin useful. We use a heavy one, about an inch in diameter, such as surveyors sometimes use, and about the same length, fifteen inches of so, as the peg itself. Drive this in the ground where the peg is to go, then pull it up and insert the peg in the same hole. A few taps with the back of the axe and the peg

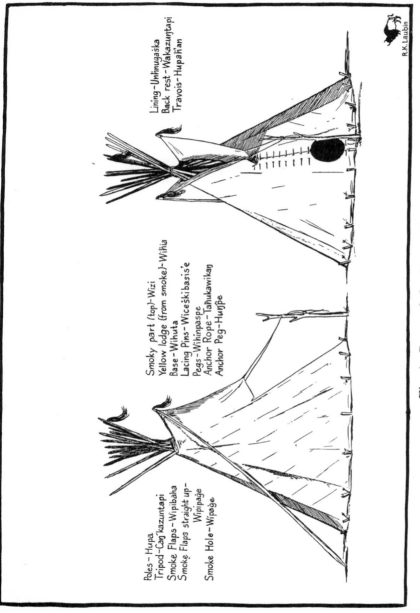

Poles – Hupa
Tripod – Caŋ'kazuntapi
Smoke Flaps – Wipibaha
Smoke Flaps straight up –
        Wipipaǧe
Smoke Hole – Wipaǧe

Smoky part (top) – Wizi
Yellow lodge (from smoke) – Wihia
Base – Wihuta
Lacing Pins – Wiceškibasis'e
Pegs – Wihinpaspe
Anchor Rope – Tahukawikaŋ
Anchor Peg – Huŋpe

Lining – Unhnugaška
Back rest – Wakazuŋtapi
Travois – Hupahʼan

R.K.Laubin

Fig. 4. Parts of the Sioux Tipi.

is perfectly solid and you have not ruined it by trying to force it through or around a rock. It is better to drive the iron pin with a small sledge hammer, or the back of an old axe, for it is likely to damage a good axe.

Now that you have the tipi pegged down, go inside again and finish the job of adjusting the poles. This time push them against the cover just as tight as they will go. If the anchor rope is tight, it will be necessary to loosen it first, but if wind is likely, be sure to tighten it again after adjusting the poles.

Even when the anchor rope is slack, it is sometimes quite a task to space and adjust the poles properly. With a yank and sudden twist they can be pulled free from under the rope. Drive them hard into the ground, so that the pointed butts bite into the earth as much as possible. If the ground is very hard, a dent can first be made in it with a sharpened stick or the iron pin.

Getting the poles spaced evenly the first time requires careful effort. But after a number of fires have been made in the tipi, the cover will become darkened with smoke except where it has been protected by the poles, so that there will be a white stripe for every pole. This makes it easy to space the poles on succeeding occasions.

In an area troubled by high winds or for any kind of a permanent camp, it is a good idea to set the poles into the ground several inches. Some Indians have told us that they set only the tripod poles, and our tipi has withstood extremely hard winds with only the tripod poles set in the ground. But other Indians set all the poles except the tripod poles in the ground. As far as getting the tipi pitched is concerned, it is much easier to plant the loose poles than the tripod poles, but for the greatest rigidity it is best to plant them all.

To plant the loose poles, raise the cover, remove a few peg loops at a time from the pegs, and dig a hole with the crowbar for each pole on the same angle at which the pole slants to the ground. Then twist and ram the pole into the earth. If the pole has bowed to a noticeable extent, it can be straightened by setting it with the bow out, and the tension of planting it in the earth will prevent it from twisting back to its former position. After the poles are planted, replace the peg loops on the pegs, tie the anchor rope, and the tipi is ready for any kind of weather.

Before Indians had iron crowbars they used a stout wooden

digging stick about 4 feet in length and 3 inches in diameter, squared off on the top and pointed at the bottom.

It is sometimes quite difficult to pitch a tipi correctly the first time. The diameter of the poles has much to do with the final size of the frame. No matter how carefully the tripod is measured, you sometimes find that the door pole is too long. I have seen Indian women just chop it off or bury it in the ground, the choice depending apparently upon whether an axe or a spade was the handiest tool. But if directions are carefully followed the error should be slight, and by making allowance for it next time, no further difficulty should be encountered. Try pitching the tipi three or four times the same day and you will master all the little technicalities.

Occasionally someone has difficulty with wrinkles in the tipi and is at a loss to know how to get rid of them. Such wrinkles come from spreading the tripod poles too far. If the poles were tied right in the first place, by following the diagrams and information so far given, it is a simple matter to shove the two rear tripod poles in toward the center a few inches to get rid of the wrinkles. If, however, the poles were tied too high in the first place, you can thus get rid of the wrinkles but the canvas will be too high off the ground. If, on the other hand, they were tied too low, the canvas will lay on the ground all the way around and even after pushing all the loose poles out against the sides of the tipi the tripod poles will still be inside the perimeter and will not be supporting the canvas. The tripod must be tied right. You have only a couple of inches of leeway if you want the tipi to look its best and be free of wrinkles.

If the tripod is tied a little too high you can bury the butts, but, if tied too low, there is not much you can do except take the tipi down and start over again. If the tripod is not spread enough the canvas will not fit right either. It will be slack on the poles and yet can not be staked out properly.

Finally, most Indians use a pole 6 to 8 feet long, for a stake set in front of the door, to which they tie the long cords from the smoke flaps. This is the pole we use for the ladder. Instead of trying to pound a long stake like this into place, make a hole first with the digging stick, crowbar, or iron pin.

Rides-to-the-Door, an old Blackfoot, saw us using an iron pin to set the anchor peg. He got very excited and warned us not to use it. Then he told us in sign language what had happened to him.

He used a short iron bar for the anchor peg one time. During a terrific thunderstorm a bolt of lightning struck the bar and knocked
him unconscious. He had been alone in the tipi. After the storm
his family found him. Wades-in-the-Water cared for him and he
recovered, but from that time on he was unable to speak. When he
saw that we were using the iron pin only for making the hole for
the peg, he brightened up and signed, "Good."

Before the introduction of the white man's steel axe the Indian
held the cover of his tipi to the ground by placing stones around
the bottom, the tipi being set to allow several inches of the cover to
lie on the ground. "Tipi rings" of such stones, left lying on the
prairie, are still to be seen in many parts of the West. Even in fairly
recent times, stones have been used instead of pegs on hard ground
and in mountain areas where stones are available. We have been
told that even canvas tipis were pitched the same way under similar
conditions. But canvas rotted out much faster than hide if allowed
to lie on the ground, so it was not a common practice and was never
done for a permanent camp.

Various types of doors were used on old Indian tipis. Some
were quite fancy, with painted designs or quilled or beaded stripes.
Others were only an old blanket hung to the lacing pin above the
doorway, with a stick tied across the blanket to stretch it over
the opening. Some doors were stretched on a willow frame, either
oval or oblong; others were stretched on two sticks instead of one.
Often the skin of an animal, such as a bear or buffalo, with the
hair left on, was used, or, in recent times, the skin of a large calf
or a steer. The hair shed water well and helped keep the area
around the doorway dry. Fig. 5 shows various types of doors and
decorations on them.

McClintock, in *The Old North Trail*, tells of a Blackfoot Indian
who, wishing to enter a lodge in which a hand game was going on,
took off the buffalo hide door as he entered and sat upon it so that
he might have the luck of the buffalo as he gambled.

Now that the tipi is up it can be plainly seen that the shape of
the interior is not circular but egg shaped. The long diameter is
approximately the same length as the radius we used in marking
out the tipi. The narrow diameter is about the same as the distance
from the tie flap to the ground.

If we had cut the tipi on a true half-circle, the ground plan
would be a circle. But the poles would be bunched too far to the
front, placing the smoke hole in front of the fire instead of over it,

and the tipi would present the illusion of being longer down the back than the front. Actually, since the length of the goods is down the front, it tends to shrink more there than down the back, where the width of the cloth is. After a few wettings a half-circle tipi has the appearance of being about to fall on its face, just the opposite of the way it should look. So, from this practical standpoint of shrinkage, if from no other, the tipi should be made tilting to the back, although this is not the reason the Indians made them so, for skins did not shrink. A tipi cut on a half-circle just makes a squat and ugly-looking lodge.

Now that you know how to make and pitch a tipi properly, you realize that it is a rather simple matter after all. Certainly you did not have to take the extreme measures employed by a group of modern Indians at one of our leading universities. The Indian students wanted to erect a tipi for a celebration on the campus, but not a single one of them knew how to do it. Therefore, they engaged members of the engineering school to do the job for them. The engineers laid the poles out on the ground like the spokes of a huge wheel, roped and chained them together at the "hub," and hoisted them into position with a derrick!

This sounds too ridiculous to believe, but we have met a number of persons who thought a tipi must be erected in such fashion. Perhaps, they thought, by a person on each pole, all hoisting them into position at the same time! In fact, that is the way it was done on one movie set. The Cheyennes have been known to move a tipi, already pitched, to a new position in this manner. It was done ceremonially at their Sun Dance.

One who is experienced in pitching tipis can do the job in a very short time. We have erected a set of poles in about five minutes and can have the cover up, pinned, and staked down in a matter of fifteen or twenty minutes more. It takes longer to hang the inside lining properly and to arrange everything inside so that it is cozy and attractive.

In taking down a lodge, you simply reverse the entire process of erecting it. The pegs are pulled up, smoke-flap poles removed, lacing pins pulled out, and the tie tapes untied; then the cover is carried around from each side of the door to the lifting pole, and folded again and again until it has the long triangular shape previously mentioned. It is then a simple matter to ease it to the ground, untie it, and roll it up into a neat, compact bundle, all ready for another camp site.

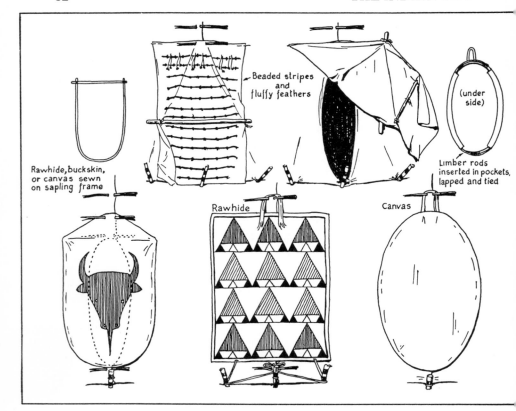

Rawhide, buckskin, or canvas sewn on sapling frame

Beaded stripes and fluffy feathers

(under side)

Limber rods inserted in pockets, lapped and tied

Rawhide

Canvas

Fig. 5. Tipi Doors.

We have already mentioned how Indians store their poles when not in use. But if you wish to keep them looking new and retain their color as long as possible, it is better to store them under cover. We have a basement long enough to contain our poles. We tell our friends we built our house just to store the tipi. Our valuable furnishings of buckskin, beads, feathers, and rawhide we store in large tin cans such as bakers have for shortening, or in the large fiber cylinders used for shipping fragile materials. These containers are moth- and mouse-proof.

Laubins' Cheyenne Tipi Beaded Door Cover. Note the Dewclaw Dangles. Photograph by Gladys Laubin.

It is a good idea to store even the cover and lining by wrapping them securely and completely in waterproof "tarps" to protect them from wear and dampness when not in use. We use the ground cloths from our beds for this purpose and pack tipi and lining in this way while traveling, so as not to chafe holes in them as they lie in the car or trailer.

5. LIVING IN THE TIPI

LININGS

WHEN YOU have pitched your tipi and pegged down the cover, you have a tent open at the top and all around the bottom, since no matter how tightly you have pegged it, the cover cannot possibly reach entirely to the ground all the way around. It should come within a couple of inches of doing so, but even a two-inch space permits a lot of draft. You have, in fact, merely a temporary shelter, just a chimney, not really fit to live in. The wind blows in at the bottom and a heavy rain will run down the poles and drip on everything inside. If poles and cover are all you have, your tipi is drafty, wet, cold—or hot in warm weather—and as cheerless as a log cabin without any chinking. One reason why so many people have been disappointed in tipis is that they thought the cover and poles were the whole thing. Far from it!

Long ago it was customary for a man to hang his painted buffalo robe behind his bed when not wearing it. This could have led to the making of the inside lining which goes all the way around the tipi, keeping drafts and dampness away from the living quarters. But there is also good reason to believe that the earliest shelter was merely a robe stretched between two poles or tall stakes set in the ground, forming a wind break. If the wind changed, more poles and more robes were probably set up. Eventually a circular uncovered shelter evolved. Then someone discovered that longer poles could be leaned together at the center and the entire structure covered. From such a primitive shelter the tipi conceivably emerged.

The lining, besides keeping away drafts and dampness, prevented rain from dripping off the poles and served a number of other purposes. It gave increased ventilation, helping to clear the atmosphere of smoke. The warm air rising inside the tipi drew in cold air from the outside, which came in under the cover and went up behind the lining, creating a perfect draft for the fire and taking the smoke out with it. Someone once said that the Indian lived in his chimney, which is literally correct, but in effect not true if a lining was used and the fire handled properly. The air space behind the lining also served as insulation, which helped to keep the tipi warm in winter and cool in summer.

War records and personal experiences were painted on the lining, so that it served another purpose, that of decoration, and it became as important to the appearance of a lodge as wall paper is to the average home. In fact, the Crows, when they set up their tipis nowadays, use fancy cretonnes for dew cloths, which serve little purpose except for decoration. Neither are their tipis waterproof. They are for show only, and the Indians always hope it does not rain during Fair week. One night there was a thunderstorm, and the next morning Robert Yellowtail announced, "I had a shower bath in my tipi all last night."

Anyone who has camped in an ordinary tent knows how wet and damp everything is in the morning after a cool night—almost as wet as if he had camped out under the stars and the dew had settled directly on him. The same is true in a tipi without a lining, but all is different with one. With a lining a tipi is almost as dry as a house—dryer than most summer cottages. The lining keeps the dew from condensing inside, and so is often spoken of as a dew cloth.

The lining also prevents the casting of shadows from the fire onto the outer wall, so is sometimes referred to as a "ghost screen." This was important to the Indians, as a matter not only of family privacy but of safety. No lurking enemy could see a shadow at which he could aim and so injure some occupant. White Bull, on his Minikonju calendar, names the year 1874 the "Killed in his Lodge Winter." The event referred to took place on the Big Dry River in Montana. One night a party of Sioux hunters were straggling in from a buffalo hunt. At the end of the camp there was a big lodge with a fire inside, which threw shadows of the occupants on its walls. A Crow warrior, who had been following the Sioux hunters, sneaked up and killed one of these men by shooting at his shadow on the wall of the tipi.

The lining was often dispensed with while an Indian tribe was on the move, for it does take time to hang it properly. But for any extended camping period it is necessary.

Figures 6a, b, c and 6d give essential details for making the lining, which is such an important feature if you are really going to enjoy the tipi in all kinds of weather. It should be made of light-weight material, but it should be waterproof. Indeed, it is more important that the lining be waterproof than the cover. We have made a lining of heavy unbleached muslin, waterproofed with a wax compound, which has lasted for years. The wax does not seem to injure the cloth if it is not exposed to brilliant sunlight. This muslin was 80 inches wide; so we had a lining fully 6 feet high, with plenty of material to turn under at the bottom. However, 6 foot material is much easier to obtain and makes a very satisfactory lining. We have included figures for both widths. It should be made in three sections, as indicated on the drawing. Otherwise you would have one piece of cloth more than 50 feet long. Imagine getting tangled up in all that, trying to handle it! Allow enough for a good lap where the sections come together, as shown on the drawing. The pattern given makes the most efficient use of the cloth and, if the figures are carefully followed, should make a lining which fits well. The only way to make one so that each seam comes down the center of a pole would be to mark each piece after the tipi is up.

Many of the old tipi linings were made in rectangular sections, but that kind is difficult to hang. Likewise it is more convenient to hang the lining to a rope extending around the poles than to tie it directly to the poles (Fig. 6b). The rope must be strung around by taking a turn about each pole—over and under—in such a way that it is to the front instead of next to the cover. We have seen the turns made the other way, so that the rope is next to the cover, but the first way gives more air space between the cover and the lining. With this rope (it need be only a 3/16- or 1/4-inch rope) stretched tightly between poles the lining can be hung very neatly.

One Bull showed us another way to hang the dew cloth on a rope. That was to run the rope around the poles inside the cover but outside the poles by fastening it on one of the door poles and running it completely around the frame and back to the same door pole (Fig. 6c). The slant of the poles prevents the rope from sliding down. The lining is hung to this rope, tied between each pair of poles, instead of to the poles, so that it does not touch any pole and water is free to run on down behind it. For preventing water from dripping inside the lodge, this method is very good, but the rope tightens and slackens with the weather, and when it slackens, the

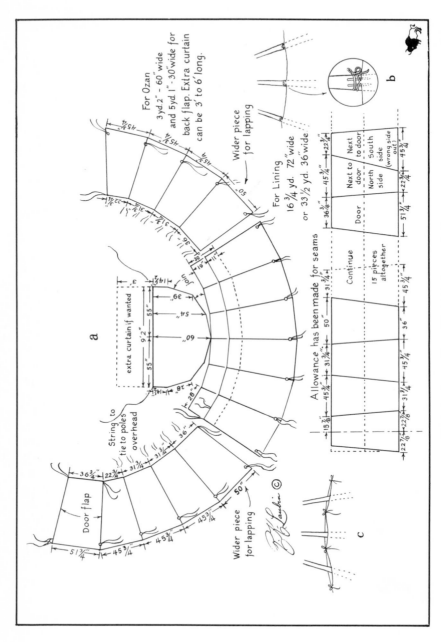

For Ozan
3 yd. 2" - 60" wide
and 5 yd. 1 - 30" wide for
back flap. Extra curtain
can be 3' to 6' long.

Wider piece
for lapping

For Lining
16¾ yd. 72" wide
or 33½ yd. 36" wide.

extra curtain if wanted

String to
tie to poles
overhead

Door flap

Wider piece
for lapping

a

Allowance has been made for seams

15⅝"	45¾"	31¾"	50"	45¾"	36"	45¾"	31¾"	50"	31¾"	45¾"	36¾"

Continue

15 pieces
altogether

Door

Next to door
North side

Next to door
South side
(wrong side out)

| 22⅞" | 22⅞" | 31¼" | 45¾" | 36" | 45¾" | 31¼" | 22⅞" | 22⅞" | 45¾" | 51¼" |

b

c

Fig. 6a, b, and c. Tipi Lining and Ozan.

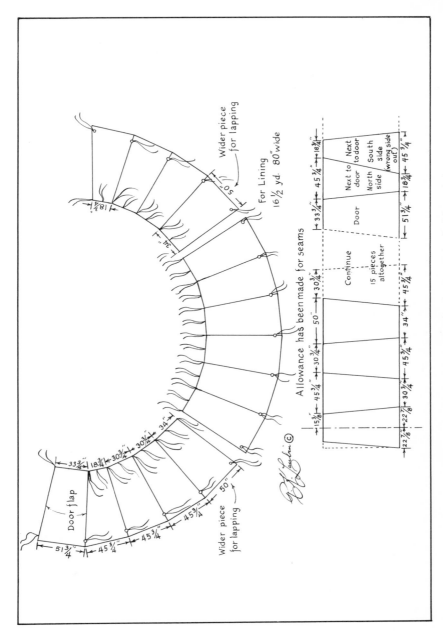

Fig. 6d. Tipi Lining made from 80 inch Material.

lining, hung in this fashion, sags more than when hung directly to the poles or to a rope with turns about the poles. However, it is a quick and easy method and good for a short camp.

For an extended stay on one camp site it is a good idea to start the rope from the lifting pole, running it around the tipi and back to the lifting pole again. Then, in case it is necessary to take the cover down for repairs, the poles and lining can be left in place, for the rope will have to be untied only from the one pole which must be moved.

The base of the lining is usually tied as near to the ground as possible and to the butts of the poles. The tying cords are attached with little pebbles in the same way that the peg loops were attached to the cover. They are attached about eight inches from the bottom, leaving a lower edge to be turned under so that ground cloths can be laid over it, sealing the interior completely from drafts and dust.

If the pieces making up the lining do not fit the poles well, use little stakes and peg the lining to the ground instead of tying it to the butts of the poles. Stakes about 8 inches long and 3/4 inch in diameter are adequate. The easiest way to hang any lining is to lay it on the ground around the inside wall of the tipi, stake it to the ground, or tie it to the butts of the poles; then raise it up and tie it to the rope. While it is laying on the ground be sure it is protected from the dirt by grass, tarps, or vinyl sheets if you want a nice clean lining.

If stones are available, as they certainly are here in Jackson's Hole, it is a good idea to lay them around the inner edge of the tipi, on top of this turned-under lining, or sod cloth; thus, even in these modern times, "tipi rings" may still be created. In breaking camp, when pulling the lining out from under these stones, they tend to roll into a smaller circle, which could account for some of the small tipi rings sometimes found at old camp sites.

When the top of the lining is tied directly to the poles, two little sticks should be placed under each tie string, against the pole (see detail, Fig. 6b) to act as a channel for water to run in as it comes down the poles during a rain. Water will always follow the poles on the inside of the tipi, no matter how waterproof the cover. This is one reason the poles should be as smooth and free from knots as possible. The water will run right on down the poles in little rivulets, following between the two little sticks, and on behind the lining.

One Bull, our Indian "father," showed us how to use the two

little sticks when we were having trouble with water dripping from the point where the tie strings on the lining touched the poles. We had devised a way of using one stick and carving a channel on the back side. How he laughed at us, and how much simpler it is to use two sticks! We have come to the conclusion that the Indians had all the important details already worked out, and that the simplest way is usually best.

These two little sticks must also be used under the turn of rope on each pole when that method is employed—and we advise using it, even if the lining is cut to fit, because the top of each panel of lining can be fastened between each pair of poles, as well as to the poles themselves, making it tighter and neater. The Blackfeet use small carved poles, slightly longer than the lining is high, which are placed in front of the lining between poles, the pointed end in the ground, upper end under the rope. These decorated poles are similar to the ones used to support the backrests, which we discuss later. They prevent the lining from sagging and add much color and interest to the tipi.

We have also given details for an *ozan,* which is an inside rain cover. This was used to some extent in early days, but few living Indians have ever seen one. The ozan amounted to another tent within the tipi and actually was an extension of the lining, with extra curtains which could be either tied, like an awning, overhead, or dropped in front of the bed, making a sort of private compartment, somewhat like a Pullman berth. We have designed it as separate from the lining, so that it need not be in use at all times, but it is a help in a hard, lasting rain, and increases warmth in cold weather, as we discovered. (See color plates 10 and 12.)

If the ozan is desired as a permanent fixture, the dotted lines can be disregarded and it can be made as part of the lining itself. An ozan in the rear of the lodge is an advantage, but formerly one was used over each bed. We do not know whether the ozan is peculiar to the Sioux or not. We use their name for it and have never heard of it anywhere else, although the earth-lodge people used a similar device. Dr. Charles Eastman, the well-known Sioux writer, knew of it and told a friend of ours about it. We heard of it from Flying Cloud, who said his mother and other old people had described it to him. Since it was not altogether essential, it was probably dispensed with during the later years of tipi living, when there was almost constant hostility with the United States troops and the Sioux were kept almost continuously on the move, traveling light and with little time for long camps. Soon after that, the tipi, as a home, ceased to exist. The few that were retained were kept mainly for ceremonial and festive use and usually were mere shells, like unceiled attics. The old-time equipment and furnishings, too, practically disappeared.

A temporary ozan can be made of "tarps." You can stretch a cord between two poles at a height of 5 or 6 feet, skipping three or four poles, so that the cord is in a line above the front of the bed. The overhead section can be made to fit the poles by tying the pebbles and tie strings where they are needed. Thus it is unnecessary to cut or damage the tarp. This overhead tarp is then stretched out horizontally and its forward edge dropped over the taut cord. To make a "Pullman" compartment, stretch another tarp perpendicularly instead of the cord.

We have included sketches of some painted lining designs (Figs. 7 and 8). Since the lining is waterproofed, it is easy to apply the color. Ordinary house paint can be used, and we have seen linings among the Crows and Blackfeet colored with wax crayons— the kind children use on their color books. If you use crayons, cover the designs with a piece of wrapping paper and go over them with a moderately hot iron. This will melt the wax color into the cloth and the paper will pick up the excess. Some linings have the stripe designs at each pole, some at every other pole, and some Blackfoot linings have stripes even between the poles. We feel that fewer stripes are more artistic and give a freer, more spacious appearance to the interior of the lodge.

Some linings—those of rectangular sections—were decorated with horizontal beaded stripes, dangles made of thongs wrapped with dyed cornhusks, and tassels made of buffalo dewclaws and dyed hair, or fluffy feathers. Only certain women were allowed to make and use such linings, however. Because the buffalo dewclaws decorating the lining and similar dangles decorating the smoke flaps and front of the tipi were supposed to call buffalo to the tribe, not just any woman was allowed to display such "medicine." Women owning such tipis belonged to a special society whose members were elected or invited to join because of outstanding character and ability as craftworkers and housekeepers.

These rectangular linings were usually used in large tipis and were hung straight down from the poles. But we have seen Crows use such linings, obtained from the Cheyennes, fastening them to the bases of the poles, then gathering the top to fit the smaller perimeter there by tying pebbles and strings and taking periodic tucks, thus compensating for the fact that they were not cut to fit the tipi cover in the first place.

In the South, where temperatures are mild, lining sections were usually hung over the beds only, not going all the way around the tipi, as was customary in the North. The section was often stretched from the pole at the head of the bed to the pole nearest the foot, skipping the poles in between, and a foot or more of the bottom of the lining was tucked under the bed instead of being tied to the base of the poles. Single lining sections were usually from 6x8 to 6x12 feet in size. When hung all the way around the tipi, the sections were overlapped so that there were no gaps between.

The Flatheads sometimes used a very narrow lining made of a single width of cloth running around the inner wall of the tipi inside the poles. When such a lining was turned under a few inches at the bottom, as was common with all linings, it might be only 18 to 30 inches high, depending upon the width of the cloth. A narrow lining like this would keep drafts from the backs of sleepers and would help clear the lodge of smoke, but it would not be so effective as the usual lining.

FURNISHINGS

It makes for more practical living in the tipi to have things placed systematically. The interior should be arranged according to one of the floor plan diagrams shown in Fig. 3c and d. The selection will depend upon the size of the tipi and the number of beds wanted in it. It is possible, of course, to arrange still more beds in either of the two patterns. Julia Wades-in-the-Water had six beds in her huge tipi at Browning, Montana, when we stayed with her.

Indian beds were usually made on the ground, although in some very large tipis, notably among the Cheyennes and Arapahoes, the beds were raised off the ground several inches. We will discuss these later on. Beds on the ground take up less room and are below the smoke, even when it hangs low from a dying fire; they are warmer and can be set back farther under the canopy of the lining, which keeps them drier. Also, there are no cots to carry, this means less packing and less trouble in making or breaking camp.

Waterproof ground cloths should be placed on the ground be-

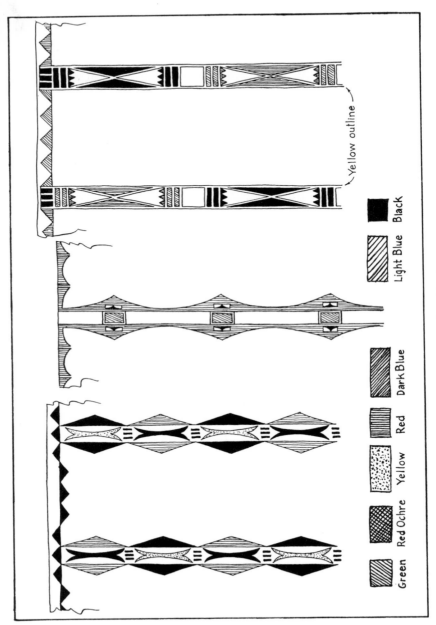

Fig. 7. Lining Design.

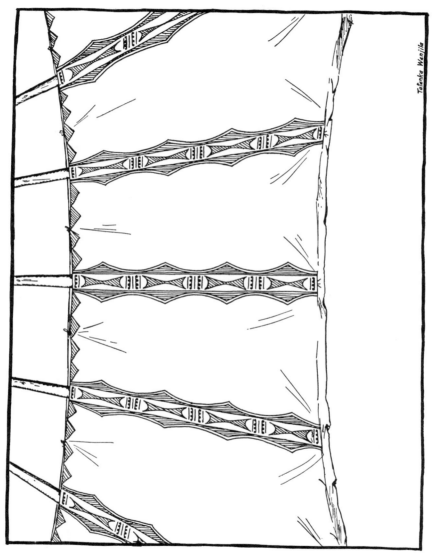

Fig. 8. Lining Design.

neath the beds. Indians had no ground cloths originally, but they did have plenty of skins to serve the same purpose. As the skins became old and worthless from too much dampness and wear, they were replaced without difficulty. Nowadays, with skins and furs at a premium, it is a good idea to keep dampness from coming up underneath by laying pieces of old linoleum on the ground all over the tipi, with the exception of the area around the fireplace, if one is to be in camp for any length of time. Even oilcloth, smooth side down, is quite serviceable, or sisal-craft paper can be used. Thoroughly waterproofed tarpaulins are all right, but are expensive, so we reserve them for the beds alone.

Heavy vinyl plastic makes an excellent ground cloth. We tried cutting one to cover the entire tipi, except for the space around the fire, but it was hard to handle. A number of pieces about 6 feet square each are better. These can be placed anywhere and made to fit the whole floor by overlapping corners. We intended to try, also, the new indoor-outdoor carpeting, which is waterproof on the under side, but could not bring ourselves to use such an artificial-looking product with its unnatural colors along with our skins and furs.

If the tipi is to be in one place for some length of time, it is a good idea to cut strips of sisal paper, vinyl plastic, or other thoroughly waterproof material about 4 feet long and 8 or 10 inches wide and place these *under* the part of the lining that turns under as a sod cloth. Such strips will keep the dampness of the ground from contacting the sod cloth. No waterproofing, no matter how good, will last indefinitely against constant wetting; so this is good insurance for a long-lived sod cloth. You must be careful, however, not to have these strips project outside beyond the sod cloth, or they will collect water in a rain and it will run under, making the sod cloth wetter than ever instead of keeping it dry.

Sleeping bags are the most convenient and efficient form of bedding. Although they were not used by Plains Indians, they are an invention of the Indians to the north. If you do not have sleeping bags, you should use woolen blankets, and remember that it is important always to have as much bedding under you as over you.

A pallet of buffalo hides, such as the Indians used, makes a comfortable bed. Lacking these, a couple of quilts ("soogans") or even an air mattress will do, although the latter is not very "Indian." Such a bed may sound hard to the uninitiated, but doctors claim that much of the back trouble from which so many persons suffer is caused by the soft beds of modern civilization.

If you are afraid of trying, for the first time, a bed such as we have described, and care to take the trouble, you might make a bough bed. It is made by laying small logs, 4 or 5 inches in diameter and 6 feet long as the sides or frame of the bed and filling in between with the tips of fir or cedar boughs. These bough tips are placed nearly vertically, butt ends down, tips up, starting against a cross log at the head of the bed. Such a bed is soft and feathery the first night, but gradually packs down and gets harder. If you want a soft bed, you must continually replenish the boughs. After our first camping trip, we decided that a bough bed was not worth the time it took to make. Besides, it is often difficult to get boughs nowadays. You are not allowed to cut anything green in any of the national or state parks. The problem of a bed might also be solved by carrying with you a bag made of ticking, the size of the bed you want, and stuffing it full of leaves and browse. But for us the Indian way is good enough. We do not even make hip holes, and we have never met an Indian who did.

On top of the linoleum, oilcloth, vinyl plastic, or other waterproof material on the remaining floor of the tipi, we place the skins we use for rugs. Raw skins, if properly fleshed, stretched and dried, unsalted, can be used on the floor if they are placed on something waterproof. It is not necessary to go to all the work or expense of soft-tanning them, although soft-tanned skins are easier to pack. Raw skins have to be rolled and take up more room in moving camp. Instead of skins, you can use pieces of old carpets or rugs to make the tipi more homelike. We have also found the large mats in which Chinese tea is shipped useful as flooring material. It looks good and wears well, too. Mexican mats are good, if you can get them. Plains Indians did not have such mats, but they did not stay in one place very long, either, except in winter, when they had plenty of skins to put on the floor. Julia Wades-in-the-Water had her tipi floor covered with burlap that she got from grain sacks. It was kept in place with long iron nails driven into the ground and was quite satisfactory. Waterproof material is really needed only under beds and articles affected by dampness—furs, skins, suitcases, or duffelbags.

The tipi should be ditched, or trenched, of course, like any other kind of tent, by digging a little gutter three or four inches

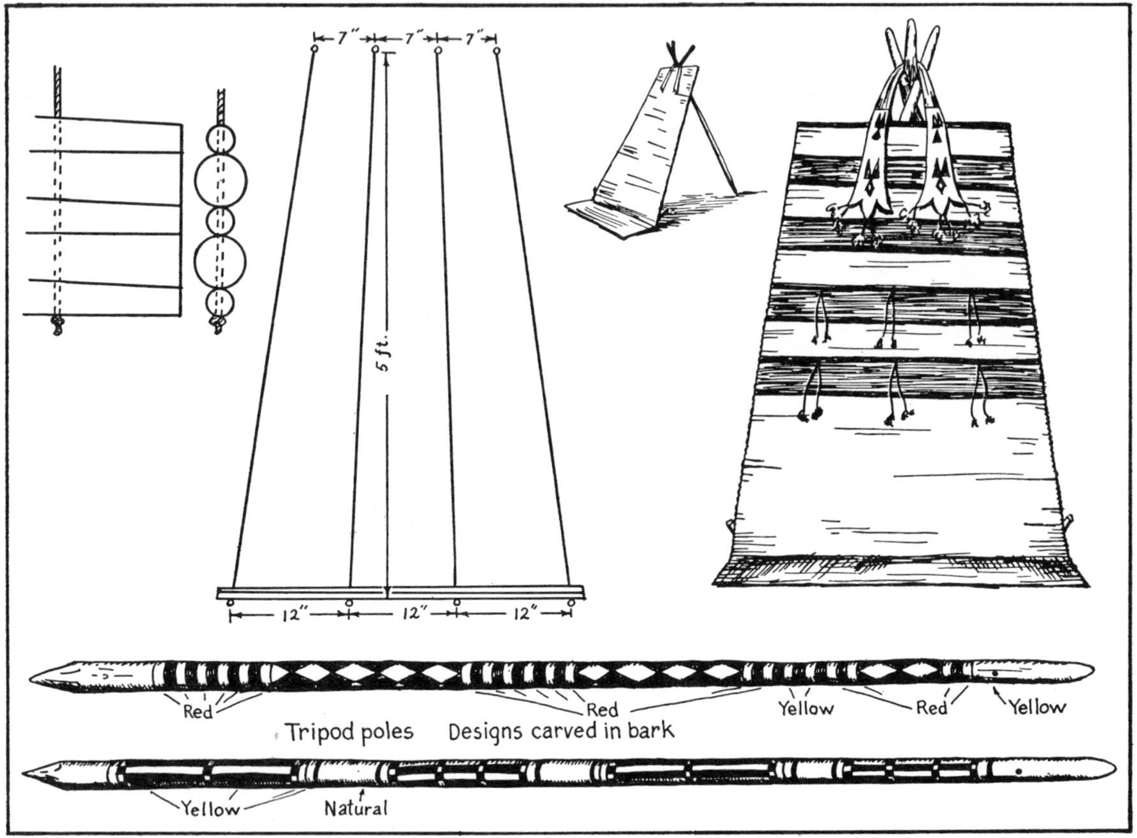

Fig. 9. Backrests.

deep and as wide all around it, with a runoff trench leading from the lowest point. We have seen people pack the dirt from the trench against the side of the cover, but this is not satisfactory. Water runs down the outside of the cover into this dirt, making a muddy mess of it and soiling the bottom of the tipi. If left to dry there it will rot the bottom of the cover. As you make the trench, place the dirt alongside, away from the tipi.

Speaking of trenches, often we are asked what Indians did for sanitary facilities. Indians answered nature's calls as nature probably intended, on the open prairie or in the brush along the river behind their camps. According to modern standards this would be considered anything but sanitary, but they were seldom in camp more than four days at a time, except in winter; so the grounds were fresh and clean again when next they arrived, and in the meantime had been enriched through the natural ecological cycle of decay and regrowth. Nowadays they have old-fashioned outhouses on their camp- and fairgrounds.

The simplest manner of disposal when camping in isolated areas not serviced by modern facilities, is for an individual to take a little shovel along. For a larger camp with several people in the party, dig a narrow trench a couple of feet deep and throw in a few shovelfuls of fresh dirt after each use. Primitive man left his junk scattered about just as modern man does today. But in early days, such junk was disposable and soon disintegrated, whereas most of our refuse today will outlast all of us, if we do not become more aware of the problem and do something other than talk about it.

Willow-rod backrests, sometimes called lean-backs or lazy-backs, are the most distinctive of all Indian furnishings (see Fig. 9). They are as comfortable as rocking chairs. We once said that the only thing we missed in the tipi was a rocking chair, but once we got some backrests were satisfied. For that matter, the Indians had rocking chairs—a bit different from the common variety, to be sure, but they served the same purpose. The simplest form was made by the way the Indian sat, with his knees up under his chin and his arms folded around his shins. This was comfortable for a while, but for more lasting comfort he sat in the same position, drew a double-folded blanket across his back, and lapped the ends together tightly below his knees. Then by rolling the top of the two lapping folds down and outward, he "locked" the blanket in position. This left his arms free and held him in a comfortable position. He could "rock" forward and back.

But the willow-rod backrests are something else again. Comfortable seats are necessary in any home. The backrests serve that purpose in the tipi. They are the most important article of furniture in a tipi. Boxes, rawhide cases, pouches, bags, and pillows, while not always considered furniture by the rest of us, are the only other furnishings, except for the robes and furs. Backrests are colorful and attractive and extremely practical. A pair of them will roll into a small bundle weighing only a few pounds. Hung from a tripod of light sticks, resting against two of the tripod legs, they will support the weight of the heaviest person with entire security.

The tripod is made of thin poles 4 or 5 feet high, and the other important part of the backrest is a tapered mat made of peeled willow rods as big around as a lead pencil. These rods are peeled, straightened in the teeth, and strung together with cords of heavy sinew, forming a flat mat about 5 feet long, 3 feet wide at the lower end, and 2 feet wide at the upper end. It is usually decorated handsomely, and the poles of the tripod are also carved and painted.

Part of the lower end of the mat is laid on the ground, acting as the seat of the chair. Backrests are much like *chaise longues,* or beach chairs. It is very difficult to find the real thing for sale nowadays, but making them is a good craft project. One who lacks time, materials, or inclination to make them might use the folding canvas and metal seats with supporting backs which are so comfortable in the football stadium or at the beach.

Backrests are not difficult to make, but like most Indian things, they do take time and patience:

1. Gather straight willow shoots about 1/2 of an inch thick at the butts, and 3 1/2 feet long. (They sometimes grow much longer.)

2. Peel them and keep them in the shade so that they do not dry out too fast. Use them while still green and soft.

3. Lay out a frame on the ground, with stakes and string, according to the drawing in Fig. 9. It is for a guide only; or you could make a wooden frame which could be set erect, so you would not have to be down on your knees all the time, and you could do the work indoors.

4. Using this frame as a guide, measure a willow rod (shoot) to the lower, or wide, end. With a very sharp, thin awl, make holes in the rod wherever it crosses the strings on the frame. Trim the rod 1 1/2 inches longer than the outer strings at each end. Cut, following the outline of the strings, with a sharp knife against a

board. The end holes should be 1 1/2 inches from either end. If the rods needed straightening, Indians straightened them with their teeth. Our Cheyenne backrests have teeth marks all over them. If you prefer, straighten them carefully with your hands

5. From heavy cord, such as that used for chalk line, or, better yet, a heavy fishing line used for deep-sea fishing, cut four pieces, each a bit over 5 feet long. Run one piece, knotted at the lower end, through each hole. (Indians strung their backrests on heavy sinew cord.)

6. Still using the frame as a guide, measure each succeeding rod, alternating small and large ends, punch the holes where it crosses the strings, trim it to coincide with the outer strings, and run the long chords through, as before. Continue until the final rod is in place, knot the cords at the top, and the backrest is finished.

7. Roll up the backrest from the wide end, tightly, then wrap it tightly with another piece of cord, and set it aside for a couple of weeks to dry before final use.

8. Backrests should be in pairs, so now make another one.

9. Decorate them like the one in Fig. 9. The wide bands are red, with dark green trimming. 5/16 or even 3/8 inch dowels can be used instead of willow rods but the holes must be drilled instead of punched and the backrests will be somewhat heavier. Also, they will be far more expensive and will not have the charm of the native material.

Alternatively, instead of drilling holes in the dowels or rods, make the frame on the ground of the same sort of cord to be used for stringing the rods together; then lay the rods on the frame and fasten them to the cords of the frame with another cord going around each rod, around the frame-cord, up over the next rod, etc. Use such a "lacing" cord around the rods at each frame-cord, so the finished backrest is fastened together on the four frame cords, just as if stringing them through four holes in each rod. The Blackfeet make backrests in this way, but they do not look as nice as when the fastening cords are hidden. Also, if you make your backrests in this quicker, easier way, they should be bound on the edges, as mentioned a little later on for Crow and Blackfeet backrests.

Perhaps the easiest way of all to make a backrest would be simply to make it from a piece of 1/4 inch plywood or from a heavy pressboard. Plywood comes 48 inches wide, so you could cut pieces the shape of a real backrest, about 27 inches wide at the base and

14 inches wide at the top and they would be 48 inches long. Although all that is necessary is one solid piece like this leaned against a tripod, it can be made even more like a real backrest by sawing off a strip 12 inches wide at the bottom and hinging this back in place with small metal or leather hinges, simulating the part of the willow rod backrest that turns and lays on the ground as the seat. This would give you a backrest 36 inches high. Although not as large as most backrests, it would be large enough for a comfortable seat and easier to handle than a large rigid one. To add to its appearance, you can also tack a decorated hanging strap to the top, or lace it in place through holes drilled in the plywood, and glue a strip of red flannel or felt down each side of the backrest for further decoration. Use strips about 2 1/2 inches wide, folded in the middle, so that they look like a binding on the edges. Rubber cement works well for this. Backrests like this look nice, are harmonious with other Indian furnishings, and are really quite comfortable. (See Color plate 13.)

Indians usually used pine saplings for the tripod poles, but we have seen a few of willow. The most attractive decoration for such poles is the carved and painted designs, as in Fig. 9. Just carve away the bark. The tripod poles should be peeled if you don't intend to carve them. The simplest decoration is to rub in some powdered yellow, red, or blue paint.

Backrests often served as the head and foot of the bed. They could be arranged as shown in either of the floor-plan sketches. (Fig. 3c and d). One Bull told us that they were used in various positions, depending upon the occasion. Indians usually rolled up all their bedding during the day, so it was simple enough to place the backrests wherever they were wanted. He said that a woman who was industrious and thought a lot of her menfolk would arrange them for the greatest convenience during the day and then set them at the head and foot of the bed at night. Sometimes, especially in winter, a tanned buffalo robe was hung with the nose on the tripod and the body of the robe lying over the willow-rod mat. This made a very warm and cozy seat.

In some extremely large tipis the entire bed was of willow rods, put together just like the backrests and raised off the ground as much as a foot on poles supported by four forked stakes. But the average family did not bother with this, as it involved too much work for the little extra comfort provided, and it took up too much room.

Crow and Blackfoot backrests are very tall and slender, Sioux and Cheyenne not so high but much wider. The decorations are different, too. Crow and Blackfoot backrests are usually bound around the edges with colored flannel, or sometimes buckskin: Sioux and Cheyenne seldom are bound, but usually have the upper ends painted and decorated with tassels.

Although it is not necessary from a practical standpoint, we prefer the old Indian equipment and furnishings for our lodge, and we have one of the few remaining tipis arranged as in early days. At All-American Indian Days in Sheridan, Wyoming, the judges pronounced ours the finest and most complete of the forty lodges on display. In it you can see beautiful parfleche (rawhide) boxes and cases, beaded pouches, bags, and containers, a painted lining, beds of buffalo hides, and skins of various kinds on the floor. At either end of the beds are Cheyenne backrests and pillows of buckskin embroidered with porcupine quills. These pillows were made for us by Mrs. Iron Bull, who remembered seeing some as a little girl. They are so rare now that they are seldom seen even in museums.

Back of the beds were stowed one — or more than one — large rawhide envelope called "parfleche," although parfleche is really the material from which it is made, rather than the article itself. These "Indian suitcases" were used for storing clothing and meat. The clothing cases were usually slightly larger than those for meat. Two such envelopes could be made from one buffalo hide, hence they varied in size. *Parfleche* was a term given by the *voyageurs*, those hardy French explorers, to rawhide. Plains Indian shields were made of heavy rawhide and could turn an arrow — hence the word *parfleche* (from French *parer*, to parry, and *flèche*, arrow). Parfleches were made in pairs, the same design being used on both. In traveling they were carried on the pack saddle, usually one pair on each saddle horn, the Indian pack saddle having two horns. Each horse thus carried two pairs of parfleches hanging on opposite sides of the saddle. Traveling bags were among the few things Indians made identically in pairs.

By following the patterns (Figs. 10–13) you can make a number of "rawhide" cases and bags. The "beaded" ones can all be made of canvas and they can be very practical. Making a set of these is a worthwhile project and they will make your tipi attractive. They can also effectively decorate a "den" in a modern home.

Special bags can be made for different things, such as one for

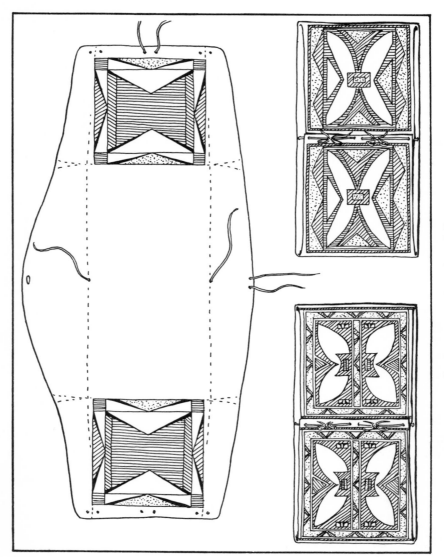

Fig. 10. Parfleches (see color plate following page 206).

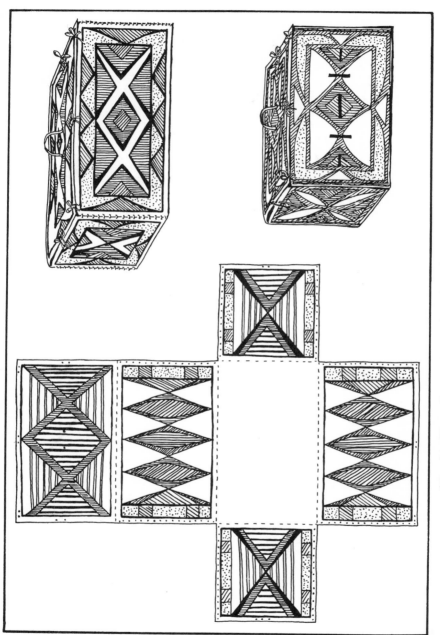

Fig. 11. Sioux Boxes (see color plate following page 206).

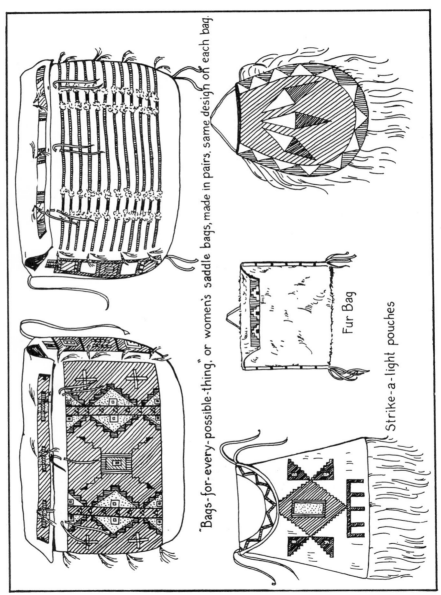

"Bags-for-every-possible-thing," or women's saddle bags, made in pairs, same design on each bag.

Fur Bag

Strike-a-light pouches

Fig. 12. Beaded Bags (see color plate following page 206).

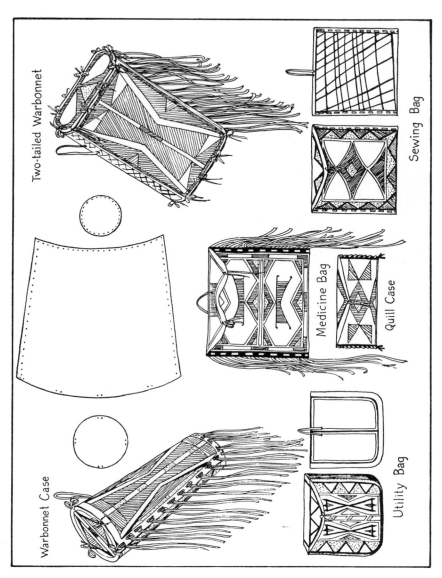

Fig. 13. Rawhide Bags (see color plate following page 206).

Making Parfleche: Using the Flesher to Clean the Hide. Photograph by Gladys Laubin.

toilet articles, another for mending materials, and so on. The "bags for every possible thing" were really women's saddle bags. Men's saddle bags were similar to regular saddle bags, but had long fringes, sometimes an entire deer skin for fringe on each side.

One can make "beaded" bags of painted canvas, fringed with felt or leather (Figs. 12 and 13). Imitation "furniture"—boxes, parfleches, etc.—can be made of cardboard, painted with tempera paint, then coated with a dull-finish varnish. They will look almost like the actual thing. Furniture like this, although not very practical, will make a lodge cozy and beautiful. If real ones of rawhide are preferred a considerable project is involved. To my knowledge, no one has fully reported the Indian method of making rawhide. It has been attempted by several authors, but they have left out im-

Making Parfleche: Using the Hand Scraper to Finish Flesh Side of Hide. Photograph by Gladys Laubin.

portant steps that produce a white and flexible rawhide instead of something hard, horny, and yellow.

Since the first edition of this book was published, other books and pamphlets have appeared supposedly reporting the process of making and decorating Indian rawhide. Not one of them, so far, has yet done an adequate job, and we are convinced that no one can make rawhide that even approaches the beautiful old Indian material in either texture or appearance by trying to follow their instructions. The authors had good intentions but apparently had never tried to make rawhide themselves and had never actually seen the Indians make it. There are few Indians today who know how to do it. The old ladies who taught us were the last with actual experience, and most of them had not made a rawhide article in twenty years before we knew them, which means that almost no rawhide work has been done in the last fifty years. On the other

Making Parfleche: Removing Hair with Wakintka *(Elk Antler Handle).* Photograph by Gladys Laubin.

hand, we have made dozens of articles that look exactly like the finest old Indian specimens, and we have letters from many people who have followed our instructions and obtained similar results.

Making Indian rawhide is not easy, but it is fascinating. The sign for "work" in Indian sign language refers to working on a hide! But the operations are simple, and working on a hide does not have to be the smelly, disagreeable work that it has often been considered. The main thing in this respect is to start with a fresh hide, obtained directly from the butcher. It *should not be salted*. Rawhide is a wonderful material to work with. You can do more things with it than with almost any other material. For Plains Indians it served the same purposes that wood, nails, string, and glue do for us.

Mrs. Goes Ahead, or Pretty Shield, whose husband had been one of the Crow scouts for Custer, showed us much about making

Painting the Medicine Tipi. Photograph by Gladys Laubin.

and painting rawhide. We got a steer hide from a local butcher and put it in the Little Horn River to soak, tying it with a rope to a stake pounded into the river bank. It was there for nearly three weeks and several times we were tempted to cut the rope and let it float down the river, we were getting so discouraged. Although the old lady had promised to help us and lived only a short distance from our tipi, we could not seem to get together. But we decided to go over to her cabin once more to see her.

Through her daughter as interpreter, we asked if she wanted to walk over to our camp, or if we should come and get her with the car. The answer was, "Yes."

Moral: do not ask a double question. Anyway, we went after her the next day. She was delighted and finally came to help us, seeming to enjoy it as much as we did.

For heavy articles, such as parfleches, boxes, and moccasin

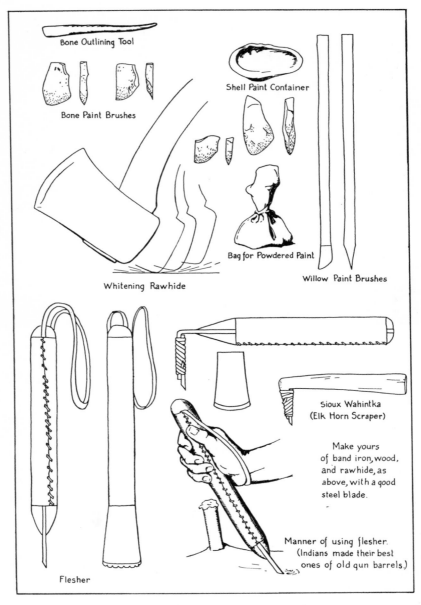

Bone Outlining Tool

Bone Paint Brushes

Shell Paint Container

Bag for Powdered Paint

Whitening Rawhide

Willow Paint Brushes

Sioux Wahintka
(Elk Horn Scraper)

Make yours
of band iron, wood,
and rawhide, as
above, with a good
steel blade.

Manner of using flesher.
(Indians made their best
ones of old gun barrels.)

Flesher

Fig. 14. Rawhide-making Tools.

Fig. 15. Dehairing a Hide.

soles, use a steer or cow hide. For small bags and cases and drum-heads use calf or yearling hide.

1. Soak the hide in water, preferably warm, a day or more, until thoroughly soft.

2. On a flat, level piece of ground, stake out the hide, flesh side up. Use stakes every 10 or 12 inches. Work from opposite points, a stake on one side, then one on the opposite side.

3. In recent times fleshers have been made of old gun barrels. Previously they were made from a leg bone of elk or buffalo. Make yours of a piece of strap or band iron. For comfort in handling, set

Steps in Making a Rawhide Bonnet Case. Photographs by Gladys Laubin.

Pattern in Green.

Yellow added.

Red added.

Black (dark brown) outlines and little triangles sharpen finished case.

it in a wooden handle. Use the heaviest wood you can get, for the heavier the flesher the better it works. That is why the flattened gun barrels were so good. The handle should be covered with wet rawhide and sewn up but, since you do not have any rawhide yet, you may have to use adhesive tape, or something of the kind, temporarily. Using this flesher, held in the position shown in the drawing (Fig. 14), scrape and hack off all fat and excess tissue. This is hard, backbreaking work, but just think of the beautiful things you can make of that finished rawhide!

4. When you are satisfied that the hide is smooth and clean, wash it thoroughly with yellow soap. (Indians used soap made from yucca roots, sometimes called soapweed.) Do this several times and rinse by pouring fresh water over it. Indians sometimes used the top cut from a tin can as a scraper to work the soap thoroughly into the hide. Stubborn bits of tissue can be removed, and soiled spots, spots where dirt has been ground into the hide, can be cleaned with this scraper. Allow the hide to dry and bleach in the sun a couple of days. *It is important that all fat and grease have been removed!*

5. If the hide is a heavy one, you need only pull up the stakes and turn it over to take the hair off. If it is light, it will need soaking again and restaking, hair side up, as it will buckle under the hide-scraper otherwise. Be sure there are no stones, sticks, or other irregularities under the hide.

6. Remove the hair with the scraper, called *wahintka* by the Lakota. This is really an adze and is used with both hands in a sort of sidewise movement (Fig. 15). The Indian ones were made of elk antler. You can get the same effect by making one of band iron, similar to the flesher, but bent at a right angle. The blade should be of good steel and very sharp. Traders used to sell the Indians iron blades, but they weren't nearly as good as steel ones and wore out quickly, encouraging the sale of new ones. You will have to touch up this blade occasionally as you work. For a few times all you have to do is stroke off the burr with the back of a table knife. But sometimes you will have to sharpen it thoroughly with a file and whetstone. If your tool is good and sharp, removing the hair is not difficult.

7. To finish the rawhide and make it really Indian-like, you have still one more process. Indian rawhide is not horny and yellow, like what we usually think of as rawhide. It is creamy white, opaque, and pliable, almost like alum-tanned leather.

Remove the stakes, keeping the hide hair side up, and lay it on a thick mat of rugs or papers. The mat should be firm, not too soft. Indians used old skins for theirs. Use a full-sized axe, one which has the back rounded rather than sharply squared. It has been reported that the whitening is done by pounding, but you could pound the rawhide from now till doomsday and never get it white and soft. Here comes the little trick that no one has explained before. The "pounding" consists of using short, glancing blows (see Fig. 14) with the back of the axe. These blows must be overlapped, so that every square inch of the hide is covered, just like planishing a bowl in metalworking. Before you get through with this job, you will probably wish you had never heard of Indian rawhide, but the results should be worth all you have put into it. You will have a beautiful material from which you can make many fine craft articles. If you can stake out a raw hide during weather when nights are frosty, you will find that a few nights of frost on the damp hide will whiten it and give it a similar texture to that of the pounding, thus saving a lot of hard work.

The best paint brushes for working on rawhide and leather are made from the spongy bone of a beef joint. Next time you have a soup bone with the big knuckle joint, save it. Boil it until it is perfectly white and clean. A little household cleanser in the water will clean it faster.

1. After it is thoroughly dry, split the joint into small pieces with a sharp hand axe. *Be careful,* for it is easy to glance off of it! With a sharp jackknife shape the pieces like the "brushes" in the drawing (Fig. 14). Keep the pores of the bone as perpendicular as possible. They suck up the paint and act almost like a fountain pen. By using these brushes edgewise, you can get a very fine line. By turning them the wide way, you get a wide line. They work just like artists' lettering pens. You can make similar brushes of willow sticks, but they are not as good because they do not soak up the paint. You have to dip them constantly. You should have at least one brush for each color.

2. You can use tempera paints as the best substitute for old-time Indian paints. The casein tempera paints are still better, for they are water resistant when dry. Indians mixed powdered pigments with water and a little glue made by boiling the tendons of a buffalo or beef leg. The Crows molded the paint into little flat, round cakes, and drew with the edges of these cakes, as well as

with the bone brushes. They added a little sugar when mixing the paint for the cakes.

3. Indians painted the hide after step 4 in making Indian rawhide, while it was still damp. Staked out flat this way, and quite hard and firm, it was almost like drawing on a table. Pretty Shield had us cut a number of straight willow sticks to be used as rulers. She insisted we use them, even though each of us can make straight lines without a ruler. She planned a whole design by laying these sticks to form the patterns.

Lay the entire hide out for the various articles to be cut from it and paint them all at the same time, before cutting them out. Work the paint right into the tissue with the bone or wooden brushes. No white man's brush will do this job properly.

4. After the paint and the hide were thoroughly dry, Indians went over the designs with the juice of the prickly pear cactus. The spines were cut off, the cactus split in two, and each half used as a sort of sponge, lightly patted on the surface, giving it a thin coat of "varnish." The easiest way to get the same results is to go over the design with a rubbed-effect or dull-finish varnish, thinned about 50/50 with turpentine. Indian rawhide designs should not be glossy. The designs should be of the same texture as the hide itself to have the charm of real Indian work.

5. After hide, paint, and varnish have dried, then the Indians turned the hide over, took the hair off, and whitened the hide with the beating process. But we have found that the rest of us poor mortals, who lack the years of experience and tradition of the Indian artist, get better results by doing the painting *after* the rawhide is fully made. After finishing step No. 7 of making rawhide, cut out the article you intend to make, dampen it slightly with water, but not enough to allow it to get soft and rubbery and out of shape, and apply your designs on the flesh side. If you run into a rough spot, one where you discover you didn't get all the excess tissue removed, use the top-of-the-tin-can scraper. Work over the spot, then wet it again and smooth it down with your fingers. After the paints have dried, varnish, as directed above.

The same bone brushes used for painting rawhide are best for painting tanned leather. First, incise the design in the leather with a bone outlining tool or a nut pick, then apply the color with the "brush." When the color has dried, go over it with glue made from a tendon. The glue can be applied with another "brush." Dried commercial hide glue can be used. Soak it in water until it becomes jelly-like, then heat it in a pan of water until it becomes thin. For painting on hide, it should be only warm, never hot, as for working in wood. When the glue is nearly dry, rub it in with the outlining tool, making four steps in the application of every color. It is tedious, but no other way of painting on leather that we have tried has been as successful.

MAKING BUCKSKIN

For beautiful, white buckskin, only the best, prime skins will do. Poorer grades can be used for smoked tan. Any soft tanned leather, especially Indian tanned leather is spoken of as buckskin, although the name originally applied only to deer skin. Doe skin is the same thing, only it is thinner and softer than buck skin. If you have a deer skin or a calf skin available and want to make buckskin you will need the following items.

You should have a beaming log, which can be any kind of wood but should be at least six inches in diameter and larger is still better. This log should be about six or eight feet long, peeled of bark on one end, and should be perfectly smooth. Let the other end rest on the ground and support the peeled end about waist high on a pair of crossed poles. These poles can be cut from an old tipi pole or from a dead lodge pole pine, or any kind of small dead tree, for that matter.

For a beaming tool the ulna, the inner bone of the deer's lower foreleg, makes a good one. A beef rib also works well, as does the back of a steel draw knife.

You will also need some brains, and some Indians also use liver in tanning. The brains and liver can come from any animal, but a deer has just enough brains to tan its own hide, which seems to be a rather thoughtful provision of nature. The Indian hunter saved the brains of whatever animal he killed for his wife to use for tanning later on. The liver was considered a delicacy. It was either not available at all, or only in small quantities, to add to the brains for tanning.

If the hide has been freshly skinned it will be soft and damp. Throw it over the beaming log, flesh side up, and scrape all flesh and loose tissue from it, using the beaming tool rather than the flesher used for heavier hides, as in making parfleche.

If it is a dry hide, it should have been well fleshed before drying, or at least thoroughly salted. Salt does not seem to adversely affect a hide for tanning as it does for making parfleche; so, if it is a dry hide, soak it in water for several days. Running water is best if a stream is near by, but a tub, or even a hole in the ground will do, as long as you keep water in it to cover the hide. If it is a fresh hide, do the same thing with it after fleshing and cleaning it.

Often this is all that is necessary to slip the hair on a deer skin, but if it does not come out easily, sprinkle the wet hair with wood ashes (from hard wood are best), roll it up, hair inside, being sure the ashes are in contact with the hair every place, and put it in a cool, shady place for a couple of days more. You will almost certainly have to treat a calf skin in this way, or you may want to soak it in a solution of 10 pounds of lime to 5 gallons of water until the hair slips. When the hair will slip readily, rinse out the ashes (or lime) in clear water, place the hide over the log, and push the hair off with your beaming tool. For a good Indian tan, push off the top scarf skin (grain) and the hair. If there is a layer of black under the hair scrape it off, too. If you run into stubborn spots, sprinkle a little dry wood ash over them and try again.

Sometimes Indians dried the brains and put them away for future use, in which case they had to be soaked in water until soft again. Whether dry or fresh brains are used, they must be squeezed and pulverized between the fingers into warm water, and stirred around until the solution is smooth. If you want to add some liver, boil it first for about an hour and mash it up with the brains, but for a pure white buckskin the brains alone are best. For a heavy hide, like buffalo, both brains and liver should be used. Both contain lecithin, which is probably the valuable material in the solution that does the tanning.

The solution should be made in a container large enough to hold the skin. After thoroughly rinsing out all the wood ashes from the skin, it should be immersed in the solution, soaked and worked around in it until thoroughly saturated, then left to soak over night.

I have seen Grandma Yellowtail make the solution a little thicker, like a mash, then smear it thoroughly over both sides of the hide (which had been well soaked and plumped up in water), roll it up and place it in the shade again for a couple of days. Next she would rinse it well in clear water, wringing it out about eight times, and hang it up in the shade until nearly dry. She then would put a pole across a corner of the fence and work the skin over it.

She pulled and stretched it in her hands, sawed it over the pole again, did more pulling and stretching until the skin came out soft and velvety and nearly white. When doing a large buck or an elk she would get some other old lady to help her and they would stretch and pull it between them, bracing each other with their feet. If they found spots that would not soften properly, they were dampened and the brain mash was smeared on them again, and the hide was rolled and put in the shade for another day. Occasionally, a difficult hide will require repeating the entire process 3 or 4 times.

Sometimes a skin was tightly laced to a square four-pole frame after the brain treatment and nearly or completely softened by using a kind of heavy wooden paddle. It is two and a half or three feet long. It is worked over the hide from both sides until it becomes soft. The paddle is held as if holding a canoe paddle, the lower edge of the blade being pressed and rubbed hard against the skin.

The earth-lodge village tribes handled buffalo hides in this way but the typical Plains Indians merely used stakes in the ground, as for making parfleche. To tan a large hide, like buffalo or elk, the wet hide was staked out, the brain and liver solution rubbed in with the hands and with a round, smooth stone, and the hide was left in the sun until nearly dry, the heat helping the mash to penetrate; then it was saturated with water, which had also been warmed in the sun, the stakes were pulled up, and the hide was rolled up and put in the shade for a couple of days. After this it was pulled and stretched by two women, then spread out again and gone over carefully with a rough stone—pumice stone when available—and, finally, pulled over a three-cornered stake, or through a heavy loop of rope or thong fastened to the under side of a spare tipi pole, set up at an angle.

Robes with the hair on were treated in the same way except that the tanning solution was smeared only on the flesh side. For ease in handling, a large hide was sometimes split down the middle, tanned in two sections, and sewed together again.

Buckskin, for any utilitarian purpose, must be smoked, as the white skin will become stiff and hard upon wetting and will never soften up nicely again. Dig a hole in the ground, oval or round, about a foot across and a foot deep, kindle a chip fire and let it burn down to a good bed of coals. Using large stitches sew up the skin into a cone and hang it from a tripod set above the fire pit and stake it down around the bottom of the cone. Do not do this while the fire is blazing, for it will ruin the skin. Before finishing the staking, smother the coals with chips of green alder, willow or birch, rotten pine or fir, sprinkle water on until a heavy smoke is produced, and finish staking the skin down. The kind of wood used will determine the color to some extent. Alder gives a reddish tinge. Dry willow makes a yellowish color and green willow will produce a more brownish color.

Still another way of smoking skins is to make a low frame, like a tiny sweat lodge, over the pit. When the smoke becomes thick and strong, lay the skin over this frame for a few minutes, until it shows a uniform shade as dark as you want it; then turn it over and do the same on the other side.

If using the sewed-up cone method, leave it over the smudge for ten to twenty minutes, depending upon the shade you want, and upon the size and the thickness of the skin. In this case you will have to check by opening the seam a trifle, and when it is right, pull up the stakes, turn the cone inside out, rehang it from the tripod and stake it down again for the same length of time. In the meantime, while making the changeover, you may have to replenish the fuel and make some more smoke.

If you prefer, you can make the fire to one side and shovel hot coals into the pit to start the smoking.

The smoked buckskin is not impervious to water but it will not get stiff. If it does stiffen up a little bit it will soften up easily again with a little rubbing, which the unsmoked skin will not do.

MOCCASINS

To really enjoy the tipi you should wear moccasins inside. Shoes just will not do. Not only are they uncomfortable to sit around in but are hard on your furs and rugs or whatever floor covering you have. Not even sneakers are a good substitute. We have heard from a number of young people who say that they enjoy wearing moccasins almost as much as living in the tipi.

There are still some people who are afraid to wear moccasins because they think they will develop flat feet, or that their feet will become too wide. Both of these fears are unfounded. In the first place, to have healthy feet they should be allowed to spread out as far as they want to; so wearing a confining shoe is of no intelligent consideration. Man originally walked on bare feet and wearing moccasins is the next thing to this. It is not what you wear on your feet that makes you flat-footed, but how you walk. If you walk with your feet straight ahead, the weight on the balls of the feet, you will not need to worry about flat feet. Use your heels only as rockers to finish the stride. I have been wearing moccasins most of my life and I do not have flat feet. I had a tendency towards this affliction before I started to wear moccasins and I overcame it by learning to walk correctly—like an Indian. I have never known an Indian old-timer who had flat feet.

During our early years on the Sioux reservations moccasins were one of the few items of Indian apparel still to be seen. Even so, there were few beaded pairs, as beads were too expensive and the people too poor to buy them. They were even rare among the dancers. Consequently, one of the finest gifts a person could make was a pair of nice beaded moccasins. Indian friends were always giving Gladys moccasins. Her feet are so small that they never had any to fit her, so they gave her moccasins that fit me. This was an Indian way of making us both happy.

We once attended a dance at Cannon Ball held in honor of Isaac Manka, who was leaving soon for the army. Gladys invited him to dance with her in the Kahomni Dance. Afterward, the Master of Ceremonies announced, "Maude Young Eagle is giving Wíyaka Wastewín (Gladys) the moccasins she is wearing in honor of her brother, the young man all of us are honoring tonight." Maude had on the only beaded moccasins at the gathering and told Gladys she would give them to her the next day.

Gladys told Flying Cloud that she did not want to take Maude's only pair of beaded moccasins, but Flying Cloud replied, "Remember, to be a good Indian you must learn to receive as well as to give."

So the next day Gladys was delighted when Maude's daughter brought her the moccasins. We have never forgotten the Indians' sense of generosity or Flying Cloud's counsel.

Almost everyone we have met has asked us either where to buy or how to make a pair of moccasins. Even if he did not want them for walking he wanted them in place of house slippers.

There are many places where you can buy beautifully beaded but expensive moccasins. Full beaded ones are now bringing fifty to seventy-five dollars a pair. For practical use you can make a pair yourself at very little cost, that will wear as well as an average pair of shoes.

The Sioux style moccasin is the simplest to make and the best for ordinary use. All Plains Indian moccasins are very much like the Sioux, only slight tribal differences in pattern and decoration being evident. Some tribal shapes did differ enough that if a full track could be found a tracker might have been able to tell to what tribe the wearer belonged, but the kind of design and appearance of the moccasin would immediately indicate its tribal origin.

Many writers have described the making of moccasins, but to our minds either they have been so limited in detail that you have to figure everything for yourself, or they have been too complicated. The Indian women whom we have watched just seem to make a pattern by eye, and when making moccasins for themselves and their families, with whose feet they are familiar, they do a perfect job. But when making moccasins to sell, for feet they have never seen, they sometimes do not do as well.

I have been making moccasins since I was sixteen years old and I also have taught at summer camps where I have made patterns for hundreds of boys and girls. So I have developed a system that seems simple enough to me and I hope I can describe it satisfactorily to you, for it has never failed. The moccasins always fit.

The true moccasin is the puckered-toe type from the Eastern Woodlands, but if a reasonably soft leather, like lightweight harness or saddle leather, is used for the soles, the Sioux moccasin will serve just as well, with the additional advantages that it is easier to make and can be resoled several times. Some writers believe the rawhide soled moccasin did not come into being until about 1850, but Lewis and Clark reported them in 1805. The Journals say, ". . . the prickly pear of the open plains, which have now become so abundant that it is impossible to avoid them, and the thorns are so strong that they pierce a soal (sic) of dressed deer skin; the best resource against them is a soal of buffalo hide in parchment."[1] Catlin, between 1830 and 1840 also mentioned parfleche soles. But they may not have completely replaced the soft-soled moccasin on the plains until about 1850, by which time the

---

[1]James K. Hosmer, ed. *History of the Expedition of Captains Lewis and Clark, 1804–6*, 332.

tribes were well supplied with steel awls, needles and knives, making rawhide or parfleche much easier to handle.

For material, buckskin is the best for the uppers, but as a cheap and satisfactory substitute you can use cowhide splits. These are available at any good leather dealer. Sheepskin suede is no good for a moccasin. Calfskin would be good but probably as expensive as real buckskin. Whatever leather you use should have a little "give" to it. On real Indian leather the grain is always removed, so to get this effect with commercial leather it should be used with the suede side out—the suede side for the good side. Some poor old Indians we knew on the reservations years ago were using canvas for uppers. You might try it as an experiment.

We have already mentioned leathers that make satisfactory soles. They should be about an eighth of an inch thick. I still prefer soles made of Indian rawhide, which has already been described, as wearing the best. If you decide to use it you must do some more to it to prepare it for soles. Cut out a couple of heavy pieces a little larger than the soles are to be. Dampen them until they are flexible, roll them, and pound them with the back of an ax; then soak them in soapy water (yellow soap), until thoroughly soft. While still wet, coat both sides liberally with neats-foot oil. Indians also use lard, or even bacon grease for this. Allow them to become almost dry; then roll and pound them some more. In other words, they are first rolled up and then pounded while rolled. Do not cut out the final soles until thoroughly dry.

For tools you will need an awl, needles, number 10 linen thread, or a good nylon thread (Eskimos now use Dental floss), and either genuine beeswax or a shoemaker's wax. The best awl is a slightly curved, three-cornered shoemaker's awl. Depending upon the way you are to do the sewing, to be explained later on, you will need either a blunt shoemaker's needle or a three-cornered glover's needle. All of these things can be obtained at a shoefinding supply house, a good leather shop or a craft supply house.

Before cutting into a good piece of leather, make a pattern of heavy wrapping paper.

1. Draw the outline of your *larger* foot. Everyone has one foot slightly larger than the other. Usually it's the right one, but I have to be different. Mine's the left. Keep the pencil straight up and down and your weight on your foot, so that you draw it and measure it full size. Before lifting the foot, measure over the instep with a strip of paper. Do this from the floor, up over the

SIOUX MOCCASINS

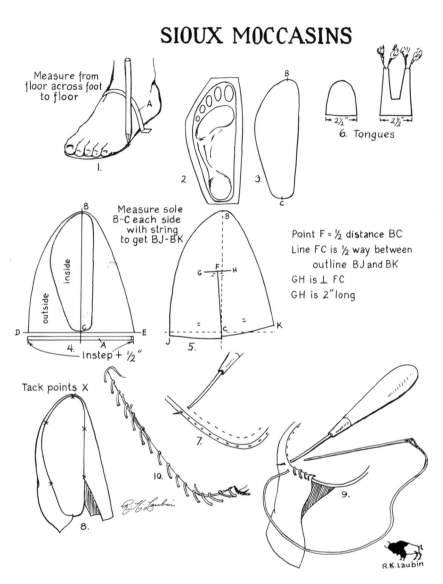

Measure from floor across foot to floor

1.

2.

3.

B

C

6. Tongues

2½"   2½"

Measure sole B-C each side with string to get BJ-BK

inside

outside

B

C

D   A   E

4.   Instep + ½"

B

G   F   H

J   5.   C   K

Point F = ½ distance BC
Line FC is ½ way between outline BJ and BK
GH is ⊥ FC
GH is 2" long

Tack points X

8.

7.

10.

9.

R.K. Laubin

Fig. 16. Making Sioux Moccasins.

instep and back to the floor again. Add half an inch to this measurement and lay this paper strip, A, aside for a moment.

2. The finished sole outline should look like the drawing (Fig. 16), about 1/8 inch wider all around than the actual outline of the foot. The line from heel to toe on the arch side is straight. Do not worry about this. It shapes to your foot as you wear it and protects this sensitive part from sharp stones and stubs.

3. The final sole pattern should look like this. Mark the center of the toe and heel, B and C.

4. On another piece of paper, large enough for an upper, draw two lines, one horizontal, DE, one perpendicular to it, BC. Lay the sole pattern on the perpendicular line, so that the center points B and C line up with it. Lay off half of the instep measurement, A, on each side of C, on line DE. This measurement, A, is the widest part of the upper. By eye, sketch the outline of the upper to correspond with the drawing. Do not make it too full at the toe. With a piece of string measure the edge of the sole, from B to C, both sides; then fit the string to the corresponding edges of the upper, BD and BE.

5. The sole measurements, checked with the string on the outlines of the upper, will probably come out below line DE on the long side of the foot and above on the short side, as indicated in the drawing by lines BJ and BK — the finished outline of the upper. A very high-arched, broad foot may come out differently, but the same procedure of measuring is followed. Locate point F half way between B and C and half way between the outer edges of the upper. A ruler laid across the upper approximately at F will indicate this halfway point accurately enough. The tongue opening, GH, is perpendicular to the ankle opening, FC. These lines, GH and FC, are cut when the outline of the upper is cut out. The points J and K are the heel points of the upper.

6. Cut a tongue pattern, as indicated, whichever style you prefer. When your patterns are complete you can cut them out of the material you intend to use. Merely reverse them for lefts and rights.

Now is the time to decorate the uppers if you care to (Fig. 17). Personally, we prefer plain moccasins for everyday wear, but if they are to be decorated now is the time to bead or paint them. Painting is easy. Use either artists oil colors, with enough Japan dryer added to dry them quickly, ten cent store enamels or acrylics. Be sure the paint is thoroughly dry before sewing them.

Fig. 17. Decorating the Mocca-sins.

Sew a tongue on each upper to the slit, GH, using waxed linen thread in an over and over stitch, the seam to come on the inner side of the finished moccasin. You will notice that the base of the tongue is 1/2 inch wider than the slit cut in the upper where it is to be attached. Center the tongue so it projects 1/4 inch beyond each end of the slit, which will make certain that there are no gaps when the moccasin is tied on the foot.

7. Trace the sole pattern on the leather you have selected, or on the rawhide you have prepared. *Do not forget to reverse the pattern for the other foot.* Cut out the soles with a sharp knife and mark the center points, B and C, just as on the paper pattern. If using rawhide, the sole should be soaked again only long enough to soften it. For a beginner, the best procedure is to punch all the holes in the sole first. Once you have made some moccasins this will not be necessary, but it helps for a start. The flesh side of the sole is to be the inside, or next to the foot. Using the awl, make holes about 1/8 of an inch apart and about 3/16 inch from the edge, pushing the awl out through the *edge* of the sole.

8. Place an upper, *outer side up,* and on it lay the corresponding sole, *inner side up.* Bring the point B of the upper over B of the sole and tack it there with a thread, tied temporarily but tightly. It will help to tack the upper to the sole at the other points marked.

These tacks should be removed as they are approached in the sewing. The moccasin is sewed wrong side out.

Indian women sew moccasins to the right, *away* from them, whereas we are usually taught to sew towards ourselves. It soon becomes obvious, however, that in moccasin making, sewing to the right helps us to see where our stitches are going. Also, there is less danger of stretching the upper out of shape when going to the right. The way you set your stitches has a great deal to do with whether the upper fits the sole or not. Making the stitches straight across keeps the sole and upper even. If for any reason it is necessary to stretch the upper a bit, pointing the stitches towards you and tightening the thread by pulling it away from you will do it. Reversing this, that is, by pointing the stitches away from you and pulling towards you, will shrink the upper.

Since you have already punched the awl holes in the sole, you can sew the upper to it with a glover's needle. It is very sharp, so be careful to push it through past the cutting edge before trying to pull it through or you will cut your fingers.

An accomplished moccasin maker does not need to punch holes in the sole first but does all the sewing at once. When using thread, you would then use a blunt, shoemaker's needle, first pushing the awl through both the sole and the upper, then following with the blunt needle and thread. The number 10 linen thread should be doubled before inserting it in the eye of the needle, so that the finished thread is four strands thick, and thoroughly waxed. Indian women sew with sinew and for dry weather this does the neatest job, but it is not good for wet weather. For the novice, thread is not only easier to use, but more satisfactory in wearing qualities. This is one of the few cases where the old Indian way can be improved upon.

9. and 10. These drawings show the sewing procedure and the way of splicing in a new thread, without knots that might hurt the feet. Note: Each moccasin is started the same way and sewn to the right, which means that on one moccasin you start on the long side of the upper, on the other you start on the short side.

The sewing starts at the heel and goes all the way around. When back to the heel again, continue up the back and the moccasin is finished except for turning. Turning is not difficult on a large moccasin but is sometimes troublesome on a small one. Indians often used a special tool, a flat stick with a rounded end about the shape of the moccasin toe, for this job, but it is not necessary. By pushing in the toe with your thumb you can gradually work in more and more of the turning and suddenly the job is done. Last step is to punch holes or cut little slits for the thongs, as shown in step 5 of Figure 16, and on the illustration of the finished moccasins (Fig. 17), and insert the thongs as shown.

A leather sole is soft enough to give no great trouble and the rawhide sole should remain flexible enough to work well too. If it has become too stiff, dampen it again with a wet hand, trying not to wet the upper, and it will usually come through all right.

A moccasin should fit like a glove. Therefore it may be hard to put on the first time, but if you have cut your pattern according to directions it should fit just right. Work in onto the toe, gradually to the instep, and then the heel will slide in without difficulty. Buckskin and some other leathers are bound to stretch, so that even though the moccasin does fit like a glove at first, it will probably loosen up a great deal. Crow women are so fond of tight moccasins that they may remake a pair two or three times, trimming a little off of the uppers each time. We don't expect you to be as fussy as that but hope you will get them to fit well. Both Crows and Sioux often put new moccasins on while the sole is still damp to help them shape to the foot.

After you have made one pair of moccasins you may want to try another—a little more fancy pair, with a welt all around the sole. The finest Indian moccasins were made this way, but we would not advise it for a first attempt. To add a welt, cut a thong about 1/4 inch wide from the same leather you use for the uppers and long enough to go generously all the way around the moccasin. Feed it in, holding it between the upper and the sole, sewing through it as you sew upper and sole together. Any excess is cut off when you get completely around and before you start sewing up the back. After the moccasin is turned right side out the exposed welt can be trimmed close to the moccasin. It hides the stitches and makes a truly neat looking job.

Sometimes we add a cuff to the moccasin, as it adds to the appearance and is some protection against sand and dirt when worn turned up. For a cuff all you need is a straight strip of the same leather used for the uppers, three or four inches wide and long enough to go completely around the top with about an inch over on each end. It is sewed on with the same over and over stitch, but with the seams on the *outside* this time.

Sioux men wear no cuffs on their moccasins. The Sioux women

do. Also, only men wear the split tongue, which represents a buffalo hoof. Gladys wanted Mrs. Iron Bull to make her a pair of moccasins with porcupine quill embroidery and the fancy split tongue. Mrs. Iron Bull said she would do it if Gladys wanted them that way, but she added, "I want you to know we women don't wear tongues like that!"

The Crow men do wear cuffs on their moccasins, turned up for practicality, down for looks. With this exception and a difference in type of design for decoration, there is almost no difference between Sioux and Crow men's moccasin patterns. Crow women wear a very high-topped moccasin, sometimes a foot high, like a boot, only the top fits the leg, much like a stocking. Kiowa and Comanche, and even some Southern Cheyenne women's moccasins are made in similar fashion, but they are buttoned in place with little German silver buttons instead of being held in place with long thongs, as the Crow moccasins are. Shoshoni women also use the buttoned high-top moccasins. Sioux, Northern Cheyenne and Arapaho women wore beaded leggings which came down over the moccasin top.

Indians sewed their moccasins with sinew from deer or buffalo. Buffalo sinew is longer and heavier and is satisfactory for moccasins, but it is not as good for beadwork as deer, mountain sheep or goat. Horse or cow sinew can also be used, and mountain lion sinew was considered by some to be best of all. But for today's moccasins, the waxed linen thread is even better, as it withstands water and is easier to handle. However, if you would like to try using real sinew, it should not be too difficult to obtain if you do any hunting or have some hunter friends.

Most non-Indian hunters destroy the sinew in butchering, but it is not necessary to do so. The sewing sinew lays along both sides of the spine, starting over the ribs and running down into the loin. To obtain it, make a rather deep cut along the spine, reach in with your fingers and locate the strip of ligament, which on a deer will be 2 1/2 to 3 inches wide at its upper end, tapering to a point in the loin, total length being as much as two feet. It is very thin and milky white, tough, fibrous and slippery. By getting your fingers under this strip of sinew you can pull it up and out, gently working it free, sometimes assisting with a sharp knife, being careful not to cut the strip. Work from the center each way, cutting the wide end over the ribs free and working the other direction to free the point from the loin. There are, of course, two such strips in each animal. Good sinew has often been ruined by cutting it off too short.

The sinew thus obtained should be carefully scraped and cleaned and stretched out to dry. When dry, it can be easily shredded into threads of any desired width, again working from near the center towards each end. The end of the thread coming from the point of the strip will itself be a fine, delicate point. The thread is then softened in water (Indians put it in their mouths), the point being left out to remain hard, for it is the needle. The thread is then rubbed on the thigh, rolling it with the palm of the hand into a quite round shape. Holes are punched with a sharp awl into the material to be sewn; then the sharp end of the thread is inserted into the hole and pulled through. Good Indian beadworkers and seamstresses can sew almost as fast in this way as most people can with a needle and thread.

Moccasins such as we have been describing are not waterproof, but if made of commercial chrome tanned leather wetting will not harm them. If sewn with sinew, the sinew will soften up and come apart. This is why the waxed linen thread is better for all around use. Indians, as a rule, did not wear moccasins in the rain. They went barefooted. Woodland Indians often went barefooted anyway, but no man was so poor that he did not carry a pair of pretty moccasins on his belt, so he could "dress up" when he arrived back at camp.

Some Indians, notably Shoshoni, took their moccasins off when smoking a ceremonial pipe, and all Indians, when holding a Sun Dance or a medicine fast, removed their moccasins.

For winter wear moccasins were often made of buffalo hide, with the hair inside. Some even wore an "overshoe"—an outer moccasin with the hair outside, which did shed water and was almost waterproof. At least, with hair inside and outside and the feet nice and warm, there was no danger of frostbite when getting the feet wet in cold weather. Nowadays the Indians wear rubbers or arctics over their moccasins in wet weather.

When moccasins were worn in bad weather they were made of smoked buckskin, which, although not waterproof, was unaffected by water. Woodland Indians wearing moccasins with puckered toes, did not get the sinew wet enough when walking on wet ground to do any harm. Even Plains Indians, prior to 1850, made a one piece moccasin of soft leather, with a seam on the side.

Now, after reading all this, if you decide you do not have time or do not care to make your own moccasins, a Navajo style moccasin is available commercially. This would be mixing tribes up pretty much, but they are comfortable and wear well, too. Actually, they are not even Navajo, but originated in North Africa and were copied by the Navajo and other Southwestern tribes from the Moorish hostlers who served the Spanish invaders. But that was nearly 500 years ago, so this footgear must have proven its worth to still be popular today. And they are still being worn in North Africa, as we saw them while on tour there.

Now that you have the materials to make furnishings for your tipi, we will return to the proper arrangement of these articles.

In our tipi, from the tripods of the backrests hang war-bonnet cases, also of rawhide, with long buckskin fringes. Hanging from the top of the lining in the rear of the lodge is a bull-hide shield, a tobacco bag, a medicine bag, and several other little pouches. In the corners between backrests are rawhide boxes, which were made in pairs. Also we have beaded saddle bags, both men's and women's varieties. These things, arranged around the inner wall and hanging from the poles make the tipi colorful and attractive.

Everything in the Indian tipi had its proper place. Indians could not afford to be messy or careless when it might have been necessary to pack and move camp at a moment's notice. Religious and sacred objects were stored and hung in the rear of the lodge, the place of honor, called the *chatku´* by the Sioux. On fine days the man's shield and other medicine articles were hung on a tripod outside, behind the lodge, and were turned periodically so that they always faced the sun. We had a "medicine rack" like this in back of our tipi when we camped with the Blackfeet. Old timers came over to look at it. They said all their painted tipis used to have such racks years ago but hardly anyone bothered any more. They complimented us on our efforts to do things "old time way."

In time of war the shield was often hung on a lacing pin above the door. Among the Crows, the woman usually took care of her husband's shield; but among the Sioux, a woman was not allowed to handle a shield. Other weapons were stored on the north side, although a quiver for bow and arrows might be slung from the backrest. Riding gear was placed north of the door, and women's belongings, food, and household articles on the south side. Wood also was stored near the door, usually on the south side.

Water might hang, in the old days, in a bucket, or more properly a bag, made of the lining of a buffalo paunch. This vessel had a small wooden hoop at the mouth to keep it open, and a stick across this for a handle. It swung from a tipi pole about shoulder height. To drink from it, the Indian put his mouth to the opening and pressed the pouch between his palms to bring the water to the top. Such a vessel might swing from a travois on a march. If kept dry or kept full, it would not rot. In hot weather a sprig of mint was often kept in the water to give it a mild flavor and cooling taste. More recently a wooden keg was used as a water container and today a forty-quart milk can is often used, along with galvanized pails.

If a tipi is made and furnished according to the descriptions we have just given, the finished lodge should be one that few Indians can duplicate today. When it is up and everything is in place, we think you will agree that man never invented a more picturesque dwelling. We particularly like the tipi because we are always in the same home, no matter in what section of the country we may be at the moment. We are not like the housekeepers who always want to try a different arrangement of furniture. We have one favorite way, and our "house" always looks the same. But we suppose the dream of the traveler is to have one home, and the dream of the non-traveler is to have as many homes as possible.

DEDICATING THE LODGE

When a new lodge was dedicated, the owners usually had a "house warming," much as we have today. They made presents to some old and highly respected man, a man known to have power or "good medicine," and asked him to make prayers for the success, happiness, and long life of the occupants, and that the new lodge might shelter them from storms and harm. White Eyes, an old Cheyenne, told us that when his people dedicated a new lodge they invited as many people into it as it would hold and gave them all a big feast. This showed the generosity of the owners and assured them that only good thoughts would be directed toward them in their new home. Presents were made to the women who had made the lodge, and they were especially honored on this occasion.

Grinnell said that when a new lodge was to be dedicated a group of old warriors was selected, who advanced toward the tipi. When a little distance from it they halted, standing or sitting in a large half circle. Their leader then walked to the tipi door and struck the south door pole (one of the three tripod poles) with a stick, reciting a coup.[2] This leader was chosen for having killed an enemy in that enemy's lodge. After counting his coup he turned and entered the new tipi, the others following in order of rank, lesser men coming in last. The new lodge owner then gave a feast to all these brave men. Previously only the women who had been making the tipi could enter it. Now anyone could do so.

Donald A. Cadzow, in his *Indian Notes*,[3] gives an interesting little dedication of a Plains Cree tipi. After the framework was built, but before the cover was put in place, a man named Rock Thunder was called to bless the lodge. He raised "his right hand aloft and facing the east he uttered the following prayer: 'Today is the day I put up my home. I leave you to the care of the four winds. Today is the day you see yourself in my lodge where you can do as you please. We cannot tell you to do this or that; we are only men. You, our Maker, direct us whether it be bad or good; it is your will. Help us to think of you every day we live in this lodge; guard us in our sleep; wake us in the morning with clean minds for the day, and keep harm from us.'" After this invocation the cover was hoisted into place and the tipi made ready for occupancy.

When a young couple was married, it was customary for the bridegroom's "fathers"—his father and his father's brothers—to provide horses for the new household, but the bride's family provided the new tipi and its furnishings. In some tribes the young couple camped with the bride's family, and her husband was expected to contribute to their support. I know this was the custom, and still is, among the Sioux. Among the Blackfeet the newly married couple live near the bridegroom's family.

Among the Blackfeet, also, when the first lodge wore out, the mother always made a new one for her daughter. Of course, a mother never entered her daughter's lodge if her son-in-law was inside.

Every year, when we put up the tipi for the first time, I always make the first fire by friction, using the "rubbing sticks" and bow, or bow drill. Before the coming of the white man with his flint and steel, most tribes made fire merely by spinning a long wooden drill

---

[2]For more information on counting coup, see Reginald and Gladys Laubin, *Indian Dances of North America.*
[3]Pages 19–27.

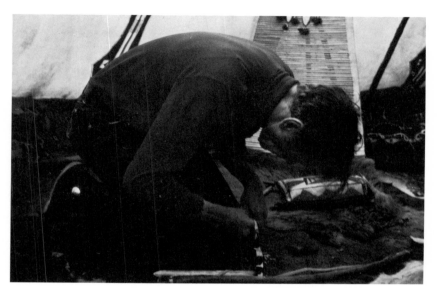

Preparing Fire Board. Cutting Notch.

Starting Socket in Fire Board.

Fire by Friction. Photographs by Gladys Laubin.

Drilling to Create a Spark.

Still Coaxing Spark.

Fire by Friction. Photographs by Gladys Laubin.

Flame for the Sacred Fire.

Fire by Friction. Photographs by Gladys Laubin.

in the hands against a flat fireboard, but this takes great strength in the arms and much practice. It is much simpler to use the method of the Indians around the Great Lakes, who used a bow to spin the drill. With a little practice one can make fire with it in half a minute. We will not go into details of this, as such information can be found in a Boy Scout manual and in a number of woodcraft books. Most Indians made a new, or sacred fire, once a year, when all old fires were extinguished, and fireplaces were cleaned out. Often this was an elaborate ceremony, part of a ritual lasting several days, but just to be a part of this ancient tradition we make our first fire of each new camping season in the old way. We did this for the old folk one time. One Bull said he had heard of it but had never seen it done. In his youth everyone used flint and a fire steel obtained from the traders, and matches were invented during his lifetime, which changed the firemaking habits of people all around the world.

Before the use of flint and steel, a special camp officer, the Fire Keeper, was responsible for carrying fire on the march. A Plains Indian Fire Keeper used a specially prepared buffalo horn in which he carried a live coal packed in punk. The horn had a little hole in the tip, so the fire could "breathe." The Fire Keeper carried this on his belt, or on a sling over one shoulder, in the manner of a powder horn. Tahan, a Kiowa, said you could always tell the Fire Keeper in the line of march because a tiny wisp of smoke came from the horn.

On arrival at the new camp site the Fire Keeper kindled a fire and the women from all the various households obtained a light from it to start the fires in their own tipis. The fire was kept alive until the next camp move. It was allowed to die down at night, and was covered with cold ashes. In the morning the ashes were scraped aside and live coals were still to be found. When burning hard wood, live coals will hold for many hours without any special attention.

TIPI ETIQUETTE

The old-time tipi was a temple as well as a home. The floor of the tipi represented the earth on which we live, the walls of the tipi the sky, and the poles the trails from earth to the spirit world— the links between man and *Wakan' Tanka*, the Great Mystery.

Directly behind the fireplace was a little space of bare earth which served as a family altar. Often this space was prepared in the shape of a square, the sod and all roots and stubs removed, and the earth within the square pulverized and brushed clean. The Sioux called this altar a "square of mellowed earth." It represented Mother Earth, and on this square sweet grass, cedar, or sage were burned as incense to the spirits. The type of incense used on a given occasion depended upon the ceremony as well as what was available, but the burning of incense was an important part of every ceremony. It carried prayers to the Ones Above, as did the smoke from a pipe. Indeed, the pipe itself was often purified in the smoke of incense.

Before a meal the host said a grace and made an offering of a choice piece of meat, either by placing it in the fire, or burying it in the earth on the altar.

Indians had definite rules of etiquette for life in the tipi. If the door was open, friends usually walked right in. If the door was closed, they called out or rattled the door covering and awaited an invitation to enter. Some tipis even had a special door knocker which could be shaken to attract attention within. It will be mentioned later on. A shy person might just cough to let those inside know he was waiting.

One morning about sunrise we were awakened by a gentle scratching on our tipi door. A Crow friend softly called to us that he had something important to tell us.

"Come in," we said, although we were still in bed. He entered and sat at the foot of our bed; then he proceeded to tell us the story of his peyote religion. It seems to be customary to tell of religious experiences early in the morning like this.

A friend of ours once went to visit an old Ute Indian. He knocked several times on the door of the old man's cabin before he got an answer; then he heard, "You guvment agent?"

"No, I'm not a government agent, just a friend," was the answer.

"You not guvment agent?" he asked three more times; then he said, "Okay, come in and eat." The old man was puzzled as to why a friend had to knock at the door before entering.

One time we went to visit Feather Earring, a reknowned old Sioux warrior. By this time we knew enough not to knock on a friend's door, but just as we walked in we caught the old man dropping an egg into the frying pan on his old iron stove. He was rather embarrassed that we saw a famous old warrior getting his own supper, but he laughed about it and said he had had no woman for a long, long time. When we left he gave Gladys a nice old pipe and a beautiful blue beaded tobacco bag which he took out of a battered old trunk in a corner of the cabin. Indians always gave a present to people they liked who came to visit them. We learned that he got his name as a young man because when he went to a dance he wore earrings made of colored fluffy feathers which hung down to his knees. We wish we could have seen him then!

If two sticks were crossed over a tipi door, it meant that the owners either were away or desired no company. If they were away, they first closed the smoke flaps by lapping or crossing them over the smoke hole. The door cover was tied down securely and two sticks were crossed over it. The door was thus "locked," and as safe in Indian society as the most strongly bolted door would be in our civilization today.

On our first visit to the Standing Rock Reservation we stopped at the home of Flying Cloud, who was to be our interpreter, and started to lock the door of the car. "You don't have to lock your car," he said to us. "There aren't any white people around here."

Generally, men sat on the north side of the tipi and women on the south. The owner's seat was against the rear south backrest (Fig. 3c, H). If he had a son, the son's seat was the other backrest, G. If he had no son, this was reserved for guests, and often both rear backrests were given to guests and the host moved farther over to the right so that the guests were on his left, or heart side. On entering a tipi, a man moved to the right to his designated place, a woman to the left. Whenever possible, it was proper to walk behind a seated person, the seated one leaning forward, if necessary. If passing between him and the fire could not be avoided, pardon was asked. In asking such pardon, a kinship term was used. This did not necessarily imply actual relationship, but was a courtesy. To an older person, one would say, "Excuse me, my father," or "my grandfather," etc.; or to a younger person, "Excuse me, brother," or "sister," or "cousin," depending upon how close the acquaintance might be.

There were exceptions to the above placements and movements within the tipi, of course. We remember seeing a sketch by "Fish" Allison, who visited Sitting Bull while he was a prisoner of war at Fort Randall, South Dakota, and we present a similar sketch here (Fig. 18). You will notice that there were occasions

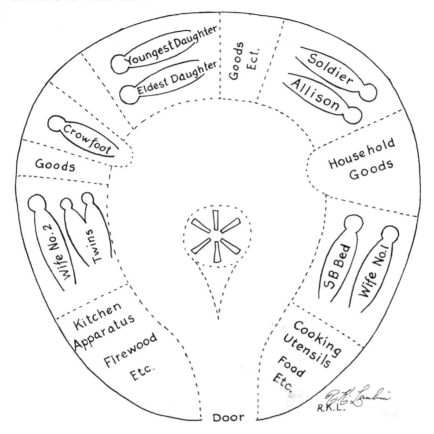

Fig. 18. Plan of Sitting Bull's Tipi.

when women occupied the north side of the tipi—especially in the case of a man having more than one wife.

A Kiowa friend said he remembered his grandfather telling him that everyone entered a tipi to the left and went out by continuing around the circle to the door, as was customary with most tribes when using the sweat lodge. However, Kiowa women were seated on the south side and men on the north, as usual. Continuing around the tipi means that they crossed the back of the lodge, whereas in many tribes the head man of the tipi was the only one to cross the back, behind the altar. Needless to say, no one ever stepped across the altar, or the fire.

We had the tipi all fixed up for a display one time, with visitors coming and going almost all day. We tried to give them brief summaries of tipi etiquette but late in the afternoon one person, paying no attention to our discourse, stepped into the altar in his effort to get to the other side of the tipi. More or less jokingly I called out to him, "You stepped in the altar. Now we'll get a storm."

"Oh, that's a lot of superstition," he said, and deliberately put his foot back in the altar and ground it with his heel.

Somewhat annoyed, but still trying to be nonchalant, we both said, "You just wait and see."

A few minutes later we all noticed a change in the atmosphere. Even seated inside the tipi, the light was different. The sun apparently had gone behind a cloud, but a few minutes before there had been no clouds. The day had been warm and now it was downright hot and stifling, with not a breath of air stirring. When I looked out the tipi door, the sky was an ugly yellow all around the horizon. The smoke flaps gave an occasional flutter, as if there was a little breeze after all; then with no further warning, the storm was upon us. The wind howled and the poles shook and rattled. Tight as the cover was staked down, it nevertheless bellowed in between the poles and strained on the anchor rope so all of us were afraid the tipi would turn wrong side out, like a big umbrella, or come crashing down over us. The lodge was full of visitors but, with the exception of a couple of close friends, everyone suddenly remembered he had left Aunt Minnie home alone, or had left a window open, or had some excuse to leave us in a hurry and head for his car.

One of the friends and I held on to the anchor rope with all our might, and as we stood there in the center of the tipi, the poles were pressing against our shoulders! They had moved in that far and were bent so much! The dust was blowing up behind the dew cloth and underneath where the dew cloth was now loose at the base of the poles, and was so thick we could hardly see across the lodge. The wind blew violently like this for only a few minutes; then there was a lull and we all took advantage of it to grab arm loads of our precious beadwork and parfleche and run to a neighboring log cabin with them. We barely got all these furnishings out of the tipi and in safer quarters, when the wind began again, and this time we abandoned the tipi. The storm blew hard for another hour or more; then it quit as suddenly as it had come.

When we returned to the tipi the next morning we were surprised to find it was still up, but the back was pushed in almost three feet and the anchor rope was so tight you could almost play a bass solo on it. The skins we had left on the floor were almost buried in dirt and the whole thing looked a mess. But we were grateful nothing was torn and no real damage had been done.

We have had similar experiences, though not quite as extreme, on at least two other occasions when people deliberately stamped in the altar after we had warned them that it was supposed to be sacred and a storm was sure to follow. Those people are as "superstitious" about it now as we are, always showing proper respect when visiting us in our tipi, and are first to warn others about this little phase of etiquette when strangers come in. When things like this happen it is easy enough to understand how Indian superstitions developed.

At a feast, the men were served first, and in an all-male gathering, as a warrior-society meeting or a religious ritual, the younger men were appointed to act as servants. The host waited until his guests had been served and had eaten before partaking of the food himself. He urged them to eat heartily and to have more. The guests were expected to eat everything put before them or to invite others to eat it, or to carry it home with them. They offended the host if they refused anything offered to them.

When invited to an Indian feast, one is expected to bring his own dishes and utensils. We think this is a wonderful custom, for it certainly is considerate of the hostess, saving her much work and dishwashing. When we went to a feast in Mrs. Two Bull's lodge, she took the meat from the kettle with a long, pointed stick and placed some on each one's plate. The broth was poured into cups and used as a hot drink. Each individual cut his meat into small strips with his own sharp knife. A strip was held in the fingers, carried to the mouth, and held in the teeth while a small bite was cut off with the knife. This way of eating is not repulsive or vulgar as the Indians do it. In fact, our own ancestors, until the recent invention of the fork, probably ate in the same manner. Indians eat with dignity and politeness.

When a pipe was smoked, it was lighted by the head man, in the rear of the lodge, then smoked to the left as far as the door, whence it was returned without smoking. In a lodge filled with men it continued around to the door on the south side, where the man nearest the door commenced smoking it again and passed it around, again to the left, following the sun, until it came to the opposite side of the door again. In other words, it was smoked only while passing to the left, and the stem was always pointed to the left, no matter which way it was traveling. This was the Indian form of communion. In some ceremonies, if the pipe went out before getting all the way around, it had to be returned to the head man for relighting.

When the host finally cleaned his pipe and laid it aside, that was a signal that the meeting was over and everyone was expected to get up and go home. The ashes from the pipe were reverently placed on the altar in a neat little pile. It was considered bad luck to sprinkle the ashes about. Thus, when Custer entered the Cheyenne camp on his campaign in Kansas to recover two white women captives, the chief, after smoking the pipe, emptied the ashes on the toes of Custer's boots to show his contempt and hostility. Custer probably did not know what this meant, but all the Indians present did. It was a prayer for bad luck for Custer.

Indians did not waste time on long farewells. When a person wished to leave an informal gathering, he just got up and went out. When visiting us, one often says, "I go now," and that is all there is to it. Sometimes, however, there were quite severe penalties for leaving an important meeting.

Women did not sit cross-legged as did the men, but with both their legs folded to one side, or on their knees, which was a practical position when cooking or tending the fire. From such a position things could be reached easily without getting up and down.

Children stayed near the door, free to run and play whenever they pleased, but not inside.

Since the backrests in the rear of the lodge were usually occupied, the women often improvised backrests for themselves from the oval netted hoops which otherwise served as the pack frame of the travois. Such a backrest was leaned against a tripod in the same way as the willow backrest.

Outside the tipi, girls and women—and men, too—when in a family group, often sat on the skirts of the tipi between two pegs, where they could lean against the tent, as on a sort of porch. So placed, they were "at home," and no one was supposed to bother them. While Sitting Bull was a prisoner of war at Fort Randall, he and his family were photographed sitting in this way on the skirts of their tipi.

In some tribes it was the custom for a popular girl to receive her admirers at the door of her mother's tipi. She stood in the slanting doorway with her feet inside, but from the knees up she was actually outside, of course. There, chaperoned by some older woman out of sight inside, she received her boy friends, who waited in line, each taking his turn in throwing his blanket around her and talking to her in privacy.

A young man who wished to marry was expected to prove his worth as a hunter and warrior by offering horses to the young lady's father. This was not a matter of buying the bride, but of prestige. The girl's choice in the matter was usually given consideration, but if the parents insisted on a marriage disagreeable to her, it was customary for her to try to elope with her lover.

Donald Deernose, one of our Crow friends, tells this story: A young man who did not have enough horses to make an impression upon his intended father-in-law decided to steal his bride. So, early in the morning, before sunrise, he slipped over to the girl's tent. He planned to coax her away, catch up his only horse, and the two of them ride away on it until they were safe from any pursuers. With his war bridle in his teeth and his knife in his hand, he quietly slit the tipi cover near the place where he supposed the girl was sleeping. Silently he crawled inside on his hands and knees. When he looked up, there sat the entire family around the fire, eating breakfast, and looking at him! The old man had decided to get up earlier than usual and go on a hunt.

Startled, the young man dropped his bridle and said, "Has anyone here seen my gray horse?"

CHILD CARE AND THE FAMILY

Since we wrote the first edition of this book many people have taken tipi life quite seriously. We have had inquiries about how Indians raised, cared for, and trained their children. Some want to live in a tipi with their own children.

Among the Sioux, new born babies were washed gently with loosely braided sweet grass dipped in warm water; then buffalo fat was applied all over their little bodies and they were wrapped in a buffalo calf skin, hair inside, or sometimes in a young beaver skin. Later, blankets were used.

The navel cord was sewed up in a little beaded or quilled "turtle" or "lizzard." These reptiles, being hard to kill and consequently living long lives, were simulated in little charms attached to the cradle while the baby was being carried in it. Later they were worn attached to clothing or to a belt. Both boys and girls wore them. A second such charm with nothing in it was also made, to fool any evil forces that might be interested in destroying the child. We have seen an old woman still wearing one of these little beaded turtles on her belt, but men did not wear them.

Instead of diapers, babies were packed in some absorbent material, the one used depending upon the season and availability. Sometimes a kind of soft moss was used. Always accessible was buffalo wool. Sometimes cattail down was used, and sometimes even pulverized buffalo chips. In springtime cotton from the cottonwood tree was used.[4] Such packing largely reduced the number of changes that had to be made. After each change the baby was usually allowed to lie for a time on a soft deer skin; then he was wrapped up again in the calf skin and placed in his cradle.

The cradle[5] was of buckskin, usually beautifully quilled or beaded, laced to a wooden carrying frame, much like a modern pack frame. Sometimes the frame for the actual cradle was of rawhide, the beaded buckskin covering it. Such a cradle with its rawhide and wooden foundation served as a protection in the same way the hoops attached to cradles of a number of other tribes did. If the cradle happened to fall forward the baby was protected by the stiff frame. Cradles were made by female relatives, not by the mother, and often the baby of a well-to-do family might be presented with several cradles, or cradle-boards as they are sometimes called, in token of the love and esteem in which it was held by all the relatives.

Flying Cloud, who in later life became a judge, was always proud of saying he had been born in a tipi. He told us that it was

---

[4]Some white people have an allergy to this cotton, but we have never heard of it affecting Indians.

[5]Every language, of course, has its own word for cradle. Lakota called it by several names, probably the easiest to say being *chanipatonpi*. "Papoose carrier" is a poor term, for "papoose" is a Narragansett word having no meaning to other tribes. One Bull thought he was talking English when he said papoose.

not unusual for an Indian woman to go off by herself to have her baby and return to her tipi carrying the baby *and* a pail of water. He went on to say, as delivery time approached a mother was warned to eat good, wholesome food, but to eat sparingly, so that the baby would not become too large and thus cause severe labor pains. After delivery she was expected to avoid heavy food and subsist mainly on broth or soup for the first few days. This induced a free flow of milk.

A new baby was fed soups and fruit juices from a sort of nursing bottle, made of a bladder, for the first four days. Since the Sioux belief was that it takes a spirit four nights to reach the Spirit World, it likewise takes a new person four suns to arrive in this world. So, on the fourth day people came to pay their respects to the new tribal member and its mother. Of course some of the visitors brought gifts for the new arrival, but the baby of a family of any standing whatever was honored by its relatives making a big feast for the visitors and giving away many presents. Another such celebration might be given when the child was a year old, but this was usually the only birthday ever celebrated. So, among the Indians, instead of receiving presents on your birthday, you give them away to your friends and neighbors!

We have never seen a Sioux or Crow baby in the old-time cradle but lately we saw a young Shoshoni mother with her baby in one, and also a Kiowa. The Kiowa cradle was made by the *father*, which is certainly a new slant. Also we saw a Warm Springs mother carrying her little one in an old style cradle, but it had a zipper on it!

Missionaries, government doctors and agency employees did their best to break down this "savage" custom, as they did all others, and seem to have succeeded. But old Indians were convinced it was the best way to start a child on life's trail and often told us of the advantages of the cradle board. They said it not only protected the baby from harm but that the baby itself felt secure in it. It also made their backs straight and strong.

We once visited old Lean Warrior in the agency hospital. He was a hundred years old and remembered seeing the first steam boat go up the Missouri River. Later he and his companions "had a fight with the boat," attacking one of these river steamers during the Indian wars. When we went to see him, sick as he was, he immediately sat up in bed to greet us, his back as straight as a young man's, his feet straight out in front of him. We were so impressed we spoke to him about it. How could such an old man sit up so straight? But he did not see anything strange about it at all. He merely said that he was brought up in the old way, and others like him could do the same. He lamented the way present-day babies are brought up, like white children, without a cradle-board. He said, "White mothers hold their babies in their arms and in doing so bend their backs and make their spines crooked. Their backs are weak, when older they walk and sit with hunched backs, soon get sick, have no strength or ambition."

The baby might be in the cradle several hours at a time, but it was periodically unwrapped for cleansing and for exercise. It played on the deer skin, or on a soft buffalo robe for a time, kicking and crawling. Babies might be carried on the cradle-board until a couple of years old while traveling.

We have heard Indians say that the longer a baby was nursed the longer and healthier would be its life. Babies were nursed at least two to three years and sometimes longer. During this period there was little likelihood of another baby arriving. Most Indian families were not large in earlier days, although they had the idea, still current among many peoples, that it was important for the tribe to increase in order to be dominant among its neighbors. The rigors of their life, coupled with a low birth rate, prevented any overpopulation which could adversely affect their resources.

Indians did not leave their children with babysitters. *Everybody*, even grandmothers and grandfathers, went to a "doings" so they took the children along. We mentioned to one mother that white people left their children at home when they went to a dance. She was horrified. "They might get up in the night and fall in the crik!" she exclaimed.

Women sat on their side of the room with little ones on their laps or tiny ones at their feet, wrapped in bundles of blankets, much like an old-time cradle, but the cradle was missing, and carefully placed on furry calf skins. These skins were cut in an oval shape, sides turned up all the way around, and looked like big shallow basins, fur inside, having been formed while the hides were fresh and wet. When a woman wanted to dance the woman next to her watched her baby. Next dance she would sit out and do the same thing for her neighbor. We have seen a line of babies under a long table at one end of the room. Older youngsters were merely placed on a skin mat and covered with blankets. The noise of the singing and drumming and of the dancers' bells bothered them not in the least. Some children played around the outside of the room but were not supposed to cross the dance circle. When they became tired and sleepy they too crawled under a table and went to sleep.

The cradle could be carried on the mother's back by a wide soft leather strap across her chest. It could be hung on the saddle horn, on a tree, or leaned against the tipi. So the baby was safe and secure and always under the watchful eyes of its mother or an older sister.

When a baby outgrew his cradle it was often carried on its mother's, or grandmother's back, pick-a-back, held in place by a robe or blanket. Indians of many tribes still do this, and sometimes make a kind of hammock by stretching a doubled rope between two trees and folding a blanket over the ropes, one fold over the ropes, one around under and the third on top again, the weight of the youngster holding all in place.

We have several non-Indian friends who brought up their youngsters on Navajo cradle-boards, which are more easily obtained these days, as the Navajo still use them. These friends tell us the boards are wonderful. The babies had such a sense of security within the cradle that they cried when they were taken out of it! They said when traveling in the car they would not have known what to do without it, for it could be placed out of harm's way, and there were no worries about baby's behavior. The Museum of the American Indian in New York has a little booklet picturing cradles of several tribes which may be obtained by anyone further interested in the subject.

Indians had no milk animals but in the east a substitute for mother's milk was sometimes prepared by crushing the meat of walnuts in a little water and adding a small portion of the finest corn meal and boiling the mixture.

Babies, when old enough, and previous to weaning, were fed soups and bits of tender meat. Sometimes the mother even chewed it for them first! They were gradually introduced to the diet of their elders, which in early days was largely meat, supplemented with wild fruits, berries and plants. Today Indian diet is usually very poor. With no wild game left on most of the reservations, and not being able to afford meat, they eat mostly bread and potatoes, with black coffee. They have had no training in white man's diet and eat what they can get. Even tribes that are faring better financially these days still have a bad diet because of never learning

Grandma Yellowtail carrying Diane Medicine Crow. A blanket was used in th fashion after a child had grown too large for the cradle. Photograph by Glad Laubin.

white man's ways and being unable to get—or now being uninterested in—the food of their ancestors.

Children were seldom punished and were never whipped or struck. To this day, the worst thing an Indian can say about anyone is that he whips his children. The Blackfeet used to say, "The Crows are bad people. They whip their children." And the Crows would say, "The Blackfeet are bad people. They whip their children." Of course, neither tribe whipped its children, but this was the utmost contempt they could show for an enemy.

A psychologist we know, who taught at one of the large universities, told us that when clients came to him asking for advice in bringing up their children, he instructed them in Indian methods, although he did not dare tell them that! His suggestions evidently were successful, for the same clients consulted him for years on these and other problems.

Children were taught by example. They were expected to imitate their elders. Sometimes a child was scolded, but seldom by its parents or close relatives. They were told what was expected of a person of standing. They were taught to love their parents, which in a Sioux family, as among a number of other tribes, included father's brothers as fathers, and mother's sisters as mothers. So it was sometimes possible to have many fathers and many mothers throughout the camp, all sharing their love. How rich they were in affection! They, in turn, were to love and respect all relatives, especially the older ones, for the aged were venerated and their wisdom respected. How else could they have lived so long?

Children early learned that obedience to parental advice and to that of other elders could be a matter of life and death in a society where enemies might slip in at almost any moment, or dangerous beasts might be encountered on the perimeter of the village. They were taught immediately, as the tiniest infants, not to cry, for a baby's crying might alert a skulking enemy. They were often pampered and petted to keep them from crying, and, being almost continually happy and contented, they seldom did cry. If they did, a hand was gently held over the mouth and the lesson was quickly learned.

On our very first visit to Standing Rock a small baby in the next room was recovering from painful burns caused by a nurse's carelessness in the agency hospital, but we never even heard it whimper. We would never have known there was a baby so near if we did not know the family.

Instead of being physically punished, a child who was disobedient, was ignored. He was not a member of society. He did not belong. He did not even exist. No one can stand such treatment very long.

Occasionally children were frightened with threats of supernatural intervention, with *djichi* (evil spirits) or some terrible consequence of their wrong doing. One of the worst threats was that a *washichu* (white man) would get them! A Zuñi friend told us that when the *shalako* came, in their gigantic, tall masks, he would hide behind his mother's dress, peeking out from behind, while they asked, "Are there any bad children here?" She assured them there were none and they would go off leaving him happy in the knowledge that his parents always protected him and the monsters would not come again for another year.

Some modern psychologists consider these scaring tactics very bad, as damaging to personality, but it never seemed detrimental in Indian society. We remember one time when a little Crow boy misbehaved, continuing against all protests and admonishments from his parents. His grandfather put him in a burlap sack and tied him up in it. He screamed and yelled, but could hardly be heard through the sack, and how everybody laughed! *He* could hear that, and Indians dread ridicule as much as anything. The youngster did look funny, or rather the sack did, tumbling, jumping and rolling about. In a couple of minutes the sack became still and quiet and only a few little whimpers could be heard. The sack was opened and a thoroughly subdued, bashful little boy crawled out, ready to be good for the rest of the day. Today he is a grown man, with a family of his own.

Tahan told us he once played in the mud and it was caked all over his feet. His mother told him he should go down to the river and soak it off, but he was tired and did not want to. Next day it was so hard that when he tried to crack it off some of the skin came with it and it took a long time to soak it off. His feet were sore and tender for several days; so the next time he played in the mud he washed his feet immediately afterward.

On another occasion his mother made him a beautifully decorated shirt and leggings, to be worn on ceremonial occasions. But it was so pretty he wanted to put it on right away. When he went out to show it off, the boys all jumped on him and rolled him in the dirt.

"Didn't your mother scold you when you came back with your new clothes all messed up?" we asked him.

"Oh, no," he said. "She knew I was already as unhappy as she was and she said no more about it. There was no need for further punishment."

Of course, for many years now, the old customs have been losing ground, the old standards have disintegrated and old values have largely disappeared. Today, Indians have the same, or perhaps more problems with delinquent children as have other Americans, for they no longer abide by the old ways, nor have they accepted white man's standards. As a result, many of them are living in chaos, hardly knowing which way to turn, confused and usually apathetic. But at the same time most of them retain a composure and a dignity usually lacking in other societies.

Indian children are still quiet, as a rule, more so than other children, it seems to us. This is not because they are not having any fun. Apparently it traces back to earlier days. We visited a family at Pine Ridge one cold evening. They were living in a wall tent, which was almost filled by an iron bedstead and a little sheet-iron "Indian" stove. There were a couple of old chairs and a trunk to sit on, which were occupied by four adults and ourselves. It was hot and stuffy inside, quite a contrast to a well-ventilated tipi of other days. While we sat and talked, four children were playing on the bed, on the mattress, as the bedding was all neatly folded on one corner. They were having the best time, wrestling, boxing, rolling over like puppies, and hardly a peep was heard out of any of them. They did not interfere in the least with our conversation. We cannot imagine four non-Indians playing in the same way.

We remember being scolded in school, "You act like a lot of wild Indians." After our years of association with real Indians, we now tell children who are admonished in this way, "This must mean that you are very quiet, for the wilder the Indians are the quieter they are."

One day, while with the Crows, we were astonished to hear some children screaming and yelling in a way we had never heard from Indian children before. We asked some of the parents what was going on.

"Oh, they went to the movies last night and they are playing Indian," was the reply.

Indian youngsters were constantly encouraged to emulate

*Rare Sioux Dolls made by Mrs. Stretches Himself of her family.
From left to right: pet rabbit, all beads with weasel tail ears. Mrs.
Stretches Himself, Mother Rainbow, baby brother (Charley Red
Beans), Grandfather Holy Horse. Clothing is beaded buckskin,
"bone" necklaces are porcupine quills, hair is buffalo, headdress is
deer and porcupine hair.* Photograph by Gladys Laubin.

some famous person, especially if that person was a relative, to be
good hunters and warriors, to be brave and generous, to be a credit
to their people. Boys played games that would train them in
strength and agility, hunted small game with toy bows and arrows,
and played war with toy weapons. Girls were expected to learn the
arts and skills associated with women, who were as respected in

their role as men were in theirs. They played "house," or rather "tipi," played with dolls, and imitated their mothers in nearly everything they did. They also had games, one in particular being similar to shinny, which helped them grow strong and built up endurance.[6]

Sometimes a group of Indian boys learned how to take care of themselves by following the leadership of a young man who had a reputation as a good hunter and warrior. They went off for several days with no provisions, carrying only their knives and bows and arrows. The leader carried a flint and steel, or in earlier days, a coal packed in punk in a buffalo horn. Such an expedition might be compared to a group of Boy Scouts on a survival hike.

Tahan said he went on such a party when he "had seen nine winters." Five other boys, only a little older, and a leader went along. The first afternoon two of the boys shot a rabbit apiece, but they made rather meager eating for six hungry boys and their leader.

On the second day the leader decided the boys had better separate and each go in a different direction. They would have more chance of finding meat this way, for they could cover more ground, and one boy would make less noise and be less likely to be seen than six would be. So they separated and agreed to meet again late in the afternoon at a place they all knew.

Shortly before sunset the boys began to come in to the foot of the red butte they had selected. They were tired and hungry and discouraged, for no one had seen a thing. Only one boy did not show up, and just as they were making plans to send out a search party, he suddenly appeared over a little rise, coming on a run. He too, was tired and hungry, but very excited.

"I found an old buffalo bull," he panted, "one who has been hooked out of the herd. I tried to kill him with my arrows but he was too mean and tough. He chased me over a cut-bank and I had to hang onto a little bush until he went away. He kept me dangling there a long time."

Of course his small boy's bow and little toy arrows were not nearly good enough to kill buffalo, especially an old bull, but now the leader suggested a plan. They would have to tighten their belts and go hungry again that evening but the next day they would all go look

---

[6]For more information on bringing up children see Royal B. Hassrick, *The Sioux.*

for the old bull. The boy who had discovered him was also the
fastest runner; so he was selected to act as a decoy to enrage the
old bull, who would charge him again. The boy would run for the
same cut-bank as before, scramble over the side and hang onto the
same bush while the others pushed the buffalo over the bank to
fall to the bottom of the gulch far below. He would be killed or so
badly crippled that the boys could finish him off.

Sure enough, they found the old bull right where he had been
wallowing before. The decoy approached and the old fellow, snort-
ing and bellowing, lowered his head and began to paw the ground
in front of him, tossing dirt over his back. The boy loosed an arrow
at him which barely pricked his skin. But it was enough to send the
old bull into a charge, and the boy ran as fast as he could, going
almost head first over the bank and grabbing the same little bush
that had saved his life the day before.

The other boys and the leader immediately came out of hiding
and rushed for the buffalo. While he snorted and pawed above
the boy hanging to the bush the others pushed with all their might
to shove him over the bank. But it was no use. He was just too
heavy for them. He suddenly realized that a new attack was being
made on his rear and whirled around. As the old bull started to
whirl around, Tahan grabbed his tail and then was afraid to let go!
The bull felt this strange thing on his tail and whirled around again,
trying to shake it off. Around and around he went, Tahan still holding on with all his strength, whirling almost parallel to the ground
and getting dizzier all the time.

Finally the old bull slowed down a little and Tahan managed
to get out his knife. It was an old stone knife that had been given
to him by his grandfather. Although the other boys all had steel
knives obtained from the hairy-faced traders that had recently
come into their country, Tahan was fond of the old stone knife
because of its "medicine," and had always been careful not to break
it or chip it.

Now that the old buffalo had quieted down Tahan quickly
sawed on his hind leg, just above the hock. He cut through the
hamstring and down went the old bull in a heap.

The other boys then rushed in, cutting and stabbing, and the
old buffalo finally breathed his last. Their leader then taught the
boys a little prayer, which they all repeated, addressed to the poor
old buffalo's spirit, thanking him for his sacrifice. "Grandfather,
we are hungry and you were made for that," they said. Then the

Reginald Laubin showing Pretty Shield (Crow) rare Sioux dolls.
Photograph by Gladys Laubin.

leader showed them how to skin and dress the carcass.

At first the boys only partially skinned the buffalo, just enough
so they could get some meat. They dressed him out, took out the
liver, and each cut off a strip to eat raw, seasoned with a drop or
two of the juice from the gall bladder. Grown-up hunters always
did this, so they must learn to do it too. Then they took the tongue
and the tenderloin at the base of the hump and broiled them over
the coals of the fire the leader had made with his flint and steel.
These delicacies were usually reserved for some of the old people,

but since the boys had gone hungry so long they felt they deserved a special treat.

When they had eaten all they could hold they finished skinning half of the buffalo, then pulled the hide out flat and piled pieces of meat on it. They wanted to turn the old bull over on his side and finish the butchering, but he was just too heavy.

When they were about to give up, they heard a loud whoop and thought an enemy war party had discovered them. Just as they started to run for cover they realized it was a party of warriors from their own camp who had been watching them all the time just to make sure they were safe and that they did not go hungry too long. These experienced warriors finished the butchering and, even though the meat was from a tough old bull, packed it all home so that the boys would feel as if they had become accomplished hunters and had brought home good meat to the people.

When the boys got home their parents sang songs in their honor and paraded them all around the village. But Tahan was honored most of all for he was chiefly responsible for the killing of the buffalo, having downed him with his old stone knife. His father gave away a horse in his honor, and he went to bed that night a very tired, but very happy little boy.

Tahan had seen ninety winters when he told us this story. He called us "his children."

Sometimes a Sioux boy would slip away to join a war party, uninvited. When he was discovered, he was given an opportunity to show his skill and courage. Some member of the party would make for him a "warrior's cup," — a buffalo bladder skin, the opening stretched on a little wooden hoop attached to a long forked stick (Fig. 19). One prong of the fork was cut short, and to the bottom of the "cup" was fastened a long cord. The forked stick was decorated, usually with magpie feathers, for the magpie was one of the first birds to arrive on a battlefield, and he warned of enemies approaching.

The boy was told to locate a spring in enemy country and fill the cup with water, which he was to bring back to the chief of the war party. To prove the spring was really in enemy territory he left an arrow from his quiver, with his personal crest, stuck in the ground near the spring, so someone could later check up on him if there were any doubts.

If the boy completed the trial, he was expected to present the water to the chief while holding the stick to which the bladder was attached in one hand and the thong in the other. When the chief attempted to take the "cup," the boy pulled the thong, splashing water all over him. Then everybody laughed, for it was as much as saying to the chief, "Well! You sent me on an errand you didn't think I could accomplish, but I did it, so now, take that!"

The boy thus proved his competence and courage, and could go along as an accepted member of a party of experienced warriors.

There was man's work and women's work—"man's business" and "woman's business," as the Indians call it, each separate and seldom overlapping. Often women's work would be considered drudgery by many non-Indians, but the women were proud of their skills and would not consider letting a man help them. James Willard Schultz wrote that he felt sorry for his Blackfoot wife doing so much hard work, so he helped her gather fire wood and bring the water. But he found her crying one day, and when he tried to console her she said all the women were making fun of her because she let a man do her work. After that he decided they had a pretty good system, which worked well for everybody.

Men's work pertained to providing for the family, to taking care of most religious matters, to hunting and to war, which may sound pleasant to people of this modern age. But if they had to depend upon the chase for a living they probably would not find it so easy or so pleasant. Both war and hunting entailed much training, great physical strength and endurance, hardship and often suffering. Training for religious duties was also involved and arduous, requiring long periods of fasting and self-denial. After a strenuous hunt or a long war path a man needed to conserve his strength and to recuperate while in camp, in order to get ready for the next expedition.

When a man was home it may have seemed as if he did nothing, merely smoking and talking with his friends or engaging in simple tasks, such as making and repairing his weapons or ceremonial regalia, while at the same time the woman may have been fleshing or tanning heavy buffalo hides or gathering and chopping firewood. But she also found time to do most of the art work. She painted and decorated most of the tipi furnishings and did beautiful, intricate quillwork or beadwork by the hour.

We hear much of lazy or idle Indians. This is largely because man's work of other days is gone and they have not yet adjusted to white man's ways. But we never found the old people idle. They were always busy with something. Old men made eagle-bone whis-

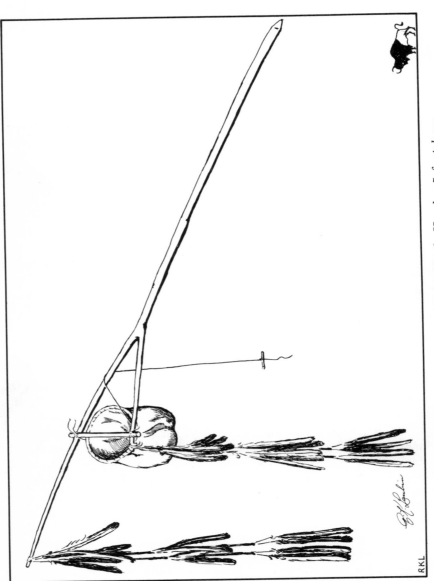

Fig. 19. Warrior's Cup made by Eagle Hawk.—5 feet long.

tles, carved diamond willow canes or perhaps made trinkets for the tourists. After One Bull gave me the club he had used as a young warrior, he at once started to make a new one for himself, although he had not used a war club in sixty years. He found a stone as near the size and shape as possible; then he sat and pecked on it with another stone, hour after hour, pecking a groove all around it to fasten it to an ash stick before sewing it up in rawhide. His daughter, Magli, said it drove her crazy to watch him sit and work like that. Younger Indians apparently acquired some of the white man's impatience, his eagerness to hurry up with everything, while in government schools.

Older men often helped women with some of the chores. One Bull and Scarlet Whirlwind went after wood together. He drove the team with a wagon for bringing back the wood, helped her gather it and place it in the wagon, and even helped cut it back home. And he was one of the last of the real chiefs!

One time, after having been away for awhile, we came back and found the old folk driving in with a load of wood. One Bull gave a little yelp and threw his hat up in the air to show how glad they were to see us. "We knew you were coming," he said. "A coyote told me so."

SIOUX CRADLE PATTERN

Figures 20 and 20a show an old Sioux cradle from about 1890, made of beaded buckskin, with a wooden slat carrier, decorated with brass tacks. The buckskin is sewed with thread but the beadwork is all done with sinew. There is no reason why the same pattern could not be applied to a present-day cradle of leather or even heavy canvas. For practical purposes it would not have to be decorated, but if painted with nice Sioux designs it would still be attractive. The beadwork on the original makes the hood so stiff and heavy that it would provide adequate protection for the baby. If made of unbeaded leather or canvas it might be well to reinforce the hood and back with rawhide, or even cardboard.

The drawings indicate how the cradle proper was laced to the wooden carrier. The carrying strap should be at least two inches wide and attached to the upper cross-piece, as shown. It should be long enough to go around the mother's shoulders and across her chest. A shorter strap was often attached to the same

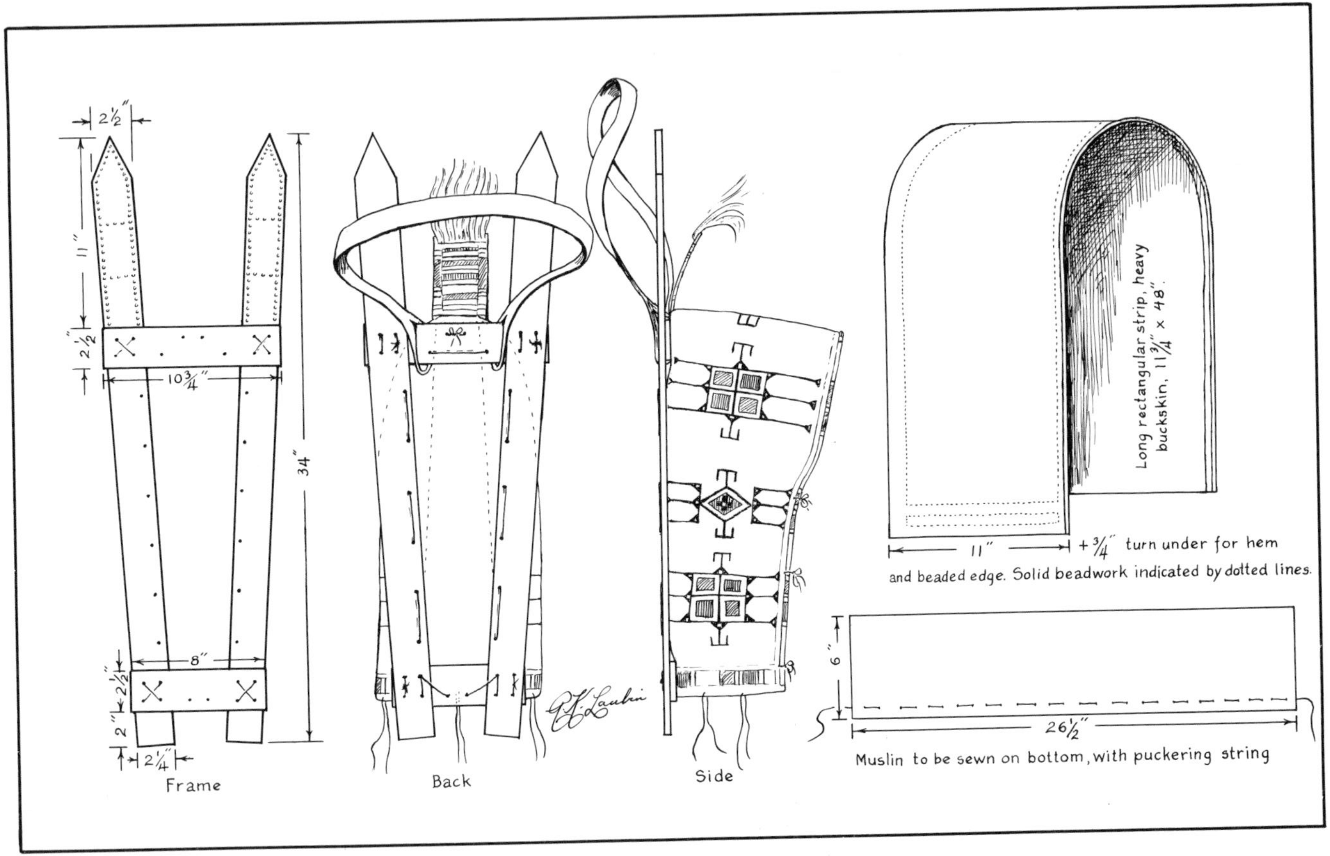

Long rectangular strip, heavy buckskin, 11¾" x 48".

+ ¾" turn under for hem and beaded edge. Solid beadwork indicated by dotted lines.

11"

26½"

9"

Muslin to be sewn on bottom, with puckering string

Side

Back

Frame

34"

10¾"

8"

11"

2½"

2½"

2½"

2"

2¼"

Fig. 20. Sioux Beaded Cradle.

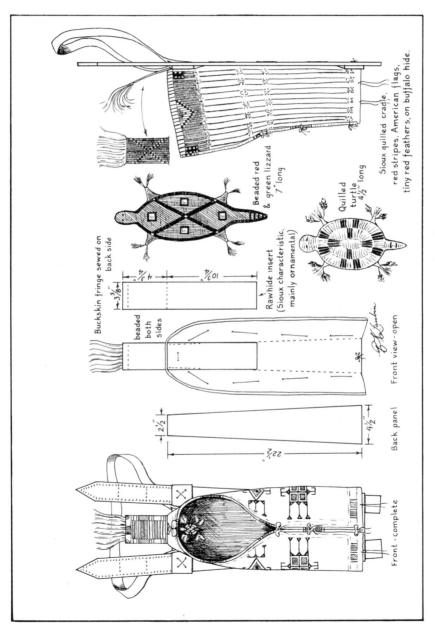

Sioux quilled cradle, red stripes, American flags, tiny red feathers, on buffalo hide.

Beaded red & green lizzard 7" long

Quilled turtle 4½" long

Buckskin fringe sewed on back side

Rawhide insert (Sioux characteristic, mainly ornamental)

beaded both sides

3/8" 4 3/4" 10 3/4"

Front view - open

Back panel

2½ 22½" 4½"

Front - complete

Fig. 20a. Sioux Beaded Cradle.

cross-piece and used to hang the cradle from the saddle horn when traveling, or from a low branch on a tree while the mother was working nearby.

The figures given for this cradle are for a new baby, up to about six months old. After that the cradle had to be enlarged, using a longer carrying frame, as much as six inches longer, and the cradle itself was extended at the bottom. The baby, though being wrapped in a longer bundle, could still be fastened in the original cradle, the bundle merely projecting farther below its base.

Sometimes an extra strip of soft buckskin or muslin was sewed around the bottom of the cradle to help hold the infant in place. A couple of thongs across the bottom served the same purpose for a tiny babe. The strip could be puckered with a drawstring, or merely tucked up around and over the baby bundle.

FIRE AND FUEL

The greatest joy of the tipi is the open fire. A tiny fire, properly laid and cared for, is enough to keep the average tipi warm and cozy even in very cold weather. A large fire is not only unnecessary but dangerous. Since today tipis are generally for show only, it is unusual to find a fire in one, but when we visit Indians who are using a fire, they generally have it right on top of the ground. A fire reflects more heat this way, but during a long stay in one place the ashes become a nuisance. When stones are available, the fireplace can be made with a ring of stones, and for a more permanent camp a shallow pit can be dug just forward of the center, i.e., under the smoke hole. The Cheyennes and Arapahoes made this small pit "square with the world," but really oblong, about 12x25 inches, longer on a line from the back to the door, and only 3 or 4 inches deep. Kiowas, Comanches, Blackfeet, and Sioux all preferred a round hole about the same depth and about 18 or 20 inches across. The fire pit in Julia Wades-in-the-Water's big tipi, however, was at least 3 feet across.

Stanley Vestal said he had seen a Cheyenne fire pit with a drainage trench leading to the door to draw off water from a heavy rain. An old Kiowa told us that his mother made a hearth all around the fireplace of boards she split from red cedar. These were polished and decorated with brass tacks.

Indians used tongs made either of a narrow fork from a sapling, as is sometimes found in red osier and other shrubs, or of an ash or willow sappling bent into a long "U," first thinned where the bend was to come. A pair of these tongs and a stick for a poker make handling the fire much easier. Often a bird wing was used for a fan to blow up the coals, although sometimes a pipestem was used for this purpose. The latter was nearly as efficient as the leather bellows of our ancestors. However, the use of either of these fire "encouragers" was governed by certain superstitions. Some families were allowed to use one method, others another. If a wing was used, it often had to be from a certain bird, because many kinds of birds were taboo. Only the wing of a bird of prey, an eagle or a hawk, could be used by some people. These birds were bold and coura-geous, and it was believed that their wings would circulate an atmosphere of bravery within the lodge. The wings of timid birds might create an air of timidity and cowardice.

Faced east, the tipi receives the morning sun and has its back to the prevailing high winds. East of the Rocky Mountains the prevailing winds are westerly, and it is very unusual to have a due-east wind. The smoke flaps can be adjusted to shield against the wind from all other directions and are handled much as a man uses the lapels of his overcoat. If the wind is driving on his left cheek, he raises the left lapel against his face; if on the right cheek, the right lapel. In other words, the flaps are set as nearly down wind as possible, or quartering down in such a way as to block the wind from blowing down the smoke hole (see Figs. 21 and 22). As an exception to the rule of facing east, the Assiniboines face their tipis south, but they live to the north, where prevailing storms come from the north.

By selecting sound, dry wood and adjusting the smoke flaps properly, one need not be troubled by smoke. The best firewood is hardwood. In the mountains we have only willow, cottonwood, service berry, chokecherry, mountain maple, and river birch (alder) to draw on. Evergreens are generally unsatisfactory for a tipi fire. They give off too much smoke and throw live sparks. Even willow, if it has bark on it, will occasionally throw sparks. Aspen gives off sparks, but it does have one advantage—it makes almost no smoke. Old pine that has lost its bark and is thoroughly dried out, so that there is no resin or pitch remaining, will do in a pinch, but it gives little heat. Farther down on the prairies, along the rivers, and throughout the rest of the country there are many good hard-

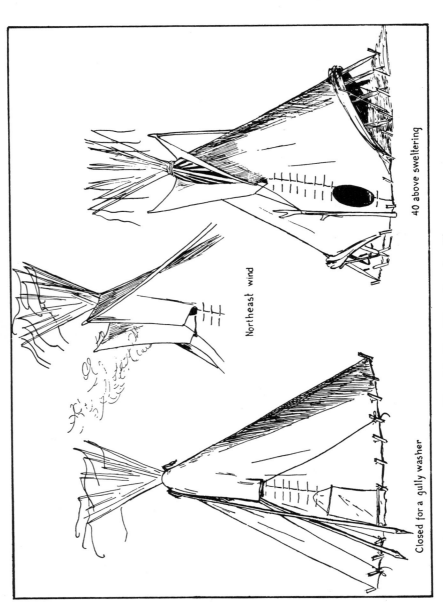

Northeast wind

40 above sweltering

Closed for a gully washer

Fig. 21. Handling Smoke Flaps.

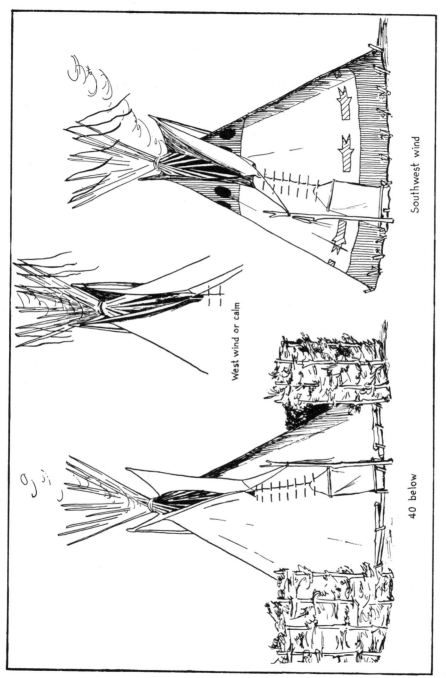

Southwest wind

West wind or calm

40 below

Fig. 22. Handling Smoke Flaps.

woods to use. Maple and ash are among the best. The only hardwood we know that throws sparks is elm, and some might argue that it is not hardwood anyway.

Walter McClintock, in one of his articles for the Southwest Museum, wrote: "Burning cottonwood smelled good but had to be watched as it continually threw sparks which might burn the blankets or skins used for bedding." We felt that he had mistaken cottonwood for aspen, but Stanley Vestal had the same experience in Oklahoma. Aspen and cottonwood look very much alike, especially when dead, but there is no aspen in southwestern Oklahoma. In our own experience we have used cottonwood in North and South Dakota, Montana, and Wyoming and have never known it to spark. This includes the long-leafed, or mountain variety. Some local or climactic difference may have been the cause of the sparking.

McClintock went on to say that burning birch has a sweet fragrance. Pine burns with a resinous scent, and alder, because of its disagreeable odor, was called "stinkwood" by the Blackfeet. Again, the alder of northern Montana must be different from that in Jackson's Hole, Wyoming, for we burn alder a great deal and consider it our best tipi firewood, with a very pleasant odor.

A supply of firewood was commonly kept just inside the tipi, to the left of the door as you entered, along with the pots and pans and the water keg. The women brought it in on their backs, but the old men and boys helped gather it. They gathered huge piles and stacked it in convenient places throughout the winter camp. This was a community project, and each family helped itself to the nearest pile.

We might add that willow and aspen are very sweet-smelling woods and that witch hazel smells much like the lotion of that name. A piece of partly rotten dogwood smells just like a dirty, wet dog. Perhaps that is why it has the name. Out on the treeless prairies when no other fuel was available, the Indians used buffalo chips.

The secret for getting a clear fire in the tipi is to burn sound, dry wood and to set the smoke flaps correctly. When the weather is sultry and the smoke hangs low, the cover may have to be raised a little on the windward side. This can be done in either of two ways: Slip three or four peg loops from the pegs and turn the cover *under*. The pressure against the poles will hold it in place. Or, use a forked stick fifteen or eighteen inches long to hold it up.

There is always some wind, no matter how calm it seems to be. One can tell from which direction it is by using the old trick of wetting a finger in the mouth, then holding it up in the air. The side first feeling cool is the windward side. Or an occasional flutter of streamers hanging from the tips of the poles will tell the direction of the wind. Such streamers, formerly long buckskin thongs, now usually strips of white cloth, are used on nearly all Crow tipis and occasionally on the tipis of other tribes. Our Cheyenne medicine tipi is supposed to have red streamers.

More reasons why the cone of the tipi is tilted should now be evident. The tilt braces the shorter length of the cone against the wind, it makes more head room in the back of the lodge where most activity is carried on, it places the poles in the smoke hole, where they belong, and it places the hole itself near the center so that it comes directly over the fireplace. The fireplace should be just a trifle nearer the door than true center, giving additional room in the rear. But a true cone would place the smoke hole too far to the front, or else we would have to redesign the hole, making it so large where it fits around the poles that it would let in a whole thunderstorm at once.

If the flaps are set right, only the heaviest rains will bother at all. Otherwise, you can still have a fire and forget about the rain. If caught in a sudden downpour, however, it may be necessary to pick up the firewood with the tongs and throw it outside, so that the smoke flaps can be completely closed. At such a time rain will come streaming down the poles, whether the cover is waterproofed or not. Usually the little sticks we mentioned will take care of the water, but until it gets to them it may cause a few drips. You can hasten its arrival by rubbing along the pole with a finger, but be careful not to rub your finger along the canvas. Even waterproofed canvas may leak if you do. If a knot or a bulge on the pole makes a drip before the water gets on down behind the lining, untie the dewcloth from the pole and let it sag at that place.

Years ago someone told us about a "drip basket" to take care of the water which sometimes drips off the poles. A long string or cord was tied high up, near the top of the tipi, to each pole, and the long hanging cords were then all brought together near the center of the tipi and tied together. The water was supposed to follow the cords and drip behind the fireplace. Recently we read of someone who suggested a similar devise but we do not recommend it. We tried it. It is a lot of work for poor results. Instead of following the cords to the center, most of the water drips off at the knots by the poles; so it actually causes more drips than it prevents. We

questioned old Indians about this "drip basket" and none of them
ever heard of it. It must be another white man's invention — trying
to improve on the tipi.

Seton reported that Missouri Indians used a bull boat as a
storm cap on their tipis, the poles being cut short to accommodate
it. But a real bull boat of bull buffalo hide on a willow frame is
quite heavy; so it must have been quite a job to hoist one on top
of the poles on a large tipi, even if they had been cut short. Other
writers mentioned the Mandans using a bull boat as a cover for the
smoke hole in an earth lodge. This would have been easier to do
since the bull boat could have been carried there by walking up
over the lodge itself. Seton suggested making a lightweight "bull
boat" of canvas and hoisting it in place with an extra tipi pole but
our experience has been that neither of these devises is necessary
if the tipi is properly made and pitched. Cutting off the poles for
such a cap makes an ugly, squat looking tipi. One Bull's trick with
the little sticks does a much better job and is so much simpler.

Our own experience has been that straight, smooth poles, a
waterproof cover, and a good lining are the best solutions to the
problem of water dripping. The little that comes in drops in the
center, where it amounts to nothing and does not even make the
fire spit. And, of course, with an ozan there is no problem at all.

Recently we heard of a couple who had to give up camping in
a tipi during a prolonged rainy spell because it dripped so much
off the poles. They certainly must have overlooked some precaution
we have mentioned. Their poles must have been crooked, or badly
peeled, or they did not have a dew cloth. Or, if they had a dew
cloth (lining) they did not use the two little sticks where it was
tied to the poles. We have camped, literally for weeks, not only in
rainy weather, but when it was raining so hard most of the time it
sounded as if we were inside a big drum. The problem of dripping
was minor. Once the little stream down each pole was established,
the difficulty was over.

On several occasions we have had the only dry and comfortable
place in camp, with constant visitors because even the main lodge
on the ranch was cold and damp. One time we were camped on
a perfectly flat piece of ground and it rained hard and continuously
for over a week. There was no place for a real run-off trench because it was so flat. So I dug a large hole, connecting it with the
little ditch around the tipi in order to prevent water running in
under the cover. It was soon filled with water. I dug more holes

and more run-off trenches all over the place. They looked like the spokes on a wheel, and for anyone trying to approach the tipi in the dark they presented a real hazard. We were as isolated as a castle surrounded by a moat. By the end of the week of rain all the ditches and the holes were full and we could not figure out what to do next. We were about ready to give up when it finally stopped raining and the weather cleared.

The biggest problem with a seige like this is getting enough dry wood. It is always well to have a sizeable wood supply on hand. The extra can be piled close to the tipi and covered with a tarp on rainy days. If you do run out of wood during a long rainy spell, cut some standing dead wood, which will be wet only on the outside. Split it, and usually it will burn well right from the start. If it is too wet to burn without smoking, pile some up around the fire a foot or more high, by building it up in a hexagon or octagon, log cabin style, crossing the ends, thus leaving an air space between all the pieces. It will soon dry out this way; then you can stack it in your usual woodpile near the door and use it as you need it.

Some people have the idea that Indians never made a criss-cross, or log-cabin style fire, but certainly they use this type today for heating the rocks for their steam baths. It is the best kind of fire when you wish to get the most heat out of a small amount of wood. It burns hot and steady. Even the so-called "Indian star fire" and "squaw fire" burn best when the ends of the sticks are crossed log-cabin style instead of just touching. These are the fires where the wood is laid on like the spokes of a wheel, the squaw fire being laid with long sticks which are gradually pushed in toward the center as they burn. When the logs are rather heavy, uniform pieces of wood, kettles of varying size can be set along a pair of them as they spread out away from the fire. When such large sticks or logs are used, it is necessary to use small pieces of "feeder" wood to keep them burning.

A friend of ours told us that years ago he had been in a Crow tipi in which the fire roared away like a blast furnace. When the owner stepped out for a while, our friend began to hunt around to try to discover why the fire burned so fiercely. He found that the old Indian had laid a regular pipe-line ventilating system under the floor of his lodge. He had dug a little trench from the fireplace to the back of his tipi, and in this laid his "pipe line." He had taken the tops and bottoms out of tin cans and laid them end to end, then covered them over with earth again. The device was not visible when the floor was covered with canvas and skins, but it certainly added zest to his fire. Later we heard of this same device from Rides-to-the-Door, the old Blackfoot, in Browning, Montana.

The question of what Indians used for lights seems to bother many people. The light from the fire usually satisfied them, as it does us. Some Indians today have gasoline or kerosene lanterns, but they have no fires. The most civilized device we use when camping is a candle, which we sometimes condescend to use when we feel we need extra light. A lid from a tin can makes a good candle tray, and we place it in a small tripod, about two feet high, so that the light is distributed evenly.

Indians threw little chunks of fat in the fire occasionally for additional light. We save suet, candle stubs, and drippings for the same purpose. Indians also made various kinds of torches — bundles of cattail rushes, birch bark folded and held in a split stick, and pitch-pine splinters.

At night the tipi glows in the dark like a great Japanese lantern. When no lining is in use, the shadows of those inside loom large against its sides. When the lining is in place, the top of the tipi shines brightly above it, leaving a ghostly half-light below. A painted medicine tipi, with its weird ceremonial figures in sharp silhouette, is a sight grotesque beyond imagination. The painted horses and buffalo on ours look almost as if they could come to life and walk right off the tipi into the dark.

FOOD AND COOKING

Before contact with the white men, the Indians of the Plains did most of their cooking without utensils. Some of the earth-lodge people made very good pottery, but the typical Plains tribes made little or none, for it was not practical in their roving life. Even in fairly recent times Plains Indians cooked in the old ways, without utensils, when off on a war party or a hunt.

For a large group, one favorite method of cooking was in a hole in the ground. A pit about two feet wide and two feet deep was dug. If stones were handy, the pit was lined with them. A large fire was built in and above this pit and more stones heated in it. Such a fire would burn for an hour or more until the stones became red hot. After the fire had burned down, the coals and loose hot stones were scraped from the pit without disturbing the lining stones any more than necessary.

Crow Woman Making Fry Bread.
Photograph by Gladys Laubin.

Baking Corn Bread in a Reflector Oven, and Frying Mountain Trout. Note Rocks for reflecting Heat. Photograph by Gladys Laubin.

Preparing a Ground Oven. Potatoes, Corn, Acorn Squash, with Ham in a Sugar Sack. Photograph by Gladys Laubin.

A fresh hide from the hunt was used to line the hole. It was laid in, hair side down, and pieces of meat for the feast were placed on the flesh side. The skin was then folded over, so that only the flesh side came in contact with the meat, the hot stones and embers were placed on top of the folded hide, and the entire hole covered with dirt. Such an "oven" was then left undisturbed for several hours until the meat was thoroughly cooked. Of course the skin so used was ruined, but that was considered a small sacrifice for the resulting flavor and pleasure of the feast that followed. When no stones were available, the same procedure could be followed without them, but more coals were needed, consequently more fire.

On the eastern fringes of the prairies, where trees grew in variety, the pit was lined with green leaves—sweet ones—maple, sassafras, basswood, or wild grape. For a modern version of this ancient Indian feast, poultry turns out exceedingly well, and so

Making a Square Cherry Pie to fit the Reflector Oven. Photograph by Reginald Laubin.

does ham. Instead of lining the hole with a fresh hide, use only the leaves, lay in a stuffed chicken, duck, turkey, or a ham, surround it with potatoes, both sweet and white, carrots, onions, sweet corn, or any vegetable you like. Do not crowd the foods. Cover them with another layer of leaves, arrange the hot stones on top, cover all with wet canvas or wet burlap, shovel the embers back on, then cover it all over with earth so that no steam escapes. Go away and forget about it for from three to five hours, depending upon the size of the meat, then come back and dig up your dinner.

While sassafras leaves make a ham taste exceptionally good,

Sweet and White Potatoes ready to eat from the Ground Oven.
Photograph by Gladys Laubin.

they give carrots a taste like medicine. Therefore, if sassafras leaves are used, it is better to save the carrots for another time.

We once cooked this kind of a dinner for friends in Jackson's Hole. We could find no sweet leaves. Cottonwood, aspen, choke-cherry, all tasted bitter and we could not find enough service berry leaves (we needed a couple of bushels). So we mowed the lawn and used the grass cuttings. Everything turned out fine. In fact, it was so good that everyone wanted us to do it again a few days later.

The first time we cooked ham; so the second time we decided to try a leg of lamb. Moving pictures were taken of us putting the ham in the ground and covering it over. Then we all went swimming while the dinner cooked. When we came back the moviemaker discovered he was out of film. So, we finished the picture on the next occasion. Everything looked the same — same place, same time of day, everyone wore the same clothes—but the picture showed us putting in ham and taking out lamb!

In the old days, Indians did a great deal of broiling. Often a whole rib section was prepared by standing it up beside a hot fire. Smaller pieces of meat were impaled on forked sticks and held directly over the coals. Hardwood makes the only good coals for broiling. In the mountain country, where no true hardwood is to be found, willow is a very good substitute.

Before the days of brass or iron kettles, boiling was done in a buffalo paunch. Chief One Bull showed us how it was done, as he remembered it from his days as a youth on the warpath. We knew that the glandular meats—tongue, heart, kidneys, liver, paunch— were the favorites of the old-timers. They wasted nothing in butchering. After they had finished cutting up a carcass, there was only a little pile of partially digested grass from the stomach left lying on the prairie. Even the horns were saved for making spoons and ceremonial equipment, the tail was used for a fly brush, and the chips were burned for fuel.

Knowing the old folks' fondness for "innards," I went to a slaughter house one day and brought them a beef paunch, turned it over to Scarlet Whirlwind, my Indian "mother." When I told One Bull what I had brought for them, he got right up and called out to her, "Don't cut up that paunch. I want to show our son how we cooked in the early days."

One Bull first hunted near the river for the proper stones to heat. He did not look for stones in the water itself, but hunted along the top of the bank and back a way where they would be thoroughly dry. Certain stones that have been lying in the water will fly to pieces when they are heated. For that matter, some dry stones will. Never use anything that looks like flint or quartz. And sandstone will crumble all to pieces when heated. If you are going to try this experiment, and do not know what kind of stones to choose, try them out first before cooking with them. Heat some of them, then plunge them into a pail of water and see what happens. If they stay whole, or merely crack open, you know they are all right.

After One Bull had gathered eight or ten satisfactory stones about as big as his fist or a little larger, he cut four green poles about five feet long and tied them into a quadripod (Fig. 23). To this he fastened the paunch, which had been thoroughly washed.

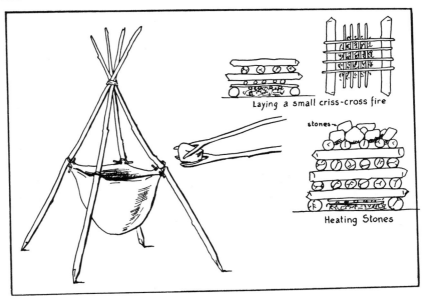

Fig. 23. Stone Boiling.

Although the paunch is like a big skin bag, he handled the opening as if it were square. He thrust four small skewers through the "corners" and, with thongs, tied each of these skewers to a pole. To one side he laid a big fire (crisscross), with the stones on top.

Water was poured in the paunch until it was about half-full, and then small pieces of meat were placed in it. When the stones were hot, they were picked up with two green forked sticks, also prepared in advance, and placed in the "kettle." The very first stone added to the water brought it to a violent boil. It was uncanny! Almost unbelievable! As the boiling died down, another stone was added, and so on. It took less than half an hour to cook the little pieces of meat. The broth made a rich soup. Because the stones had been carefully selected, there was no grit or sand in the bottom.

The nice part about this kind of a dinner is that there is no kettle to wash. Next day we ate the kettle. The Indians surely had the right idea!

Indians did a similar kind of boiling out on the prairie, where there were no trees or poles: a little hole, the size of the paunch, was dug in the ground and the paunch placed in it. The stones were heated with buffalo chips. The meat and soup were just as good this way, but the "kettle" was ruined because of resting in the dirt.

One of the most familiar sights in an old tipi village was meat drying on racks all over the camp. "Jerking" meat is becoming a lost art, along with the rest of tipi life. One can see much jerked meat at Indian summer camps today, but only the older women still make it. The young ones now depend upon local stores, refrigerators, or even the deep freezer, for their meat supply.

The way the old women do this work does not look very difficult, but it requires skill and can prove to be a big job for a novice. Jerky, or *ba pa*, as the Sioux call it, may not be quite as tasty as fresh meat, but it has much food value and actually is very good. It has the advantage of being light in weight and of keeping indefinitely, so long as it is kept perfectly dry. For flavor, we prefer it to commercially dried beef.

In butchering, the Indian followed the natural contours and muscle layers. He did not cut cross-grain or saw through bones, the way the white butcher does. Indians, and early mountain men, refused to eat cross-grain meat in former times.

Jerky can be made out of almost any piece of meat. The piece can be small, only a pound or so, or large, up to several pounds in size. Of course it must be removed from the bone and kept in chunk form. A very sharp butcher knife is required. A hunting knife is too thick-edged and usually too short for the job. An Indian butcher knife is sharpened on one side only, beveled on the top edge as you look at it while holding it in the right hand with cutting edge to the left. This method of sharpening seems to be advantageous in jerking the meat.

First, cut straight through the center of the piece, stopping within a quarter of an inch of going clear through. Then the process is practically like unrolling the meat, first one side of the chunk and then the other. The drawing in Fig. 24 will help you understand this. Hold the meat on the palm of the hand and work the knife carefully along through the meat, parallel to the surface of the palm. Be careful you do not cut yourself, and don't be discouraged if at first it seems very slow. We have seen two Indian women jerk an entire steer carcass in a day. By the amount of meat they hung up it looked as if they had done four carcasses, for one little chunk opens up into a long, thin slice, many inches in length. We have seen pieces five and six feet long! You will end up by discovering

Fig. 24. Cutting and Drying Jerky.

that you have only about one pound of jerky for every five pounds
of fresh meat you started with. But, you still have the real meat
and all of its food value. All you have lost is water.

Skewers, usually of plum or cherry wood, are made to keep the
long strips spread while drying. These are pointed at both ends
and merely caught on each side of the strip. The strips are then
hung in the hot sun on poles of the drying racks, which are made
in various forms, high enough so that the dogs cannot reach them.
Bruce Yellowtail made a big fuss when his grandmother hung some
of her jerky on his radio aerial!

Pretty Shield, wife of Custer's scout, Goes Ahead, demonstrating to Reginald Laubin how to make Jerky. Photograph by Crandall.

You need not worry about flies. The meat is cut so thin, not much over a quarter of an inch in thickness, that flies cannot "blow" it. And the cleaner the camp is kept, the fewer flies there will be. Very few flies will even alight on the meat. Even if they do, sunlight is a good disinfectant, and most people prefer the jerky cooked, further eliminating any danger of contamination.

While drying the meat, make sure that no two surfaces touch. In hot sun, jerky will dry hard in a couple of days. It should be removed at night, piled up on a clean canvas and covered, so it will not absorb moisture from the atmosphere. In cloudy or rainy weather, the meat may be hung indoors, tying cross poles high up to the tipi poles. This is the only time the meat is smoked, and it is unin-

tentional then. Real Indian jerky is neither smoked nor salted.
When it is properly cured, it is nearly as hard as iron, about the
consistency of sole leather, but we can assure you that it does not
taste like it. Real Indian jerky is a far cry from the stuff now on
the market, sold with misleading labels to make you think it is
Indian. It is highly salted, smoked and full of additives, so has
neither the flavor nor the food value of the genuine article.

Jerky was packed in the flat, rawhide cases known as parfleches. It can be cared for just as well by keeping it in cloth sacks
which are in the air and dry all the time. For an extended period of
time it can be kept in a big tin can, like a lard can. If the meat gets
damp, or is unprotected in a dark place, it may be attacked by
weevils.

Jerky is sometimes eaten "as is," but is best when cooked. One
method of cooking is to break it up into little pieces, barely cover
them with water, and simmer until soft. The jerky will never re-
gain the original plumpness and texture of the meat, but it will
become quite tender, depending upon what cut of meat it was made
from in the first place. Salt the stew to taste, and, if you like,
thicken the broth with a little flour for a rich gravy.

The Sioux made a soup, usually a winter dish, using all dried
materials. They call it *washtunk'kala*, and it is very good. The
ba'pa is cooked with dried prairie turnips *(ti'psinla)*, dried corn
(wakimi'za), and dried squash *(wagmu)*.

Prairie turnips still grow in great numbers in parts of the
prairie country of the Dakotas, Nebraska, Montana, and Wyoming.
They are gathered in June or early July, dug with a crowbar sharpened to a flat point, like a spear point. They are peeled while still
fresh, then braided together by the root tails. The braided strings
look much like the strings of garlic seen in Italian shops and will
keep indefinitely. Fresh, the "turnips" do taste like a mild turnip.
After being dried, then soaked and boiled, they have something
of the texture and flavor of mushrooms. The center core is woody
or pithy, but the remainder is delicious, especially when cooked
with other vegetables.

Perhaps the best "iron ration" ever discovered is the pemmican
of the Plains Indians. U.S. soldiers in the field so preferred it to
their hardtack and other emergency rations that they made all
sorts of swaps with the tribesmen to get it. Today the army uses
a modern variety of the old Indian pemmican which has proved to
be very satisfactory. It has been used in great quantities by polar

exploring expeditions. But we do not think it tastes nearly as good as the old Indian variety, though it may have even more food value.

To make pemmican, first roast jerky over coals until the grease begins to show and it takes on a rich brown color like seared fresh meat. This in itself is a good way to prepare jerky for eating. It is rather crunchy but very tasty. To continue with the pemmican, pound the roasted jerky fine.[7] This is done on a clean canvas or oilcloth, using a smooth, flat stone for an anvil and the back of an axe for the pounder. Formerly a stone hammer, set in rawhide, was used.

Now dry fresh chokecherries just enough to take out the excess moisture, then pound in the same way, enough to reduce the pits to as fine a pulp as possible. Mix some of this cherry pulp with the pounded jerky, pour melted suet over the whole mass, mix it thoroughly, and then pat into egg-shaped balls. These balls can be preserved in oiled silk or in a plastic bag. In the old days, the pemmican, instead of being made into balls, was stored in cases made of bladders or of rawhide, with melted suet poured over it, and sealed completely.

When we went to Europe with our Crow dance troupe, Grandma Yellowtail insisted that we take a big sack of jerky and another of pemmican with us.[8] She was afraid we might get stranded and have nothing to eat. And, indeed, this old Indian food came in very handy on several occasions when we had a tight schedule and no time to stop for meals.

The cherry pulp, when not used in pemmican, was made into little flat cakes and thoroughly dried for future use. Service berries, or June berries, sometimes called squawberries, can be used in the same way. Sometimes nowadays the pemmican is made without any fruit, a little sugar being added instead. But it is not so rich or tasty as the old kind.

The dried cakes of fruit were later soaked in water until soft and made into *wojapi*, a sort of pudding. The softened cherries or berries were gently simmered for an hour or so. Nowadays a little sugar is added and a bit of flour to thicken the mixture. Honey or

---

[7]This pounded jerky is spoken of by the Sioux as *wasna*, although *wasna* usually has marrow added to it. The completed pemmican, with berries and suet, is *wakapanpi*.

[8]See Laubin, *Indian Dances of North America*.

maple sugar, instead of granulated sugar, makes the *wojapi* still better.

In Paris, a famous restaurant wanted to feature an Indian menu while we were there; so we donated some of our precious jerky and dried chokecherries to the cause and the Indian ladies showed the French chefs how to prepare them. But to our amazement and that of the Indians, they served the cherry pudding *on* the meat, which certainly made a different dish from anything we had ever had before!

An Indian friend in Oklahoma once invited us to have dinner with him and asked, "Have you ever had any Indian food?"

"Well, yes, some," we answered.

"What did you have?" he wanted to know.

"Oh, raw liver, jerky, pemmican, marrow guts, prairie turnips," we replied.

"You have?" he said in astonishment. "That sounds like old time. I never even had those things."

After that he would introduce us to his friends and say, "These folks have eaten *real Indian* food," and then he would ask us to name them all off.

We cannot say we enjoy raw liver, even though it is recommended by some modern doctors for certain ailments. But once while trying to help an old Crow Indian butcher a buffalo, when the Crows still had their buffalo herd up in the Big Horn Mountains, Bob Yellowtail came along and said, "One Bull, if you want to be an Indian you'll have to eat some of this," and he cut off a strip of the fresh liver and handed it to me.

He ate it with apparent relish, so I ate mine, although it was something like chewing a piece of wet rubber. Next year in a conversation with some of our friends this subject came up and they all laughed.

"What's so funny?" I asked.

"It made Robbie sick," they said. He had never eaten raw liver before either, but did not think I would take him up on it when he offered me a piece.

The other Indian delicacy, marrow guts, does not sound very appetizing either, but when we were camped with Julia Wades-in-the-Water, she introduced it to us. In her huge tipi she had a little sheepherder's stove, which is a small version of the old-fashioned iron kitchen range, oven and all. Knowing we never had a stove in our tipi when she visited us, she kept apologizing for hers and said, "When fair is over and ever'body go home, I throw stove out and we have nice fire, like old time." Then one time she asked, "You like marrow guts?"

"You bet," we answered, although we had never tasted them and were not even sure what they were.

She was constantly cooking for visitors, who came from tribes all over the west, so the little stove was almost essential. She even wanted to serve us at a table, with a table cloth and all, but when we told her we really preferred to eat Indian style, sitting on the ground with a big oil cloth spread in front of us, she was highly pleased. She sometimes served as many as twenty people, ten on each side of a long oil cloth.

After the first stormy night we spent in Julia's tipi the weather cleared and we were able to put up our own tipi. One evening we went over to visit her but she was gone. Her son told us she went to town to get a "hamburg." She had been serving visitors all day and had run out of food. No Indian hostess eats while her guests are eating. For that matter, neither does the host. We waited for her and by and by she came back, loaded down with more groceries, happy as a child, laughing and chuckling, seeming to be completely delighted as she told us, "Lots mo' people comin' tomorra from Canada."

When the "doings" were over, Julia kept her word and threw the stove out, making a nice fire ring of stones, and she cooked us the marrow guts. These are a section of intestine heavily coated with fat. It is thoroughly washed and cleaned, but the fat is not removed. It is turned inside-out, so the fat is inside, and washed again. It is broiled over the coals and I do not think we have ever smelled anything more tempting. It tasted delicious, too, but it does take a lot of chewing.

The Indians used all the glandular meats. Although they knew nothing about vitamins, they learned early that if you have an almost completely meat diet it is essential to eat the glandular meats as well as the red muscle meats. The pioneer Whites scoffed at the Indians for eating "guts," but had they been willing to eat them they never would have suffered from scurvy and other ailments that beset them on their long journeys across the prairies. When on a hunt, if someone helped you butcher your game he was entitled to the liver and heart—a special reward for his assistance!

In the *Lewis and Clark Journals* is a report of an occasion, shortly after contacting the Shoshonis, when the Indians as well as

the entire expedition went hungry for days until one of the white
scouts killed a deer. When the Indians heard about it they all
rushed to the scene but amazed the explorers by taking only the
parts the hunter had discarded. Lewis wrote: ". . . though suffering
with hunger they did not attempt, as they might have done, to take
by force the whole deer, but contented themselves with what had
been thrown away by the hunter." Actually they took what they
wanted but it just so happened that the white men did not care for
the glandular meats anyway.

One Bull told us they could not live on deer or elk alone. He
said they would starve to death with nothing but those meats for
the winter because they do not have enough fat, and what little
they have is indigestible. But buffalo! That was the meat of all
meats!

Eastern Indians, of course, had many foods unknown to those
of the Plains. Without attempting to list them, we were once invited to a feast among the Cherokees where they served thirty-five
different Indian dishes, ranging in anything from bean bread, which
is made of corn meal and fresh beans, wrapped in a large grape leaf
and boiled like a dumpling, to mountain trout, squirrel, and roast
corn on the cob. And they really have "roasting ears," a special
variety of exceptionally sweet green corn, left in the husks and
roasted directly across two green logs with a bed of hot hardwood
coals between. We watched George Owl prepare this, and could
hardly keep from telling him, "You're burning it." But he purposely
roasted it until the husks were charred almost black, turning it
about four times, so all sides of the ears were equally heated. It
takes about five minutes for each side, or 20 minutes in all. And
is it ever good!

Anyone further interested in Cherokee cooking can obtain a
little Cherokee cookbook from the Cherokee Historical Association
in Cherokee, North Carolina.

Woodland tribes prepared corn in many different ways. In fact,
most of them had several varieties of corn, each being raised for
a specific use and purpose. In New England they had a type of
large-kernel corn, similar to modern field corn, which was parched
and pounded very fine with a stone pestle in a hickory mortar.
Mohegans called this *yokeg.* In other Algonkin dialects it was
known as *nokeg* and *hokeg,* called by the English "no cake" and
"hoe cake." So we think the so-called "hoe cake" had nothing to do
with being baked on a hoe but was merely an English corruption

of a native word. Indians of Connecticut and Massachusetts made a kind of cake from corn meal which they carried on a journey. New Englanders called this "Johnny cake" because they could not pronounce the "r" in "journey."

The *yokeg* powder was also carried on a journey in a little pouch on the traveler's belt. A small quantity of this in the palm of the hand, mixed with water, made an entire meal for the traveler, serving as a substitute for the pemmican of the western tribes. The powder could not be eaten dry because it would choke anyone who tried it. Not too many years ago, while the Mohegans were still holding an annual fair near Norwich, Connecticut, they served the yokeg on ice cream, with maple syrup. It made quite a sundae! Yokeg has a rather nutty flavor.

Another variety of corn was used to make hominy. The kernels were soaked in a lye solution made from wood ashes until the hulls came off. The hominy was boiled to prepare it for eating, and it was often served with maple syrup or maple sugar. It was also used in soups and stews, or served with meat broth.

A third variety was used as green corn for roasting ears, and still another was our familiar popcorn. Indians popped it by stirring it in a clay pot set on the coals. They parched the corn for yokeg in the same way. Today they do it in an iron skillet.

A fifth type of corn was ground into meal such as most of us know today, but of course was far better than most of what we now find in the stores, which has been de-germinated, de-nuded, de-vitalized, then "enriched" by adding chemical preservatives and a small amount of synthetic vitamins. Yellow corn was used for meal in the north, white in the South.

Indians made a mush by boiling the meal in water, then ate it with marrow fat, maple syrup, or both. To prepare the mush it is best to mix the meal with cold water into a batter, then stir this slowly into boiling water, about twice as much water as meal. It must be stirred almost constantly until thickened, or about ten minutes, then should be hung high above the fire, to cook very slowly, for about an hour, being stirred occasionally. If it needs thinning before it is done, use boiling water. Sometimes the mush was boiled in thinned maple syrup instead of water. For this kind of cooking in the tipi there is nothing better than a tripod of wooden poles with hooks of different lengths for hanging the kettle at varying heights.

After traders brought molasses to the Indians it was also used on hominy and mush. When the Sioux first received molasses as part of their rations from the government, they thought it was some new kind of hair oil and smeared it on their heads![9]

Succotash was made in many ways. Best, to our way of thinking, is the way it was made in New England with fresh green corn scraped off the cobs, fresh shelled *scipio* beans, and a little bacon or salt pork, all simmered together in enough water to cover. Most Indians never cooked with salt, but if you like salt you may add it to taste. The cobs were cooked with the succotash for extra flavor, then later discarded. Even the silk was sometimes included, and some Indians saved and dried the silk for future use. *Scipio* beans are pinkish in color, with dark spots or specks. Chili beans would be a good substitute if they could be obtained fresh. Otherwise, any fresh beans can be used. Such succotash was also made with venison, beef, and even fish. Another succotash can be made of dried materials, first soaking them in water overnight, then cooking them together, but of course it has an entirely different flavor from the fresh ingredients.

Lake Indians make a corn soup, nowadays using beef short ribs for the stock. The short ribs are boiled, or rather simmered slowly until the meat is tender enough to slip from the bones. The soup is then cooled until the grease collects and hardens on the top, which is then skimmed off. The stock is then re-heated, the corn, freshly scraped from the cobs, is added and cooked a few minutes in the broth. Today they even use canned cream-style corn. Formerly dried corn was also used.

Corn can be dried by scraping it carefully from the cobs, being sure to scrape them clean, then spreading out the fresh kernels on a cloth, oil cloth, or in trays and setting them in the sun. They should be stirred occasionally so as to dry evenly. Trays of fresh corn can also be dried in a very low, open oven if there is no sunshine.

Fresh green corn is also boiled for three or four minutes on the cob, some of the husks being left on; then the husks are peeled back and the ears hung up by the husks to dry. The only disadvantage of this method is that it takes up a lot of storage space. To use the corn, it is placed in boiling water until tender and eaten as fresh corn on the cob.

---

[9]Flying Cloud told us that when first issued frying pans, everyone, young and old, used them for sleds to slide down the hill.

A quicker way of drying corn is the way a Caddo friend described to us. After scraping fresh, juicy corn from the cob, as previously explained, place it in a shallow pan about 8 inches square, and mix about a tablespoon of melted bacon grease in it. Add a little salt if you care to. Treat it just as if you were making corn bread, placing it in a Dutch oven, or a reflector oven, at what you think would be about 425 degrees. That is the temperature to use if baking in a modern oven. In the old days, before oven thermometers, the cook tested the heat with the back of her hand. With a little experience you can tell at once if it is hot enough, too hot or too cold. Bake the corn for thirty-five to forty minutes, until it is crisp and brown on top. It can then be broken up into small pieces and stored for future use. When you want to serve it, cover the amount you need with twice the amount of water and simmer it for half an hour or so. It is delicious and tastes almost like fresh corn.

Squash and pumpkins were sliced and the circular slices hung on a pole to dry. Another method was to peel a thin-skinned variety of squash around and around, something like paring an apple, making as long a "string" as possible. These strings of squash were then woven into a mat and dried. Either way, the dried squash or pumpkin was soaked, as other dried foods, and used in stews, soups, etc., as mentioned for *washtunkala*. Squashes were also baked whole in a ground oven. Little acorn squashes are delicious this way, and you can bake them in a modern oven at home just as well. After they are baked cut them open and take out the seeds, not before. The seeds add a nutty flavor.

Lewis and Clark brought some dried squash, which they had obtained from the Mandans, to the Shoshonis. Sacajawea's brother, Cameahwait, declared it was the best food he had ever tasted except for a small lump of sugar he had received from his sister.

Many kinds of berries can also be dried, rather than canned, for future use. We have dried blueberries, huckleberries, service berries, chokecherries, rose hips, wild plums, haw-apples, and elderberries and found them all delicious.

After talking so much about Indian foods, some people who are acquainted to some extent with Indians are going to say, "But you haven't said anything about fried bread!" One would certainly be led to believe that this is a typical Indian item, for Indians all over the country make it and have been doing so for many years. You can hardly go to an Indian "doings" when "fry bread" is not important on the menu. We first ate fried bread with our Sioux "relatives" in South Dakota, then later with Crows, Blackfeet, Arapahos, Chippewas, several tribes in Oklahoma, Winnebagos in Chicago, with Navajos on the lawn of the Fine Arts Museum in Dallas at the Fabulous West exhibition, and finally with Shoshonis and Bannocks at the Yellowstone Park Centennial celebration. But fried bread was not Indian originally, for it is made of white wheat flour and is fried in deep fat. Indians knew nothing of wheat or of such frying in early days. Just where it actually came from is a mystery that, as far as we know, has not been solved. In North Dakota we were told it came from the Norwegians, but we have never heard of Norwegians who knew anything about it. Perhaps it came up from Mexico via the Spanish trail, but it is not Mexican, for they use corn meal for everything. Perhaps white pioneers made it. It is certain that somewhere along the line the Indians learned to make it from white people, passing it from tribe to tribe, and it has been a staple with them ever since.

Flour was one of the first things issued as rations to the Indians. At first they just threw it away, dumping it out of the sacks and using the sacks for storage and for cloth on anything from a war bonnet trailer to articles of clothing. Nor did they take to bacon much quicker. An old Sioux said to his people on ration day, "Don't eat that meat with the blue marks on it. That's a dead white man. I have seen those blue marks (Government stamps) on white men (tattoos). These white men are bad people. They are cannibals. Do not eat their meat!" But the time came when they had to eat the rations or starve, and once they learned to make "fry bread" with the flour and fry it in the bacon fat, it was not so hard to do. If made well, it is delicious, even though it may not be the most healthful of foods.

A young man who just returned from serving in the Armed Forces overseas came to visit us. He said he just could not wait to make a tipi (which he did from our instructions), and go visit the Indians. They were kind to him and taught him to make fried bread, mixing it right in the bag of flour. He had so much fun that he sat up most of the night frying it and eating it.

Fried bread is made from a mixture almost exactly like baking powder biscuits. It is pulled and stretched and kneaded like a biscuit dough. Some women make it in large cakes almost the size of a large frying pan. A slash is cut in the center, so that it cooks all through in the hot grease, and the final result is like a great big doughnut. Others make smaller cakes, but unless very small they are also slashed in the center.

For many years the dough has been fried in lard in an iron skillet, but before the buffalo were gone, or while they still had beef rations, they fried it in melted buffalo or beef tallow. If you do not like the idea of using lard there is no reason why you can not use a vegetable shortening, but most Indians prefer lard. Whatever grease you use should be heated enough that a drop of water sizzles in it. The dough is usually cooked on one side, then carefully and quickly turned over to brown the other side. A typical recipe would be about like this:

    5 cups flour
    2 tablespoons baking powder
    1 teaspoon salt
    1 tablespoon melted lard
    Water enough to mix the dough.

Some women do not add melted fat to the dough. Others, nowadays, use melted butter or margarine instead of lard. Sometimes they also add a little sugar, and sometimes they mix it with about two cups of milk instead of water. Canned milk may be used, mixed with equal amounts of water.

There seem to be almost as many recipes for fried bread as there are women who make it, but in recent years the favorite among some Indians is a fried yeast bread rather than a baking powder bread. A Shoshoni friend gave us these recipes, one for regular "fry bread" and the other for fried yeast bread, which came from his grandmother. She called them both "moccasin track bread."

For the baking powder type she uses a large mixing bowl and

(1) mixes 3 cups of flour, 3 teaspoons of baking powder, and 1/2 teaspoon of salt;

(2) adds water or milk to make a dough that can be rolled out; lets it set 15 minutes to half an hour;

(3) flours a bread board, rolls out the dough, cuts it into squares, and stretches and pulls each square into a rounded flat cake, which she then fries in deep fat as before mentioned.

For the yeast type, use your favorite wheat-flour bread recipe, but instead of using sugar, use corn syrup or honey and before setting the dough to rise, add two eggs. Let the dough rise twice, 30 to 40 minutes each time, kneading as for ordinary bread. Have the frying fat hot, put some cold grease on your hands and take a ball of dough, stretching it to shape. If you want large cakes, slash the center. For smaller cakes this is not necessary. Drop the cake into the hot fat until brown on one side, turn it over with a fork and brown the other side. Let it cool a bit, but eat it while still hot. Fried bread is best eaten hot, and if you like it really good, pour maple syrup on it, as the Chippewas do.

We saw an Indian girl recently, who had more training in nutrition that most Indians, using whole wheat flour, wheat germ, honey, butter, milk, and eggs in mixing the dough for her fried bread. She told us, "The white man took away our buffalo and gave us in its place white bread, which has no nutrition in it, so instead of remaining strong and healthy, we became sick and fat."

A more nutritious bread, and really more Indian than "fry bread," because it was native to Indians of the east and south, is bread made of corn meal. To be at its best, the meal should be whole-ground and fresh. If not used soon such meal must be kept refrigerated or in a cool basement. This is why it can not be procured from the average grocery, because it has no shelf life.

A typical recipe would be:
  1 quart meal
  1 teaspoon salt
  1 pint warm (not scalding) water
  Stir together until light. The "bread" will be still lighter if a couple of well beaten eggs are added. Some people think it is further improved by using milk, either fresh or canned (50/50 canned milk and water) instead of water.

This batter can be baked as one flat loaf on a greased tin or in a shallow greased pan in a reflector oven or in a Dutch oven. Do not use extreme heat, but rather use moderate heat and bake at least 45 minutes. If using the Dutch oven, take the oven out of the coals when the bread is done and let it set and "sweat" for about 15 minutes (cover on, of course). If using the reflector, get the same results by removing the bread from the oven and setting it to one side of the fire, covered, for the same length of time.

Indians sometimes added walnut meal, hickory nut meal, or pecan meal to this batter. You can also use raw peanut flour, sesame seeds or caraway seeds, which are not Indian but a substitute for the nut flour, which might be hard to get, although pecan meal is available. Indians also used lots of sunflower seed meal and pumpkin seed meal. Any of these things would make delicious changes from the original recipe.

This same kind of bread can be baked in hot ashes, and is called "ash cake." Early New England Indians mixed corn meal dough with dried berries made into cakes, wrapped in leaves, and baked in hot ashes. How about using foil instead of leaves? If the dough is rolled in the hands into little cylinders and fried in deep fat it becomes "corn dodgers" and might be considered a close relative to "fry bread."

Another recipe for corn pone calls for
3 cups white corn meal
1/2 teaspoon salt
1/2 cup nut meal (as mentioned above)
1/3 cup corn oil
Boiling water
Slowly pour a little boiling water and a bit of the oil into the meal, stirring thoroughly and adding the rest of the oil and more water as needed. Use only enough water to make a firm dough. When cool enough to handle, form into cakes and bake on a greased tin or shallow pan 35 to 40 minutes at moderate heat (about 375 degrees).

Any of these corn breads can also be baked on a hot flat rock. Indians in the southwest still bake in this fashion.

If you really want something good, try what some of our visitors call *Glad's Fluffy Extry-Scrumptuous Pancakes*, which is an adaptation of some Indian recipes.

1/2 cup wheat germ
1 1/2 cups whole ground
   cornmeal (finely ground)
2 eggs
3/4 teaspoon salt
2 tablespoons corn oil
   (or butter)

3 level teaspoons baking
   powder
1 teaspoon molasses
1 tablespoon honey
1 3/4 cups milk (half canned,
   half water)

Sift dry ingredients and mix well
Separate eggs, beat yolks, add milk, honey, molasses, and stir well
Pour 1 cup of this liquid into dry ingredients, stirring quickly

Add corn oil (or melted butter) and beat well
Pour in remaining liquid and beat again
Gently fold in beaten egg whites
Lightly grease a not too hot griddle with corn oil
Use about two tablespoons of batter to each cake.
Serve with real butter and real maple syrup, or with choke-
cherry, rose hip, or haw-apple syrup for still more special.
Yum! yum! Come and get it!

This same batter can be baked for a delicious corn bread. Merely double the oil (or butter) and do not separate the eggs. Pour into a well greased pan (9″ x 9″), bake at 425 degrees for 20–25 minutes. With coarse meal use half flour and half corn meal. (Set a reflector oven close to the fire. If it browns too quickly, pull it back a bit.)

Before white men came it is doubtful if any Indians cooked with salt and even today many do not. In the early days they got salt from salt licks and other natural deposits, but they used it only sparingly, as a luxury. Some of these licks are now known to contain calcium chloride, rather than sodium chloride. The La-kota word for salt, *mniskuya*, means *sweet* water. A little salt was used now and then about like candy.

Olaus Murie, famous biologist and ecologist, and our neighbor, told us that while he was in Alaska he noticed that the natives did not seem to be bothered by mosquitos whereas white men were almost eaten alive. He came to the conclusion that the difference lay in the fact that the natives ate no salt. He tried it for himself and found that he was not nearly as troubled by them as before.

While on the subject of Indian foods, perhaps we should make some mention of the camas root, which was a favorite food of Indians living on the plateau in Idaho, Washington and Oregon, many of whom became tipi dwellers during the early 1800's. Jack Williams, superintendent of Nez Perce Park, sent us information on the camas, which we pass along.

First, there are two varieties of camas, one edible, the other very poisonous. So, for anyone interested in this Indian food it will pay to learn which is which. The edible camas always grows in big, swampy meadow lands. When it is ready to harvest it has a blue flower and the blooms almost cover the area so that it looks like a beautiful blue field. The death camas, on the other hand, grows on higher, arid and rocky land and the flowers are cream colored or pale yellow.

The camas bulbs can be eaten raw or cooked but most people think the flavor of the cooked is better. Indians still prepare bushels of camas bulbs by roasting them in a pit oven, such as we have already described. Sometimes these pits are six to ten feet in diameter and about three feet deep. Firewood is laid to a depth of a foot or more all across the bottom of the pit and stones are placed on top of the wood. When the wood has burned down and the stones are hot, they are spread level across the bottom and covered with a thin layer of earth. Grass is placed on top of the earth; then the camas bulbs, having first been cleaned by removing the black outer layer with the fingers, are dumped in making a conical heap. These white inner bulbs are also covered with a layer of grass. Water is poured on until steam begins to rise, then everything is covered with a few inches of dry earth. The bulbs are thus steamed anywhere from twelve hours to three days, depending upon the quantity.

When the pit is opened the cooked camas is allowed to dry, where it lays, from the heat of the still warm stones. Then the bulbs are removed and placed on scaffolds for further drying.

The bulbs are no longer white, but by now are black again and much sweeter than when raw. Some are eaten at this time, but the majority are preserved. Longer keeping requires further treatment. The now soft bulbs are pounded into a sort of dough and formed into little loaves, which are rolled in grass and steamed in the pit again. Of course a new fire must be built and the stones heated again. The loaves are then interspersed with fresh camas, which now gets a first steaming while giving the loaves their treatment. The loaves are removed and broken into smaller cakes and dried in the sun, or over a campfire if the weather becomes bad. The cakes are irregular in shape and about an inch in thickness. If kept dry they will remain edible for a long time. When the camas is steamed for longer periods it comes out a sort of dark brown or black mass. Gruel is made from this for immediate use and loaves are made from it and dried for later use.

HOUSEHOLD HINTS

Before white men brought metal tools, pots, and pans, cooking equipment was simple, as we have already described. In other parts of the country both stone and pottery pots and dishes were used,

but twenty-five years after the coming of the white man you probably could not have found any in use. But even after the introduction of metal containers, they remained few and simple.

While we were on the reservations most families we knew
usually possessed a large kettle, a frying pan, and a coffee pot.
A government extension worker once came to Standing Rock to
teach the women how to prepare better meals. At the first session
she handed them paper and pencils and told them to write down
what they needed for the course—a large kettle, medium kettle,
small kettle, large and small frying pans, colander, sieve, mixing
bowls of various sizes, measuring spoons, dippers, ladles, salt and
pepper shakers, spices, and so on. The Indian women wrote them
all down, looked at each other, got up and went out, and that was
the first and last session of the course in home economics. Not one
of them had ever heard of all these things, and they were completely frightened off by the very first lesson.

We do not intend to suggest anything quite so complicated,
but we have done all this talking about foods and cooking and have
said very little about what to cook in. We formerly had a set of
granite enamel kettles or pots—a large one, medium-sized one and
a small one—which nested together very well. All, of course, had
handles, or bails, for we used to do most of our cooking in the tipi
with a tripod for a stove. A small tripod of light poles about 4 feet
long was tied within 5 or 6 inches of its upper ends and from it
hung a "dingle hook," a hook made from a forked branch and sus-
pended by a cord or thong from the tripod (Fig. 25). These hooks
can be made of different lengths to accommodate kettles of various
sizes or to hang them at varying heights above the fire.

Over the years the old granite kettles finally wore out and we
have been unable to replace them. So we have acquired a set of
enamel pans, with side handles, which cannot be hung over the fire,
of course, but are all right on an iron grill. We still prefer enamel
to aluminum or steel, and we also have some old fashioned iron
kettles, "spiders," and a Dutch oven, which, although heavy, are
hard to beat for really good cooking.

Naturally, cooking over an open fire makes the outside of the
pots black, but do not worry about that. If you do, of course you
can spray them before putting them over the fire with an oven
cleaner or some other modern product supposed to keep food from
sticking. Instead of using it on the inside, as the directions say,
use it on the outside and the black soot will wash right off. Or you

can coat the outside with soap or grease. Actually, the blacker
the pot is, the faster and better it will cook the food; so all you
really need do is wash the inside after using; then put it in a paper
sack or some old canvas saved especially for the purpose. In this
way you can even stack the kettles of a cooking kit without getting
everything else black.

Indians made beautifully beaded buckskin carrying bags for
their cooking utensils. Of course, they got black on the inside, too,
but the outside was the part you saw.

We also made a canvas bag for carrying our kettles and cooking
kit and we carry knives, forks, spoons, etc., in another cloth bag.

A set of enamel, or even plastic bowls, and cups that nest
together are almost a necessity for good camp cooking, and one of
the most essential and convenient articles is a long-handled dipper.
You might also include a measuring cup. Also, at least one bucket
for carrying water, as well as a covered container to store it in
should be included in any outfit where transportation is not an
important consideration. Another bucket for waste water is also
handy. Folding canvas buckets are still available and save space
in packing. All of these things should have lids, for the kettles to
make cooking faster and more efficient, for the buckets to keep
the water clean.

Some campers seem to think that cleanliness is unnecessary,
but it actually is very important. An old sailor friend told us that
on one voyage everyone got terribly sick and the ship had to make
for the nearest port. There the doctor informed them that the ill-
ness was caused by uncleanliness on the part of the kitchen help,
who did not wash and rinse dishes and utensils thoroughly. There
is no more reason to be a dirty camper than to be dirty any place.
So we suggest having three good-sized basins that will nest—two
for washing and rinsing dishes and one for personal use. We do not
recommend plastic because it cracks in the cold. Towels, wash-
cloths or sponges, and soap should be in your kit also, and if you
want to be really Indian, a razor should be included.

Indians despised hair on the face but they were fortunate in
not having much. The little that appeared was plucked out with
tweezers, originally made from fresh water mussels. They referred
to white men with whiskers as bear faces, hairy faces, or old buffalo
bulls. So, even when camping in the tipi, I shave religiously every
morning.

Both men and women of many tribes wore their hair long, but

they did not allow it to hang loose, falling all over and getting in the way. It was kept braided and often the braids were wrapped with otter skin strips, or ribbons, not only to decorate it, but to keep it under control and from becoming frayed and disheveled. Only for certain ceremonies was the hair worn loose, certainly not ordinarily, when engaged in daily activities. Most men and women prided themselves on beautiful hair, keeping it well combed or brushed and neatly plaited. Combs, or brushes, were made of porcupine tails, skinned out and sewed around a foundation of wood, or of dried buffalo tongues. Some were carved from wood. Husbands and wives sometimes brushed and braided each other's hair. The hair was occasionally washed with the suds made from yucca roots and then oiled with fats of various animal origins such as bear, raccoon, and goose, or sometimes with vegetable oils from sunflower seeds, pecans, or other nuts.

There is no excuse for not having plenty of hot water when you have a fire so handy as that inside the tipi. A sheet of oilcloth to place on the ground in lieu of a table is also handy. Or an extra piece of clean canvas will do, but the oilcloth is easier to keep clean.

If you use soap powder, carry it in a jar or covered tin can, as it draws moisture from the air in its original carton. If you are camping in one place for any length of time you will also find that covered metal or plastic containers are good for storing foods that mice or chipmunks are likely to get into. We hide all such "civilized" things either behind or inside of our rawhide boxes and cases when they are not in use and we want the lodge to look its best.

In a big tipi Indians sometimes used a crane above the fireplace made by setting two tall, heavy forked sticks into the ground, one on each side of the fire, with a pole across the top, from which hung hooks for several kettles. They even had blacksmiths make adjustable pot hooks of iron, like our pioneer ancestors had in their kitchen fireplaces. Sometimes they used a swinging crane, made of a short pole with a horizontal branch left on for the arm. The pole was set in the ground deep enough to support considerable weight, but it could be turned to hang a kettle or two in different positions above the fire.

Recently we have made good use of a folding metal grate or grid, about 12 by 24 inches, above the fire, but we cut off the legs so that it stands only about 6 inches above the ground instead of the foot or so high as originally designed. On it we can cook with

several kettles at once. But we are glad we have had the experience
of using the tripod, for it is really elemental.

Most of the grids, as well as most of the built-in fireplaces
found in parks and recreation areas are far too high. You need a
cord of wood to make fire enough to heat anything set on them and
wood is one thing hardest to find in these places.

Two of the handiest tools for any kind of outdoor cooking have
already been mentioned—tongs and a stick for a poker. A third is
a pot hook, or lifter, which can be simply a long forked stick with
one prong of the fork cut short for a hook (Fig. 25).

We have fared very well when camping in hot weather, although we did not have an icebox or a refrigerator. We simply dug
a deep hole in a shady spot (you can find some shade even on a sage
brush flat), about 2 feet across and the same depth, lining it with
stones when available. We poured water over the stones, for further cooling, set our milk, eggs, butter and other perishables in
the hole, and covered the entire thing over with a tarp, on top of
which we placed a pile of brush. Then we came home one day to find
a big skunk asleep on the remainder of our supplies in the hole.
He had eaten a dozen eggs, a pound of bacon, a pound of lard and a
pound of butter. No wonder he looked so fat! So we learned the
hard way, and after that we set a big lard can, obtained from a
bakery, in the hole and kept the cover on tight.

We showed this refrigerator trick to some Indian friends and
they were delighted with it. They have to depend upon such foods
themselves nowadays, but many of them still have no refrigerators,
and no one has ever showed them how to make the adjustment to
our way of life. They have had to learn the hard way—by experience.

We also showed them how to bake in a reflector oven (Fig. 25),
for in those days most Indians had a stove made of a 50 gallon
oil drum, with no oven. The girls went to school, learned to use
sophisticated electric or gas stoves and ovens; then they came
back home, often to a dirt floor and the primitive stove. We found
them trying to bake bread on top of the stove. Of course it was
burnt on the bottom and raw on top. So we got the idea of showing
them the reflector oven. A good folding one can be bought from any
camp outfitter, but we made ours from a five gallon can, cutting
the can diagonally, thus actually getting two ovens. We inserted
a couple of metal rods on which to place the pan, and propped the

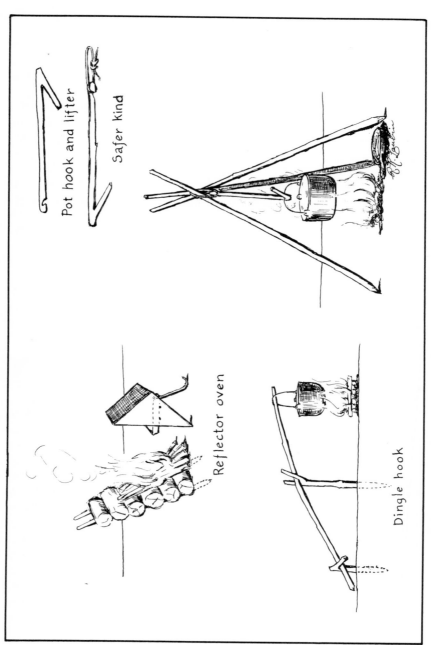

Pot hook and lifter

Safer kind

Reflector oven

Dingle hook

Fig. 25. Cooking with an Open Fire: Reflector Oven, Dingle Hook, Pot Hooks and Lifters.

oven up with a stone in front of the fire. You can braze a strip of band metal for a stand on the back of the oven, if you have the facilities, but in this case we were lucky to find the can, a pair of tin snips, the rods and the drill for our rudimentary reflector.

An old lady came over to watch us make the biscuits. She watched us mix the dough and place it in the pan, then the pan on the rods in the oven, but kept remarking, "I don't believe it." As she saw the biscuits puff up, then come to a golden brown, her eyes got bigger and bigger. When the biscuits were done (they take the same time to bake as in any other oven) we handed her one and she ate it. Then she believed it!

You might also like to try a stone or clay oven sometime. When we were camped in parts of the country where flat stones or clay were available, we sometimes made one of these. It is easier to build one of stones and plaster it with clay, but one can be made of clay alone. The principle is the same as that of the Spanish ovens now used by the Pueblo Indians, or the ovens at the sides of fireplaces in old Colonial kitchens.

As a boy I made an oven by just digging a hole in the clay of our backyard, with one large flat stone across to cover the main oven, another to cover the front of the hole, which I used for the door, and a smaller stone to cover the little opening at the rear of the oven which served as a chimney and draft.

Making the oven above ground takes more work but is more convenient to manage. You make a fire in it for about an hour, then scrape out the coals, put in your material to bake, put a stone over the chimney and another at the door, sit back and wait. The hardest part is not to peek too soon and let out your heat at the wrong time.

We started off with a blueberry pie. After we raked the coals out, put the pie in and closed the door and chimney, we worried about how long to leave it in. Too long, and it would be burnt. If not long enough, it would not be done. We sat and waited until we could not be quiet any longer, then decided to take the stone off the chimney and look in. It was a beautiful golden brown! We have never seen a prettier pie. We left the chimney open, to cool the oven down a little and finish the baking of the berries. It takes some experience to have things come out right every time, but we never had any real trouble and this first experiment was so encouraging that we baked not only pies, but bread, puddings, cakes, and all sorts of things this way. You soon learn how long to make your fire, according to how much heat you need, how long to leave the goods in, etc.

If you have no Dutch oven, no reflector, and do not want to make an earth oven, maybe you would like to try an even simpler way of roasting. Cut a pole just long enough to go across the tipi about as high as your head, tying it to two opposite tipi poles. Stuff a chicken, or leave it unstuffed for that matter, truss its legs and hang it by a long cord to the pole so it will come just in front of the fire. Give it a spin every once in a while. It will wind and unwind, roasting slowly. It takes about three hours. Set a pan under it to catch the drippings and baste it occasionally. This is one of the most delicious ways of cooking, and is a rewarding way to spend a gloomy, rainy day while visiting with friends.

A few other suggestions: a couple of flat rocks, when available, on the east side of the fireplace in the tipi come in handy for setting down black kettles. Some kind of shovel is an important tool and the easiest to carry around is a little folding army shovel. A child's broom helps in keeping the tipi neat and clean. If you can't find one of these a whisk broom is better than nothing. To be really civilized a roll of paper towels comes in handy and a couple of bandanna handkerchiefs make good pot handlers, as well as serving a variety of other uses. And of course, do not forget your matches, an axe, a good paring knife, and a butcher knife. A light, full-helved axe is best, but even a little hand axe comes in handy. One of the new little camp, or "bow" saws just can not be beat for getting firewood in a hurry. Last, but not least, it is always a good idea to have a little first aid kit along, just in case.

We take for granted you will have some kind of camp dishes, metal, or even plastic, with knives, forks and spoons, including some large table and mixing spoons. Here again the Indian utensils were simple, few, but often beautiful. They knew nothing of forks, and any knife would serve as a table knife, but many tribes made exquisite spoons and ladles of wood, buffalo horn and mountain sheep horn. I have a big ladle made of mountain sheep horn given to me by "father," One Bull. It was made for him by his father, Chief Makes Room, when One Bull "had seen five winters." It served as both bowl and spoon for soup. Most adults had spoons of buffalo horn, not nearly as large, of course. The smaller the boy, the larger the spoon!

Most everyone had his or her own wooden bowl, too. Some of these were beautifully carved from maple, beech, or birch burls.

Sioux warriors who had counted coup were permitted to use bowls of snapping turtle shells. Tribes of the Woodlands also made family trenchers of wood, often nicely carved, into which the entire family dipped at once. Some of these were boat-shaped, with clan totems carved at each end—heads of foxes, wolves, bears, eagles. Some of the burls from which they were carved weighed as much as seventy-five pounds, and it required an unbelievable amount of work and patience to finish one of these big trenchers, which was polished to a mirror-like finish after being thinned down to less than a quarter of an inch in thickness.

Men were the carvers and so made the spoons and dishes. We have two buffalo horn spoons, one nicely carved, one rather poorly made. It so happens that the poorly made one has a nicely beaded handle, which distinguishes it as a man's spoon. It looks as if the man made a nicely carved spoon for his wife but he evidently practiced by making his own first, and did not do so well. So his wife took pity on him and decorated the handle of this spoon with the pretty beadwork so that it would not look so bad.

We mentioned earlier that at a feast the men were served first, but there were exceptions. At any feast, if old people were present, they were served first, both men and women. Sometimes a feast was held in honor of the women and children, and at such times they were served first.

As with most of our families, when home alone, the mother did the cooking and serving, but was often assisted or sometimes relieved by an older daughter.

LIST OF THINGS HELPFUL FOR
AN EXTENDED CAMPING TRIP

Buckets with lids, at least one, two are better
2 basins, better if not plastic
Dipper
Towels
Dish cloth, or sponge
Soap, and a can of soap powder
Kettles, large, medium, small, with lids and bails
Frying pan
Coffee pot, if you want one; but if you must have coffee the best can be made cowboy-style in one of the kettles
Knives, forks, spoons, table-spoons, a good butcher knife, paring knife
Oil cloth, for a table
Plates
Bowls

continued on next page

Cups, and a measuring cup, if these are not full cups

Large can for storage, with tight lid, like a baker's lard can

Reflector oven, or a Dutch oven

Small sieve and eggbeater, for fancy baking, but not really necessary. You can use a fork or a bundle of sticks for an eggbeater

Folding grate, tongs, poker, hooks for hanging and lifting pots — you can make these yourself. Also a couple of bandanna handkerchiefs, or other

pot holders

Matches, in waterproof container. Or if you prefer, flint and steel, fire drill, or glass lens — some way to make a fire

Small broom

Paper towels, facial tissues

Canvas or denim bags for carrying some of above articles, and save paper sacks for same purpose

Small camp or "bow" saw

Axe

First aid kit

YEAR-ROUND CAMPING

We have camped in our tipi at some time in every month of the year. No tent is so sturdy against wind and weather as a good tipi — the tilted cone with its back towards the prevailing storm winds, braced by the long slope of the forward poles; the weight of the poles themselves with their pointed butts piercing the earth; the taut conical cover offering no hold to the wind, no pockets or folds to catch water; the anchor rope taut from the apex to the ground inside the tent; the pegs pinning the cover firmly to the ground — all these things make the tipi a strong, dependable protection.

It is the best possible outdoor shelter, whether the temperature is above sweltering or below freezing. When it is just ordinarily hot, the lining acts as enough of an insulator to keep it quite comfortable. When the weather is extremely hot, the cover and the lining can both be raised three or four feet on the sides and propped up on forked sticks. The tipi then is like a huge umbrella, with the extra ventilation of the smoke hole at the top. In such weather the cooking is done outside.

If the days are hot but the wind is too strong to make it practical to raise the cover, except perhaps for a few inches on the lee side, willow, cottonwood, or pine boughs may be leaned against the tipi on the south or west to break the heat. Sometimes an extra

Color plate 1. The Laubin Tipi. Photograph by Bill Stone.

Color plate 2. Drying Tipi Poles. Photograph by Gladys Laubin.

Color plate 3. Camping in the Snow. Photograph by Gladys Laubin.

Color plate 4. Reginald and Gladys Laubin in their Tipi. Credit: The Laubin Collection.

Color plate 5. Shadows in the Tetons. Photograph by Gladys Laubin.

Color plate 6. Blanket, Buffalo Robe, Wolverine, Coyote, and Fox Furs on Drying Rack near Laubins' Tipis. Photograph by Gladys Laubin.

Color plate 7. Good Feather (Gladys Laubin) Making Moccasins in the Laubin Tipi. The dress is Blackfoot. Credit: The Laubin Collection.

Color plate 8. Altar at the Rear of the Laubin Tipi. Photograph by Gladys Laubin.

Color plate 9. Cooking in the Tipi. Photograph by Gladys Laubin.

Color plate 10. Red Ozan cut from the Top of an Old Tipi, above a Beaded Inner Lining. Photograph by Gladys Laubin.

Color plate 11. Buffalo Hide Bed between Backrests, in front of Inner lining. Notice Anchor Rope behind Fireplace. Photograph by Gladys Laubin.

Color plate 12. Winter Camping showing Red Ozan, Beaded Lining, Buffalo Hides, Kiowa bonnetcase, Porcupine Quilled Pillows, Fox and Coyote Skins. Photograph by Gladys Laubin.

Color plate 13. Wíyaka Wašteẃín (Gladys Laubin) and Igomo enjoying the new Plywood Backrest and the Fire. Photograph by Reginald Laubin.

tarpaulin is stretched against the outside of the tipi to add more insulation. We have seen both done together—the boughs leaning against the tipi on top of the tarpaulin. Sometimes the tarpaulin is placed inside, between the cover and the poles, instead of in front of the poles like the lining. The purpose of any of these devices, of course, is to increase insulation and help keep out the heat.

In the old days, during hot weather, a special kitchen tipi was pitched. An old tipi, the bottom of which had become worn and rotten and had been trimmed off entirely, was erected at its usual height, the bottom thus being two or three feet off the ground. This gave the same effect as raising or rolling up the cover of the family tipi, but was more convenient. The dwelling could be left undisturbed, and in case a sudden wind came up, the kitchen tipi could be taken down quickly. Or if it happened to be damaged in the storm, it was small loss anyway.

When camped for several days during a hot spell, Indians often made a brush arbor, referred to as a "wicky," a shade, or a "squaw cooler." These are common today, a part of almost every Indian homestead, even though the people live in houses or cabins. The "wicky" is made by setting four or more strong forked posts in the ground at the corners of a rectangle, laying stout poles from fork to fork, with other poles crossing these every foot or so, and covering the entire structure with fresh-cut leafy boughs. This makes a kind of airy outdoor porch for cooking, eating, working, loafing, or napping. To hold the brush down in a wind, more poles are laid across the tops of the boughs. Such a shade is still serviceable even after the boughs become brown and dry. Sometimes a piece of canvas is stretched and tied across the windward side from post to post, and often the south and west sides are built up and enclosed with more boughs.

Sometimes a willow frame is made, as for a sweat lodge or an eastern wigwam, by setting long willow shoots in the ground in a circle 8 or 10 feet across. The shoots, 10 feet or more in length and as big around as a man's thumb, are bent over and twisted and tied together in pairs, forming a domelike structure. Across the top of this, a piece of canvas is spread and fastened. This is more like a true wickiup and not nearly so large or pretentious as the arbor, but makes a pleasant shady place under which several people can gather. Sometimes the ground plan of the wickiup is square or rectangular, each opposite pair of willows being bent together and making a completed shape something like the top of a covered wagon. Sometimes it has brush or boughs leaned against it instead of canvas.

Old timers could predict the weather by the color of the clouds. Rain clouds are dark black; snow clouds are greyish white; hail clouds are white. Sun dogs forecast cold weather. Old Indians said the sun had campfires on each side, and consequently the Indians prepared for a very cold winter. We agree that sun dogs predict cold weather, but the one winter when we had the most sun dogs, although each appearance was followed by very cold weather, the winter as a whole was extremely mild.

The Blackfeet believed that sun dogs foretold the death of a chief and two ex-Presidents took the Spirit Trail following these appearances.

Cold weather was also predicted by aimless and unprovoked stampeding of horses or by senseless chasing of dogs. "When horses chased each other round and round or when they stampeded like wild horses, we knew there was a snowstorm on the way and that the winter would be cold. Indians would say to each other that they had better prepare for a cold winter. The old men would tell their wives to weight down the edge of the tipis with plenty of rocks to keep the tipi covers down and thereby the cold out. The same thing was said when dogs chased each other round and round."[10]

Our experiences in severe dust storms have each been introduced by ominous yellow skies shortly before the storms arrived.

In the old days, when a violent storm threatened, older people tried to drive it away, the women screamed and shook blankets at the dark clouds and the old men fired guns at it. Some medicine men claimed to have power to divide the storm so that it went around the camp. Meanwhile, the younger people closed smoke flaps, tightened anchor ropes, and drove down pegs. Short sections of logs were laid around the bottom of the tipi cover, resting on the peg loops and against the cover. These, in addition to rocks and stones, kept the wind from getting under it and lifting it off the pegs. The Indians took no chances.

A storm makes it plainly evident why a tipi should have its back to the prevailing storm winds, with the doorway and the long smoke hole down the front facing the opposite direction, usually

[10]Bureau of American Ethnology Bulletin 148, *Arapaho Child Life*, 93.

but not always east. At Jackson's Hole we have been tempted to face our tipi north, for the winds blow from the southwest or west all day and at night swing around and blow from the east.

The best solution to a situation of this kind seems to be the one offered by Gilbert L. Wilson in his report on the Hidatsa Indians. The Hidatsas used tipis only for summer, probably rather small ones, and, according to Wilson, when they were bothered by a change of wind, they merely turned the whole tipi around. This was accomplished by five to seven people. Entering the tipi after loosing the cover from the pegs outside, four persons took a foundation pole each and one the lifting pole, and swung the tipi to its new position. Then the loose poles were moved around where they belonged. The work of more than five people made it possible to move some of these other poles at the same time.

The Hidatsas, relatives of the Crows, are four-pole people, as you see. They said that their neighbors, the Mandans, had an easier time moving a tipi like this, for they had only three main poles. They did not think the Mandan setup as good, however, believing that four poles tied together made a stronger frame than three. The reverse is really true, as we have shown, but everyone to his own opinion!

Also, it seems that the Hidatsas did not anchor the quadripod when pitching the tipi, as the Crows do, for in case of high wind they ran a lariat around the four quadripod poles from the inside, under the cover, threading it through the honda, or eye, to make a loop, and pushing it up to the crotch with long forked sticks.[11] Then it was pulled tight and pegged to crossed stakes behind the fire. The Flathead way sounds easier. These Indians put the rope around the poles, from the inside, in the same way, and simply pulled on the rope, which forced the noose to tighten and work its own way up to the crotch.

Sometimes two, or even three or four, outside guy ropes were used on the four-pole tipi. This was entirely unnecessary in the three-pole type. The only time we have ever found it necessary to use an outside guy on our tipi was an occasion at the Standing Rock reservation, when we borrowed some very old, short poles. They were barely long enough for our tipi, and a high wind cracked

[11]G. L. Wilson, "The Horse and Dog in Hidatsa Culture," *Anthropological Papers of the American Museum of Natural History*, Vol. XV, Part II.

the door pole. Since the poles were so short, it was a simple matter to lasso the tips with a lariat and then fasten the rope to a long stake driven behind the tipi. This straightened up the tipi where it had begun to sag, and we had no more trouble.

Otherwise, our tipi has weathered storms of tornado force and suffered no damage. When we were teaching at a summer camp in the East some years ago, the tipi was pitched on the top of a hill where it took the full brunt of a hurricane that blew in one day. The wind toppled every tree in an apple orchard, knocked over all the wall tents in the boys' camp, and blew the roof off of the girls' mess hall. Small cedar trees near the tipi were bent to the ground during the gale, but the old tipi withstood it all and did not even pull a peg!

We were traveling through the White Mountains in New Hampshire one time, and when we pulled off the road to camp had just started to unpack when the sky got black and the wind began to howl. We knew there would be no time to get our little twelve foot tipi up before the storm hit us. So we hastily unrolled the cover, fastened a long rope to the tie-flap and threw it over the top of the car, pulled the cover almost across the top, and staked down the rope on the other side. (Cars in those days were a good deal higher than they are today.) Then we stretched the cover out like a big fan around the car and staked it down, having barely finished when the storm was upon us. But we were snug as could be. We could open the car door right inside our "tent" and reach in for whatever we needed. How it did rain! We have seen many "gully-washers" but this was one of the worst and it continued to rain hard all night. We felt well protected in our improvised shelter, however, and except for being jolted awake occasionally by an extra-loud clap of thunder and bright flash of lightning, slept soundly until daylight. By then the storm was over. Not having had time to ditch around the edge we found that water had run under one side and the ground was soaking wet for four or five feet there, but it never quite reached our bed.

Another time we arrived in a howling wind and dust storm in Browning, Montana, when we went to visit Julia Wades-in-the-Water. We could hardly see the front of our car. Julia's tipi was one of the largest we have ever seen, about 24 feet across. The smoke ears were flapping and the poles rattling—22 poles in the frame of this huge lodge—the whole thing sounding like an old square-rigger in a gale. We helped Julia pile logs around the back of the tipi, on the windward side, to help hold it down. Julia sent me out every once in a while to take another twist on the smoke flaps, to try and keep them from snapping so hard, and between times we tightened the anchor rope on the inside.

Mrs. Yellow Owl was trying to make the wind stop blowing. She said she was a medicine woman. She sat on a little stool, a bowl of hot coffee at her feet, a little stone-bowled pipe in her hand. She would hold the pipe up above her head, the stem pointing to the apex of the tipi, then smoke it and call out, sometimes in Blackfoot, sometimes in English, sometimes in both. She wailed, cried, beseeched, and commanded in turn. "I am a medicine woman. This is medicine pipe. You, Thunder, we don't want you. We don't need you. Wind, leave us. Too strong. I offer this pipe. Medicine pipe." Then she drank coffee, smoked again, prayed again. It went on and on.

No one paid much attention to her. Night finally came, and she went to her own tipi. We turned in, but all night long the tipi seemed to rock in the wind. Those long, heavy poles vibrated so that the ground shook under us like an earthquake. But we eventually went to sleep, and in the morning we awoke to find everything still in place and the tipi over our heads. It was calm and the sun was shining brightly. We heard Julia muttering to herself, "They're no Indians." At first we thought she meant us, because we were the only ones there. But she meant the Indian visitors from other tribes who had been staying with her in the same tipi. "They got scared and went home," she said. "They're no Indians."

We enjoy camping at all seasons. Each one has its particular attraction and activities. In the spring there are many wet, cold, and disagreeable days, but the bright ones are more than adequate compensation. One spring we camped on a little knoll that proved to be a delightful place. It was sandy, covered with soft, dry moss, and was almost exactly the same size as the tipi. It was unnecessary to trench it, as rain could not possibly run under it, and because of the sandy soil, it never got damp inside.

We discovered violets growing beside our wood pile one day, right inside the tipi at the foot of our bed. Later we were even more amused to see mushrooms popping up near the fireplace. They first appeared in the morning as tiny white buttons pushing up out of the moss. By noon they had grown to be an inch tall. In the afternoon they had distinct stems and heads that opened up as big as silver dollars. By evening they were three or four inches high. The next morning they were shriveled and black, and by that noon had practically disappeared.

Tenderfeet are likely to say—especially the ladies who have never been camping—"This is so beautiful and cozy, but aren't you afraid of ants and bugs? Or snakes?"

The tipi, with its lining tight to the ground and turned under, and ground cloths laid over the floor, is better protection against snakes than any kind of a tent except one with a sewed-in ground cloth. As for ants and bugs, they are something that every camper has to combat; even city dwellers have a constant fight against them in warm weather. The tipi protects against mosquitos, and we have never found ants or other insects bothersome as long as we store food in containers that keep them out. If it is hot in the evening, we hang a mosquito net over the doorway instead of the usual door cover. We still have the smoke hole for ventilation but mosquitoes almost never come down through it, for they do not like the smoky smell. When mosquitoes are very bad, the smallest smudge will drive them out.

Probably fall is the most enjoyable season of all. The air is sharper then, clear and invigorating, the nights crisp and bright. The insects are gone. It is a joy just to be alive on days like this, and when we come back to the tipi, after a long ride or a hike in the mountains, the little fire is more cozy and cheerful than ever. The moon rides high in the late fall nights, and when it is full it shines right down through the long oval smoke hole to the buffalo hide bed in the rear of the lodge. Its pale white light on the furnishings, added to the rosy glow of the dying fire, is beautiful beyond description. It is fascinating to watch the long streaks of moonlight and the shadows from the poles across the smoke hole move from one pole to the next inside the tipi, then fade away as they fan out over the backrests.

We listen to, and breathe in, the deep silence of the wilderness and finally fall asleep watching the stars sparkling above as brilliant Jupiter darts in and out between the poles.

Sage hens whistling and clucking to each other awaken us to find a blue sky with wisps of white clouds floating overhead as dawn gradually fills the tipi with soft yellow light. Pink sun rays creep slowly over the red tipi top and slide down the new poles, spreading into a warm glow as they hit the buffalo robe where the moon beams were previously resting.

A Cheyenne-Arapaho winter camp with cane windbreaks around the Tipis. Credit: Western History Collections, University of Oklahoma Library.

The sun coming up over the horizon bursts through the tipi door in all its glory, throwing a round ball of sunlight across the tipi and onto the lining at the back of the lodge. Meadow larks singing bring pleasant memories of camping on the South Dakota prairie and hearing old Two Shields and Makes Trouble singing to the dawn.

This is the time the Indians used to begin preparations for the long winter ahead. At the time of the great fall buffalo hunt, in October or November, the hides were prime and were tanned for winter robes. Great piles of meat were dried and stored in parfleches. This would be the principal food supply during the long winter months. Occasionally it was necessary to make new tipis at this season, for tipis had to be in good condition to withstand the winds and cold. But summer hides were preferred for tipis because they are thinner, and new lodges were usually made in the spring. Once the winter camp site was chosen, huge amounts of firewood were gathered and stacked in convenient places to be used as community fuel supplies.

Even winter camping holds fascination for us. In some ways it is the most thrilling part of the game. It is a challenge to all one's knowledge and camping skill. We have lived in our tipi at twenty-seven degrees below zero and kept perfectly comfortable.

Winter camp sites were selected for as much shelter as possible, usually in the timber along a river bottom. Indians often made a windbreak of poles and brush, 10 to 12 feet high, around the tipi in winter. In the South they made a circle of posts filled in with dried, upright sunflower or ragweed stalks, bound securely with horizontal withes.

The old Blackfoot, Rides-to-the-Door, told us that sometimes, for extra sturdiness when in a permanent camp, slim willows were bound to the poles inside the tipi, all the way around at a height of five or six feet, or just under the height of the lining. This had the effect of bracing the poles with a huge hoop. Roan Bear, a ninety-seven-year-old Sioux, told us the same thing.

Sioux Indians also braced the poles from the inside in a severe wind with long, forked branches of box elder. The forks were cut short, so as not to puncture the cover, placed against the poles above the lining, and the long branch set into the ground at an angle.

For winter use, the lining was usually hung nearly straight up and down, reducing the area of the interior of the lodge but making heating easier. When hung in this way, it was, of course, fastened to pegs in the ground instead of to the butts of the poles. Old-timers have told us that in severe winter weather they sometimes used two linings, one tied to the bases of the poles and another inside, almost perpendicular and pegged to the ground. The space between the cover and the outer lining was filled with prairie grass or hay. The space between the two linings was used for storage. It seems to us that it might be better to hang both linings together, nearly perpendicular, and stuff hay between them, but this is the way we were told it was done. The extra door flap, pictured on the lining pattern (Fig. 6) gave added protection during this kind of weather. When it was not needed, it was folded behind the lining so that it did not show. An ozan also added much to the comfort of the winter lodge.

Naturally a canvas tipi is harder to heat than were the old

ones of buffalo hide. To partially compensate for this, often an extra layer of canvas, six to eight feet wide, was laid over the poles just under the cover itself. This was usually made by cutting off the lower part of an old tipi cover. We sometimes call this our "outside lining." Adding a double layer of canvas all around the tipi in this way adds quite a bit to the heating of the interior.

When it snows during the night, you can tell something is different, even before you open your eyes. Everything is so still. Even a branch creaking or a tree rustling sounds soft and far away. When you do look out from under the covers, you see shadows of the lacing pins through the canvas, and they look thick and fuzzy. The light that comes through the cloth is pale and diffused. You peek out beneath the door flap and discover the whole world covered with a beautiful white blanket, each tiny snowflake sparkling like a diamond.

On bright days like this we can not resist going for a hike and we snowshoe down to the Snake River. There are a few places along the river where the snow never gets deep and we can take our snowshoes off and walk right on the bare earth along the shore. There we can make a fire and make tea and cook some meat.

A hike in other directions, where the snow is deep, presents problems in making a fire. To build one on top of the snow means that if you can keep it going at all it drops farther and farther away from you and you are presently tending a fire in a deep hole.

One winter day, with a group of friends, we took a hike along Ditch Creek, where the snow was nearly six feet deep. We carried supplies on a toboggan and there was plenty of standing dry willows for firewood. When we arrived at a place that looked like a good picnic spot we used our snowshoes as shovels and soon excavated a hole in the snow about ten feet across. About eighteen inches from the ground we left a shelf, or bench, all the way around. On this we placed a couple of old blankets, then proceeded to build our fire in the center of the opening. In a few minutes we had a warm and cozy fireside seat. To one side we made another fire, which we allowed to burn down to a nice bed of coals for broiling our steaks and making soup and tea, while keeping the first fire burning brightly for heat.

To save space we brought along only cups, to serve also as bowls, planning to wash them out after having the soup, only to find it was so cold that some of it froze to the sides. But we had a good time, feasting and singing around the fire, feeling sheltered and at home in the wilderness, even though it was 25 degrees below zero. Our friends said they enjoyed it all immensely but it was the first time they ever had tea with noodles!

Sometimes we leave a set of tipi poles up, just in case we have an opportunity to do some winter camping. One day the sun was nice and bright, so we decided to have a cookout. But we found it was also cold and windy; so we just tied a tipi lining all around the poles, on the outside, for a windbreak. It was 26 degrees outside, but in about ten minutes with our little fire we had it up to a sizzling 52 degrees inside! We enjoyed cooking our supper sheltered from the gusty winds, and looking up through the naked poles as the puffy white clouds rolled over the Teton Mountains.

Igomo, the cat person, could crawl under the lining any place, but no, he had to climb up the poles and look down upon us, as much as to say, "What are you all doing down there?"

We used to camp in the tipi on winter weekends. Carrying our sleeping bags and a hand drum stuffed full of beefsteak, we trudged through the snow for miles to our camp site. One time, when we arrived, the snow was piled high and had drifted up above the door cover. It took quite a bit of shoveling to clear it away enough to enter and build a fire. In a few minutes it was warm and cheery inside, but we were able to relax only a few moments before we nearly knocked each other over rushing for the door.

We had burned up most of the oxygen in the tipi, which resulted in a stuffiness worse than smoke. The snow was packed so tightly around the outside of the lodge that no fresh air could get in. This, of course, happened only once. After that we always cleared away a little snow on the windward side, allowing a draft to go up behind the lining. When you use a lining with the extra door flap, it can be closed and the outer door raised, so that fresh air enters behind the lining without creating a draft inside.

Later we discovered that the idea of a ventilating pipe underground to the fireplace helps a great deal towards insuring a clear lodge and adequate heat. We used sections of 4-inch stove pipe and laid them just to one side of the door instead of to the back, for our night winds are easterly in Jackson's Hole and night is the time of severest cold. However, when the air is heavy, or the wind changeable and it is difficult to make the smoke draw, it may still be necessary to raise the cover a trifle at one place. There may be a slight heat loss because of this, but it is better than a smoky atmosphere.

Winter Picnic in the Laubins' back yard. Credit: The Laubin Collection.

We have read about Indians removing the earth from the center of the tipi and piling it on the cover outside for insulation. It has been reported that the beds remained on the normal ground level but the earth within the circle thus formed was removed, so that the fireplace and working space were six to eight inches lower. This may be true enough but we fail to see how they could keep the lodge free of smoke with no air coming up behind the dew-cloth unless they used the ventilating pipe idea we have mentioned. Before tin cans or stove pipes were available, a trench only, covered over with boards or hides, would have worked just as well. Leaving the door open a little would also make the fire draw but would cause an uncomfortable draft.

Perhaps the dirt was piled all around the outside except for one little space from which air could enter. The old earth lodges were constructed by digging out the entire inside area but they had an entryway similar to an Eskimo igloo and a smoke hole sometimes six feet in diameter; so the ventilation would be considerably different than in a tipi that was air tight all around the bottom.

Another thing that added comfort to a winter tipi was hanging buffalo robes on the backrests. We have a pair of such robes, given to us years ago by two nice ladies. They were prepared especially for use on the backrests. A strip about one foot in width was cut out all the way down the center of each hide, from nose to tail, and the two remaining pieces were then sewed together again. This left the hides long and narrow. The nose is hung over the tripod and the hide hangs down over the entire backrest and onto the floor. We can sit against the backrest, pull the fur around us, and be comfortable in the coldest weather.

Of course, if you want to go somewhat civilized, you can use a stove for winter camping. Either an old Sibley stove, which was formerly used to heat army tents, or a sheet iron stove, still called "Indian stove" on the reservations, serves very well. In a large tipi the stove can be set a little forward towards the door and the open fireplace made behind it. This way, you can still have the cheer and light of the open fire and the more efficient heat from the stove, in which almost any kind of wood can be used. The 4-inch pipe can be extended only a few feet if using wood that does not spark too much. The little sheepherder's stove in Julia Wades-in-the-Water's big tipi had a pipe that stood about six feet in the air.

We once used an old Sibley stove in our tipi in very cold

weather, not because we felt we needed it but because good fire-wood is at a premium where we live. In case you have never seen one, a Sibley stove is an old Army stove developed by General Sibley during the Indian wars. It stands about 3 feet high, is an open cone of sheet iron and looks like a big ice cream cone upside down. The fire is made directly on the ground inside the cone. A small opening at the base of the cone supplies a draft and can be closed with a stone. A small door in one side is used to feed the fire. It uses a standard 4-inch pipe. In the Sibley we could burn anything, but it sent up such a shower of sparks that we extended the pipe to go up into the smoke hole and wired it to hold it between the two door poles, so as not to set them on fire. We have been comfortable at 27 below zero with the open fire, but it does take lots of wood. With the Sibley we could be sparing of our choice wood but we would never give up the open fire for the stove alone. You might as well stay in any old kind of tent if you do that!

We just heard of the ultimate in tipi living. A family in California is living in a tipi with a basement under it, dug into the side of a hill. The basement is big enough for a small wood stove, with a space to store the wood. The ceiling (or the floor of the tipi), has a trap door into the center of the tipi. We were not told whether the pipe went up through the tipi too, or whether it went out behind. But they had no open fire! If we were to go that modern we would go one better and lay a piece of heavy asbestos in the center of the floor, with some sand on it, so we could enjoy an open fire too.

In addition, they have a water bed!

Speaking of fires, civilization offers another thing that may be appreciated if pressed for time. That is what most people here in Jackson's Hole call "goop." Fill a can, like a tall coffee can with a lid, with sawdust, then pour about a cupful of fuel oil or kerosene on it—just enough to moisten it. Keep it covered for safety reasons. It gives all the benefit of kerosene as a fire starter without the danger, for it will not flash or explode. About a tablespoon of this goop will start any fire you want, instantly, and you never have to make shavings or kindling.

We go the two extremes. We make our first fire in the old Indian way, with the rubbing sticks, and subsequent fires with this quick starter. How tied down to time we are. It takes only about thirty seconds to get a fire with the rubbing sticks, once one is in practice. A flint and steel fire takes about the same time, or a little less. Then comes the match, but all of these depend upon good kindling. The goop even eliminates this!

We made no attempt to keep a fire all night, but discovered that if you burn hardwood the fire will hold coals all night. We keep a little pile of shavings and a few twigs for kindling right beside our beds. In the morning all we have to do is put one arm out, place the shavings and kindling in the center of the fireplace, a few larger sticks on top, and in a few moments we have a fire burning merrily away, while we are still in bed! Furthermore, if the tipi-dweller is fortunate enough to have some furs on the floor, as we have, when he does get up, he can put his bare feet on them and feel perfectly warm and comfortable. Fur is much better than a braided rug, such as our ancestors had beside their beds. We know another trick which is better than using the old brass warming pans to warm the bed. Take a couple of hot stones from the fireplace, wrap them in papers or an old towel, and put them in your bed before you turn in. They hold heat all night.

One day we were surprised to come upon sister Magli heating some nice smooth pebbles, about the size of large marbles, in an iron skillet over a small open fire in back of the cabin. When the pebbles were hot she put them in a cloth sugar sack, which served very well in place of a hot water bottle for father One Bull. The same idea could be used to warm the bed in the tipi. Cloth bags are hard to find in this day of plastics, but paper bags are even better because they retain the heat longer. Sand could be used, too, instead of pebbles.

We are convinced that Indians, in their buffalo-hide tipis, with plenty of warm furs and robes, were far more comfortable than the pioneers in their log cabins, heated with fireplaces only. The old-time tipi is a decided contrast, at least, to the way some of our Sioux friends spend the winter nowadays—40 degrees below zero in wall tents with only flattened corrugated cartons for flooring, stifling hot above, ice cold beneath, and no ventilation!

The only trouble with camping in the winter is that you should spend all summer cutting wood. Or you might keep warm all day by cutting wood for the night.

One morning Gladys woke up and said, "I feel so sorry for all the people in the world who have never slept in a tipi. You know very few folks who have visited us have enjoyed it to its fullest or have seen all its beauty."

"What do you mean?" I asked.

"Oh!" she replied, "They come in and look around and say how pretty it is. But then they ask about snakes and bugs and fail to see the tipi's complete beauty."

"Most people would think the tipi dull, all right, this morning, without the sun shining through its red top," I said.

"Oh, heavens!" she replied. "I don't mean that, or even the lovely things *in* the tipi. I was thinking of the beauty of the straight yellow pine poles reaching up to the sky, forming such a beautiful pattern; the way the smoke flaps are sewed so smoothly and simply down the front of the lodge; the stripes of the seams running around the cover in a rhythmic design; the beautiful way the lacing pins close and button up the front, to say nothing of the roundness and simplicity of it all. The tipi is just a beautiful structure."

"I guess they didn't stay long enough to appreciate all that," I commented. "One has to sleep in the tipi at least one night and spend a day in it in order to catch just a little bit of its atmosphere."

Then she said, "I'm glad the anchor rope is the same tawny color as the poles, canvas, backrests, grass mats, Nez Percé bags, and the mountain-lion skin. And look how the dark green pine needles around the stone fireplace bring out the yellows and reds all around us."

Just then the sun came out and shone down through the smoke hole, making each tipi pole a stripe of turquoise reflecting the sky. The yellow sunbeam hit the top of the painted lining and we knew it was trying to tell us how high the sun was in the heavens. Gladys said, "Gracious! Look how late it is! To think that a couple of weeks ago, when the sun hit the floor, it was only seven o'clock. Now when it hits the floor it's eight. We should be up and doing! Whoever heard of Indians sleeping so late!"

Soon the sun picked up the individual soft hairs on the mountain-lion skin and a shift of wind sent a breeze down the smoke hole, making each hair ripple and dance before our eyes. This led us to name all the various hides and furs in our lodge. We counted sixteen different kinds—buffalo, mountain lion, wildcat, red and gray fox, coyote, dog, black and brown calf, wolverine, bear, faun, 'possum, horse, elk, and moose. There were three black calfskins, one of which was given to us by Mrs. Returns-from-Scouting, who took it off of her own bed to present to us. Two dog skins came from Mrs. Iron Bull. There were two wildcat skins, and an old buffalo coat we had ripped up and sewed back into its original shape as a pelt, and our two good buffalo robes. They are Indian-tanned and were brought back by an army officer in the 1870's. Another buffalo hide was a wedding present, and our very best one is a painted one we did ourselves in the old Indian way, with willow sticks for brushes. Five buffalo hides in all! The wolverine was given to us by Yellow Brow, an old Crow Indian who told us his "granpada's pada get him in high timber l-o-n-g time ago."

So we lay there thinking how unfortunate it was that so few people could enjoy a lodge like ours. Why, even the chipmunks find it fun to run around inside the lining, and the birds like to perch on the tips of the poles. Their shadows, flitting along the wall of the tipi as they fly, always fascinate us. On cold, sunless mornings a tiny fire warms our hearts and makes breakfast an enjoyable occasion. Sunny or cloudy, it is good to be in the tipi.

The Kiowas had a charming custom of leaving a "gift to the place" when moving on from a particularly pleasant campground, where there had been plenty of good water, grass, and wood, and everyone had enjoyed himself. Individuals who felt especially grateful left little presents, like strings of beads, little beaded pouches, or small offerings of tobacco hanging on near-by trees or bushes. Other Indians would never molest such offerings, but the same thing cannot be said for wandering white men who chanced upon them.

One day a man whom we all called Tropical John came to visit us. He had spent a great deal of time in the Bahamas, hence his nickname. He was much impressed with the tipi and made many enthusiastic and complimentary remarks about it. "It's just like home," he said. "The only thing I miss is the bathroom."

"Ah! We have a surprise for you," we told him. "Come out in back of the tipi with us, and we'll show you our bathroom."

So we took him to see our sweat lodge, our Indian steam bath over by the stream. It was then that we learned he was a faddist on steam baths; he had tried them all over the world—Russian, Swedish, Turkish, Finnish. All, that is, except the Indian.

"Have you ever tried an American steam bath?" we asked him.

"If this is what you mean by American, no. I never heard of one until now. I never knew an Indian took any kind of a bath. But this looks interesting to me. I'd sure like to try it."

"All right," we said, "come back any time and we'll see that you get a real steam bath—the best there is."

6. THE SWEAT LODGE

nO EARLY-DAY Indian camp was complete without a sweat lodge, and on many reservations, even today, the frames for sweat lodges are common sights on the Indian landscape. It seems that most of the Indians from Alaska to Tierra del Fuego used the sweat lodge in one form or another. The nearest thing to it in the white man's world is the Finnish *sauna*, which is a sort of sophisticated version of the same thing.

The sweat lodge was an important part of Indian religion, and anything pertaining to Indian religion was frowned upon by the missionaries and government officials. Sioux Indians were even punished by the Indian police and government representatives between 1900 and 1934 for using the sweat lodge. Some other tribes were not so oppressed, but the Sioux had been such fierce fighters and had caused the army so much trouble that every effort was made to break their spirit and "civilize" them.

Even during this period of oppression, a few of the conservatives continued to take steam baths in the sweat lodge, but they were always people far away from the agencies. An old man named Twin, from Standing Rock, first told us about them.

Essentially the same ritual is followed today in sweat baths as in the old days, and the sweat lodges are built in much the same fashion. The type of framework erected was universal among the prairie tribes except for very minor variations. Here is the way to build such a lodge:

For the average frame, twelve to fourteen willow shoots, as large at their butts as your thumb and eight to ten feet long, are used. They are set upright in the ground to form a circle roughly seven feet across. The door for every sweat lodge we have ever seen, regardless of tribe, always faced east. In building the frame, then, two willows are first set to mark the doorway, one on each side, about two feet apart. Holes, six to eight inches deep, are made in the ground with an iron or wooden pin, and the butts of the willows are set in these holes. Opposite the doorway—on the west—

191

two more willows are placed in the same way. You can set a peg to mark the center of the lodge and use a cord from it to measure the distance to each willow. The other willows are set to complete the circle — in pairs, one willow shoot opposite the other across the circle.

When all the willows have been placed, each doorway shoot is bent toward the center, its opposite shoot at the west bent to meet it, and the two twisted together to form two arches about four feet high. The remaining shoots, making the north and south sides of the lodge, are then bent perpendicularly across the east-west arches and twisted together in the same way, forming a dome-shaped structure like a small wigwam. If the arches do not hold where they are twisted and crossed, they are tied with bark stripped from the willow shoots, or with twine.

The average sweat lodge will accommodate four to six people. In the center a pit about fifteen inches in diameter and twelve inches deep is dug, and the earth taken from it carefully placed on a piece of canvas (formerly hide) and carried out to the east of the doorway. About six feet in front of the door this earth is piled into a little mound, which represents the earth on which we live. Some of this same dirt is spread to make a path from the door to the mound — the Good Road. In important ceremonies a painted buffalo skull was used in the old days, placed either upon the mound or to the east of it, depending upon the ritual. It symbolized the great herds upon which the people were dependent and the belief that all things come from and return again to the Great Mystery; it was a prayer for plenty and for long life.

The floor of the sweat lodge is carefully covered with sweet sage and the framework with canvas "tarps" or old quilts — formerly old hides were used. The framework is completely covered, so that it is absolutely dark inside. No light must show anywhere. The covering is raised on the east, or front of the lodge, to allow for a little doorway. Eight or ten feet east of the mound of dirt a large fire is laid for heating stones.

The stones are gathered from a hillside, not from a river bed. They are selected to stand heat without splitting, crumbling, or exploding. Stone of a volcanic variety is considered best because sandstone or granite crumble and flint or quartz explode when heated and then touched with water, thus being liable to cause severe burns. In the old days, the holy man in charge of a sweat-lodge ritual selected four virgins to look for the stones and bring them back to the site of the lodge. The stones should be about the size of your two fists, and a dozen or more may be used for a ceremonial sweat.

The fire is laid by placing four pieces of firewood, about three feet long and a few inches in diameter, parallel on the ground and pointed east and west. Kindling is laid between these, then four more pieces of firewood are added, crossing the first layer at right angles—north and south—with more kindling and small sticks placed between them. The stones are now arranged on top of the upper layer of wood, and other pieces of firewood leaned against the four sides of the pile, beginning at the west side and going around "with the sun." The fire is lighted on the east side first, regardless of which way the wind blows, for that is the direction where the sun first appears—the source of light. It takes from three-quarters of an hour to an hour for such a fire to burn down, and by the time it does, the stones will be almost white hot.

Two stout wooden forks are used for handling the hot stones. These forked poles are about four feet long and as thick as a man's wrist, with prongs about six inches long, sharpened flat to be slipped under a stone. With one fork under a stone and the other crossed over it to clamp the two together, the stones are carried from the fire to the pit in the center of the sweat lodge.

When the fire has nearly burned down, the participants, naked except for breech clouts, enter the lodge, going to the left, with the sun, the leader being last to enter and sitting left of the door. All sit down cross-legged, tailor fashion. The leader then offers a pinch of Indian tobacco, or *kinnikinnik*, called *chanshasha* by the Sioux, to the sky, the earth, and the four quarters, beginning to the west. He then places the tobacco in the pit, to the west, and adds another pinch to the north, another to the east, and another to the south. A coal from the fire is passed in by an assistant and placed in the center of the pit. A little bunch of sweetgrass is laid on the coal to permeate the lodge with its pleasant odor.

The leader purifies himself in this sacred smoke, rubbing it over his arms and body, and also purifies his pipe in the smoke. The pipe is then passed to the left to the man in the rear, who offers it to the six directions—sky, earth, and four quarters. He then lights it and smokes a few puffs before handing it to the man on his left. Each man, as he passes the pipe to the next, utters a brief prayer. The pipe continues around, crossing the door in this ritual (which it does

Fig. 26. The Sweat Lodge (Crow).

not do when smoked in a tipi), until it returns to the man in the rear. He cleans it, places the ashes west of the pit, and lays the pipe down, stem pointing east.

The assistant outside now begins to bring in the hot stones. He lays one beside the pit, and then the leader places it in the center of the pit, using two more forked sticks, but only about eighteen inches long. The first stone represents Wakan´ Tanka, the Great Mystery, who is at the center of everything. More stones are added in the same way, the second one being placed in the pit to the west of center, the next one to the north, then east and south; and each time a stone is placed, the man in the rear touches it with the stone bowl of the pipe. A sixth stone is now added, representing the earth, and a seventh, so that finally there are seven stones to represent the Seven Council Fires of the Sioux Nation. All the remaining stones are added on top of the first seven, until the pit is completely filled.

A bucket of water is next handed to the leader, who sets it in front of him; and, with a sort of dipper made from a bunch of sage and willow sprigs whose tips are bent back, twisted, and tied to form a shallow cup, he sprinkles a few drops of water on the hot stones to clear the air of any smoke resulting from the tobacco or incense, or from any hot coals which may have been carried in with the stones. Different kinds of dippers may be used. They could be of buffalo horn, a buffalo tail, or a horsetail. Sometimes water is taken into the mouth and squirted on the rocks.

As the next step of the ritual, a bowl of water is passed around, and each participant thoroughly wets his hair and face and takes a drink if he likes. When the bowl has been around, the leader sets it in front of him, next to the bucket, and the door is closed from the outside. It is pitch black inside, with only the glow of the hot stones to relieve the darkness. Suddenly there is a report like a pistol shot as the leader splashes a little water on the stones. The lodge is instantly filled with hissing, stifling steam. It is terrifying in the darkness. The heat becomes almost unbearable. Everyone bends forward as far as possible, until his head is almost on his knees, for the heat is terrific near the roof. Then everyone calls out, *"Hi-ye! Pilamaya!* (Thank you, thank you!)" and tells how good it feels.

Four times the water is poured gently on the stones. The red glow disappears, but there is no doubt they are still hot. Each time the hissing increases and the heat becomes more intense. Some writers have reported temperatures of 140 to 170 degrees Fahrenheit, and we can well believe them. The sweat streams from every pore of the body. The noise of the steam, the heat, the lack of air, the bitter taste of sage in the mouth, and the sting of sweat in the eyes, all in pitch blackness, is frightening. The urge to escape is almost uncontrollable. At the end of the fourth "dipper," when the limit of endurance has been reached, the leader calls out, and the assistant raises the cover over the door.

Fresh, cool air was never so welcome. How good it smells and tastes! You sit there, breathing it in, absorbing it, wondering why you ever thought you would like to try such a thing as a sweat lodge. Your skin is already as red as a lobster, and you have only started! You know now what old Chief White Bull meant when he said, "The sweat lodge makes men brave!" But you cannot quit now. Here comes the bowl of water and then the cover comes down and you are enveloped in darkness again.

This time four more dippers of water are poured on the stones, but at briefer intervals, so that the heat increases even faster than before. You are told that if you cannot stand it, to turn on your side and lie close to the ground. You may even put your nose near the edge and lift the cover a crack. But you hate to do that if no one else does. Surely you can stand it if the others can. You realize now how important it was to wet your hair and face and drink a little water. The sweat is running off as if you had poured on the whole bucket. Wetting your hair and face enables you to stand the intense heat at the top of the lodge without feeling as if you were drying up. But even though the lodge seems hotter than it did before, you seem to be able to bear it better. In fact, there is something pleasing about it, even though you feel as if you are being physically and mentally cooked. When the door is opened again, you are grateful, but this session seems to be over more quickly than the first.

There are two more sessions, or periods—four in all. In the third session seven dippers of water are used. The stones are getting colder. The leader sings a sacred chant as he begins to put on the water. During the fourth session he sings again, and all the remaining water is used. The stones have definitely cooled, but the heat of the lodge seems as intense as ever.

When the cover is raised for the fourth and last time, all file out, moving around the lodge to the left. Outside they rub themselves with handfuls of the aromatic or sweet sage and plunge into the river. You would think it would be a terrible shock to plunge into nearly ice-cold water after enduring such heat, but there is almost no shock at all. You feel wonderful! Like an angel, with no bones, and about to fly away. You are completely relaxed and at peace with the world.

When no stream is near at hand, you can create much the same result by pouring pails of water over each other. Often Indians today must do this, for many of them live miles from any river or stream. For such people, one of the best things about the sweat bath is that they can get so clean with so little water. One pail in the sweat lodge is enough for several people, and another pail will rinse off two or three more.

Although the steam bath is the best way in the world of cleansing one's body, it still has a great deal of religious significance and ritual associated with it. It is supposed to purify internally as well as externally, spiritually as well as physically.

According to the legends of the Sioux, the small, dark lodge represents the womb of Mother Earth. The darkness is the ignorance of men's minds. The hot stones represent the coming of life; the hissing steam is the creative force of the universe coming into action; the cover is raised to the east, the source of life and power, the dawning of wisdom upon the minds of men. The elements of earth, air, water, and fire are all represented in the sweat lodge, which is called *initipi*, the "new life lodge," by the Sioux. The fire which heated the stones, *peta owihankeshni*, is "the fire that never dies," the light of the world, eternity.

On many occasions we have been invited by our Crow friends to take steam baths when visiting them in Montana. They never gave up the sweat lodge. They were always friendly to the whites and served as scouts for the United States Army. Therefore, although much pressure was brought to bear on them to give up their old ways, they were not actually punished when they persisted in them. One big difference in the Crow sweat lodge is that the pit, or hole for the stones, is not in the center but just inside the door to the right as you enter. So the framework can be made slightly smaller and yet give enough room that there will be no danger of getting burned by the hot stones.

Among the Crows, even many young people still take steam baths. When a Crow is preparing a bath, he calls out to his neighbors so that they may join him if they care to. The Crows prefer evening as the time for a steam bath, and they take it before eating their evening meal. The lodges open toward the east, but there is no little mound of earth. The fire is laid in the same way as that of the Sioux, and usually east of the lodge, but not always. Men and women go in together when they are relatives or close friends. Otherwise, the men prepare the fire, heating enough extra stones so that after they have had their bath the women can follow with a session of their own.

Inside the lodge they place mats of old canvas, blankets, or even pieces of corrugated boxes. The men enter, wearing only short cotton breech clouts. One remains outside to handle the stones. As the fire burns, a couple of pails of water are set close to it so that they become slightly warm. A pitchfork is used to take stones out of the fire and put them in the hole (Fig. 26). This is easily done since the pit is near the door. No one speaks as the first four stones are put into the hole, and everyone is supposed to think only good thoughts, to think of pleasant things, and to wish good things for his friends, neighbors, and all mankind. Later, in one session I attended, Goes Together said, "I wish that all of us may be here together again next year, in good health and in this same place, for another steam bath." He added, "In the old days they used to sing a song. They repeated it four times before making the steam. Then they sang a different song for each part of the bath. Nowadays, unless some old man conducts the bath, we no longer sing the songs."

After the stones are all placed in the pit, a bucket of the warm water is set inside beside it, and the man who has been handling the stones comes in and sits by the door. He acts as leader. With a metal dipper he sprinkles a little water on the stones, just as the Sioux do, to clear the lodge of any smoke. The dipper is then passed around, and everyone wets his hair and face and takes a drink. Each one has also prepared himself with a switch, made of osier or willow sprigs and sage, bound together with twine at the butts to make a handle.

The door covering is pulled down from the inside and tucked snugly around so that no light shows anywhere. Four dippers of water, one at a time, are carefully poured on the stones, just as in the Sioux lodge, and everyone lightly brushes himself with his switch. We think it is an improvement over the Sioux bath, for the light switching not only has the effect of stimulating the body and bringing the blood to the surface but also spreads the heat evenly throughout the lodge. Recently we have learned that the Kiowas and Navajos also use switches, so it may be that a number of tribes have used them for a long time. The Southern Cheyennes preferred eagle wings or feathers for this purpose.

After the fourth dipper, the cover is raised for a few moments, then seven dippers are used. The Crow bath is in four periods, also, but the third uses ten dippers of water, and the fourth they call "a million," which means they keep putting water on until the lodge gets as hot as desired.

Before leaving the lodge, after the final raising of the cover, everyone lathers himself with soap. We thought this was a modern innovation, but were told that the Indians used to use yucca, or "soapweed," roots. They also said they had always used the switches. After cleansing with soap, all plunge into the river, the Little Big Horn—only thirty miles from its source in the snow fields of the mountains! But still there is no shock, although the water itself is close to the freezing point.

We have been in the sweat lodge of the Arapahoes also. Here the pit for the stones was in the center, as it seems to be with most tribes. They told us that they use thirteen "poles" in the construction of the sweat lodge (thirteen are also used in the Sun Dance lodge), and prefer alder to willow. They use thirty-two stones, but could not give a reason for this number. They put cattail rushes on the floor of the sweat lodge and use switches of willow and sage, but they do not employ them as vigorously as do the Crows. They also use soap. All entered the lodge from the left and a pipe was smoked before the bath began, but it did not cross the door, and the leader sat to the right of the door on entering. In leaving after the ceremony, the Arapahoes did not "follow the sun."

Some of the old Sioux ceremonies we have been told about were much more involved and complicated than the one we have described, and must have lasted for hours. Today a sweat bath lasts from half an hour to an hour, plus the time for preparing it and heating the stones. We participated in an Arapaho ceremony recently when we were in the sweat lodge more than two hours. That same afternoon we all went for a plunge in a local hot pool, temperature 112 degrees Fahrenheit. Talk about "dirty Indians"!

In early days larger lodges to accommodate as many as twenty men were sometimes made. Some of these used as many as one hundred willows and a like number of stones. These lodges were usually elliptical in shape instead of round. Some observers have reported that the average sweat lodge was elliptical, but it was probably not intentionally so. Sometimes lodges were not laid out with a cord on a center pin and, being made by eye, would tend to be oval rather than truly round. But several old Sioux Indians told us that they always used a cord to plan the circle, and the ones we have seen them make were made this way. The circle is a sacred symbol and so was part of the ritual.

Some of the Crows take steam baths two or three times a week, and many of them take them all year round. The Little Big Horn River is so swift that it never freezes. Those who have to use some other pond or stream cut holes through the ice in order to plunge in after the steam bath.

The Indians used to take steam baths for every kind of ailment, and perhaps there were some occasions when they did more harm than good. When epidemics of smallpox, a disease strange to them, broke out among them years ago, they resorted to their only known cure-all, which only helped to kill them off. The same thing might be said for tuberculosis, another disease with which they were un-acquainted. Heat and moisture would encourage the spread rather than the cure of these diseases. But we believe, with enthusiasts for other types of steam baths, that they are beneficial in many ways. They have helped us to break up colds and to ease pain from sprains and strained muscles and from rheumatism or arthritis. And they are so thoroughly relaxing that you go to bed afterward and sleep like a baby.

Once, on a visit to the Yakimas, in the State of Washington, we learned that they take a mud bath before the steambath. They dig a hole in the earth about as big as a washtub, fill it with water, then put some of the loose dirt back in, so that the result is a "tubful" of not-too-heavy mud. Into this they put a couple of hot stones, until the mud becomes as hot as one can stand. The "patient" sits in this hot mud for awhile, then goes into the sweat lodge proper for the final cleansing.

We still do not understand how one can go into cold water after being so overheated in the sweat lodge, without feeling a shock or suffering some undesirable results, unless the secret is in that very overheating. Perhaps you do heat the surface of your body to such an extent that it heats the water that comes in contact with your skin. Anyway, we have enjoyed the sweat lodge so much that we think it should be experienced by everyone who likes the out-of-doors and the tipi. Regardless of how many benefits there are sup-posed to be, or actually are, from the sweat lodge, the fact remains that there is no other way in all the world in which you can get a more thorough cleansing. Tropical John admitted that the Indian steam bath was the hottest and best he had ever had.

7. OTHER TYPES OF TIPIS

HIDE TIPIS

IN THE EARLY days all tipis were made of buffalo hides, but since the last large herd of buffalo was destroyed, tipis have been made of cloth. The only hide tipis remaining today are to be seen in a few museums. Before the first edition of this book was printed, even canvas tipis were becoming curiosities.

A small tipi, like the ones used for hunting trips, about 12 feet in diameter, could be made of eight to ten buffalo hides. A lodge of the size we have been making would take twenty-two to twenty-five hides. The average was said to be between twelve and fourteen hides, making a lodge between 14 and 16 feet across. The average family dwelling was much smaller when made of hides than when made of canvas, although families rich in horses usually had tipis about the size we have been discussing. A few tipis were large enough to require from thirty to fifty hides for their covers.

A skin tipi would last a number of years if well cared for, but sometimes, owing to constant use and travel, the covers had to be replaced every year. Summer-killed hides were best for tipi covers because they were thinner and lighter in weight. Buffalo cow hides were preferred to bull hides because of their more uniform thickness. A woman collected the hides her husband had obtained on the hunt, tanned them, and then invited her friends to help make the new tipi cover. From inquiries we have made among several tribes, the procedure seems to have been much the same everywhere. The woman wishing to make a new tipi prepared a feast and invited other women to attend. If they accepted her invitation and ate of her food, they signified their willingness to help.

Because of the size and weight of the skins and of the finished cover, it was necessary to make this a community affair, much like an old-time quilting bee. An older woman of experience and cheerful disposition was chosen to superintend the work—one who would think only good thoughts. Otherwise, it was believed that the tipi would smoke and be vulnerable to high winds.

201

Alice Fletcher, in her study of the Omahas,[1] says that one hide was so placed in the cover that its tail formed the tie flap, and the lifting pole was called "the pole to which the buffalo's tail is tied." We think this is strange, for the weakest part of the hide is near the tail, whereas the toughest part should be chosen for a place receiving so much strain. This would, of course, be the neck. But the Omahas were not primarily tipi people anyway. They used the tipi only for summer hunting trips.

Old photographs of hide tipis of the Comanches, Apaches, Kiowas, and Cheyennes show tails dangling at the *bottom* of the hides which formed the upper part of the tipi cover. The Arapaho hide tipi in the National Museum in Washington plainly shows that the neck was used for the tie flap. Wissler's drawing of the hide tipi also shows the neck of the hide at the center of the cover at the top.[2] A buffalo tail was often tied to the tip of the lifting pole for decoration, just as a horse's tail or large imitation scalp was fastened to the lifting pole of a chief's tipi.

A new hide tipi was pure white, and when it was pitched for the first time, it was pegged down tightly all around and the smoke flaps crossed over in front so that the smoke vent was completely closed. The pegs for a skin tipi were driven through holes cut in the hide around the bottom of the cover. A smudge fire was built inside in order to make the smoke permeate the entire hide cover. This helped to make the tipi waterproof and also kept it from getting hard and stiff following a wetting. Smoked skin retains its softness even after a complete soaking. Unsmoked skin does not, and water will ruin it. Regardless of this preliminary smoking, the cover did not absorb enough smoke to change its general appearance, and new lodges were a beautiful cream color. As they became older, they darkened considerably at the top, which eventually looked quite black, as will the top of a canvas tipi.

Old lodge covers were used for moccasins and other articles of everyday clothing which might be exposed to rain.

Figure 28 shows a Sioux hide tipi of the same proportions as the pattern included earlier for a canvas tipi, and it would

---

[1] "The Omaha Tribe," Bureau of American Ethnology, *Twenty-seventh Annual Report*, 1905–1906.

[2] Clark Wissler, "Material Culture of the Blackfoot Indians," *Anthropological Papers of the American Museum of Natural History*, Vol. V, Part II, 103, Fig. 63.

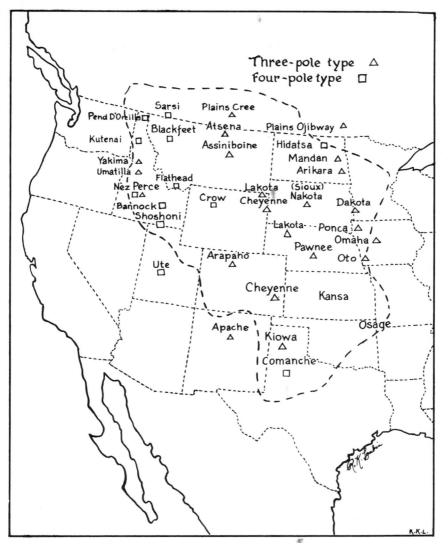

Three-pole type △
four-pole type □

Sarsi   Plains Cree
Pend D'Oreille□ □   △
Blackfeet   Atsena   Plains Ojibway △
Kutenai □   □
Assiniboine   Hidatsa □
△   Mandan △
Yakima △   Arikara △
Umatilla △   Flathead
Nez Perce   □   Lakota (Sioux)
□△   Crow   Cheyenne   Nakota
Bannock □   □   △   △   Dakota
Shoshoni   Lakota   Ponca △
□   △   Omaha △
Pawnee   Oto △
Arapaho   △
Ute   △
□   Cheyenne   Kansa
△
Osage
Apache   Kiowa
△   △
Comanche
□

Fig. 27. Distribution of the Tipi.

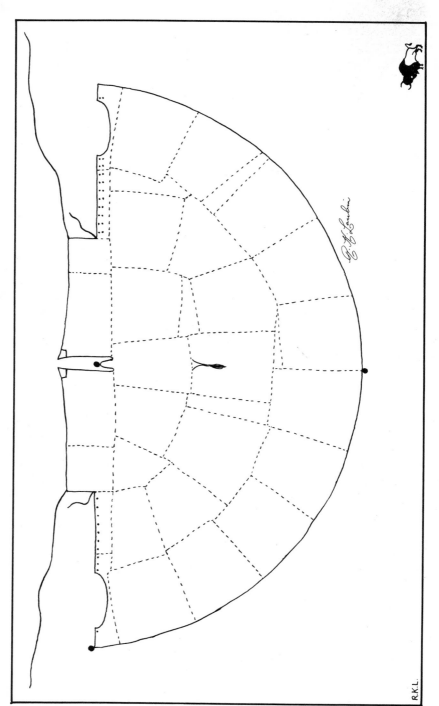

R.K.L.

Fig. 28. Sioux Buffalo Hide Tipi.

take 18 to 24 buffalo hides. Can you imagine the enormous amount of work this represents? Every hide had to be staked out, cleaned and fleshed, then dried for several days, turned over and the hair scraped off. Then it was turned again flesh side up and the heavy, thick skin on the shoulders and hump had to be scraped and flaked until the entire hide was of uniform thickness—all strenuous, back-breaking work. Next it was soaked in water for a couple of days, and when thoroughly softened, was treated with a preparation of brains and liver, thoroughly worked into it. Rolled up and laid aside for several days, it then had to be dried by stretching, pulling, and sawing over a sharp-sided stake, or through a heavy rawhide rope loop, until soft and velvety. The main ingredient in Indian tanning was elbow grease and lots of it. As mentioned earlier, the sign for work in the sign language of the Plains refers to the scraping of a hide!

When the Cheyennes laid out the hides for a special, or "medicine" tipi, an old warrior counted coup as he walked across them. After that the women were free to sew them together and to handle them in any way that was necessary as the work progressed.

Sometimes in laying out a skin tipi, three stakes were driven into the ground—shown on Figure 28 as black spots—to mark approximately one half of the cover. The hides were trimmed and fitted into this triangle and the other side then matched to it. The skins were sewed together on the wrong side (flesh side), using an over and over stitch almost as fine as that used in making moccasins and clothing. They were sewed with heavy sinew from the buffalo's back, and an awl was used for punching holes to insert the sinew thread. The stitches on the Arapaho tipi in the National Museum are so fine that it is almost impossible to see the seams, or to define the number of hides in it from the observer's view outside of the display case. The tipis we see in the movies, dark brown and with great long stitches, would either put a capable Indian woman into convulsions or embarrass her to death.

When the cover looked nearly complete it might be folded in half and the stake that had been set where the tie flap would come was moved out another couple of feet and the arc of the bottom marked by using a long cord attached to the stake and a piece of charcoal. This seems to have been the custom rather than swinging an arc for the entire tipi cover, as is usually done with canvas. The cover could be cut at this time but often the tipi was pitched first and the cutting done while it was set up.

The smoke flaps and the strips down the front where the lacing pins were to go were added last. From the few available photographs of hide tipis it seems that the pockets for the smoke poles were patches added to the corners of the flaps rather than the added pockets used on canvas tipis. Leather, stretching more than canvas, would soon assume the same elongated appearance from the tension of the poles pushing against the tips. Also because of its stretch, the cover would fit the poles without the addition of the gores necessary on a canvas tipi.

It took several days, working long hours, to sew up a big tipi like this. Even for a ten to twelve hide tipi three women might work as much as four days.[3] It was much work, but during the time the women amused themselves with songs, stories, talking, and gossiping. They took pride in their work and were honored and admired by the rest of the village.

Lieutenant James H. Bradley, who wrote about the Blackfeet of the middle 1800's, said, "From six to twelve skins were ordinarily employed . . . The number rarely exceeded twelve but occasionally reached eighteen or twenty, and Major Culbertson relates having seen one of forty skins that would hold one hundred people. A six-skin lodge was ten feet in diameter, holding six people, while a twelve-skin lodge was about fifteen feet in diameter and afforded shelter to eight or nine persons. The cover was stretched over eight or twelve lodge poles, in the larger lodges from eighteen to twenty, standing in a circle and inclining inward till they joined near the tops at a height of from eight to twelve feet from the ground."[4]

Most of the writers gave the impression that the average lodge was rather small, yet the artists of the period always showed tremendous tipis. So it is hard to know just what to believe. Since the large tipis were most attractive, the artists probably preferred to show an entire camp of large ones. Apparently they were more impressed with their size than with their details, for very few ever showed a tipi properly constructed.

Even among actual observers there seems to be considerable discrepancy as to lodge sizes and the number of skins required

[3]Royal B. Hassrick, *The Sioux: Life and Customs of a Warrior Society,* 184.

[4]James H. Bradley, "Characteristics, Habits, and Customs of the Blackfoot Indians," p. 258. Cited in *B.A.E. Bul. 173.*

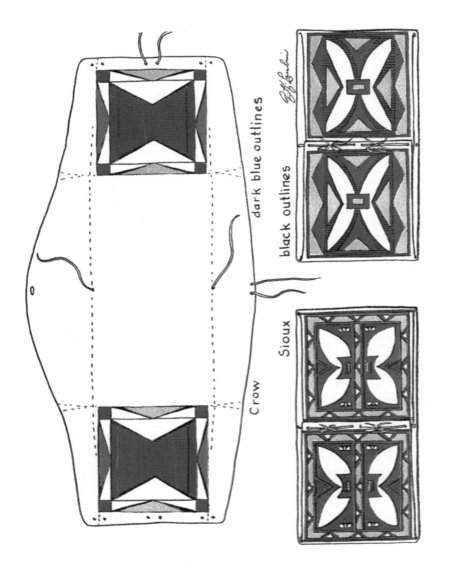

Color plate 14. Parfleches.

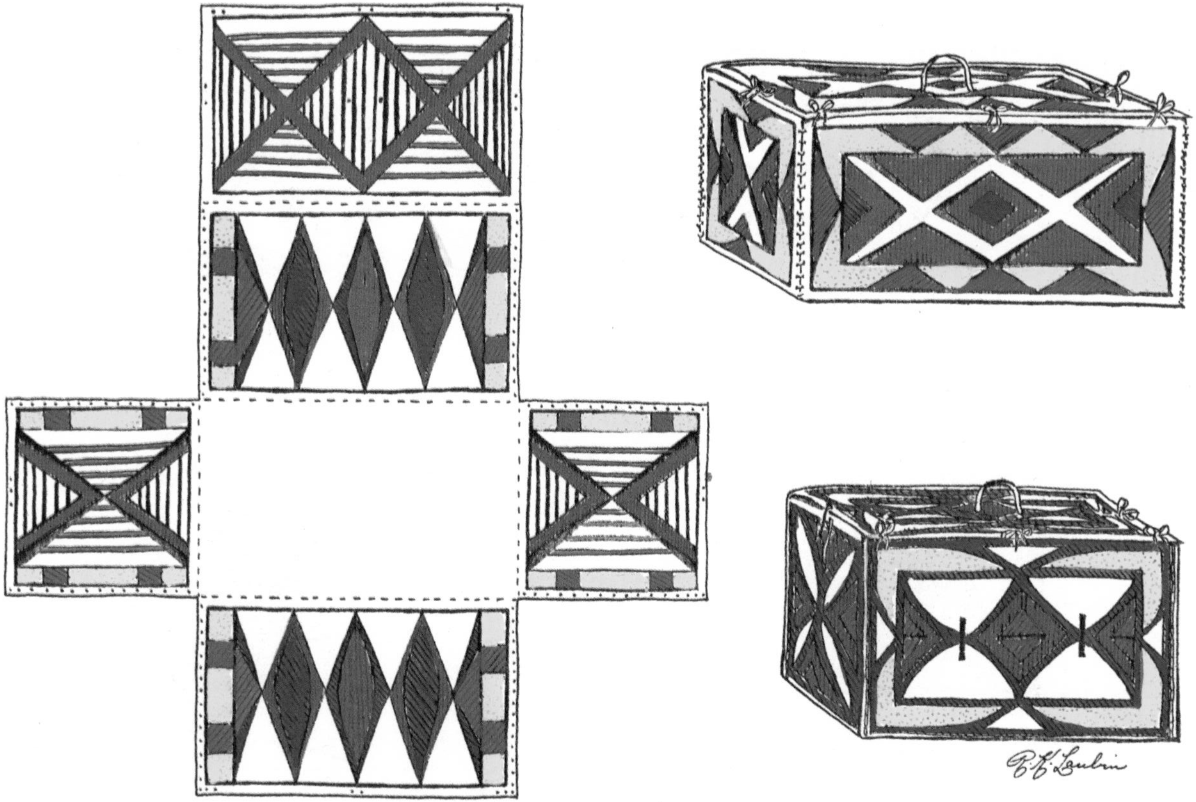

Color plate 15. Sioux Boxes.

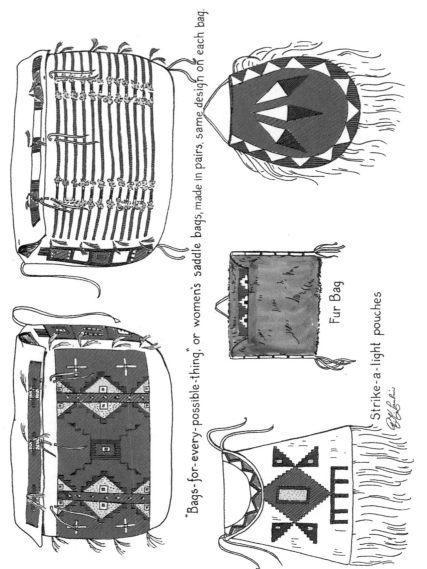

"Bags-for-every-possible-thing," or women's saddle bags, made in pairs, same design on each bag.

Fur Bag

Strike-a-light pouches

Color plate 16. Beaded Bags.

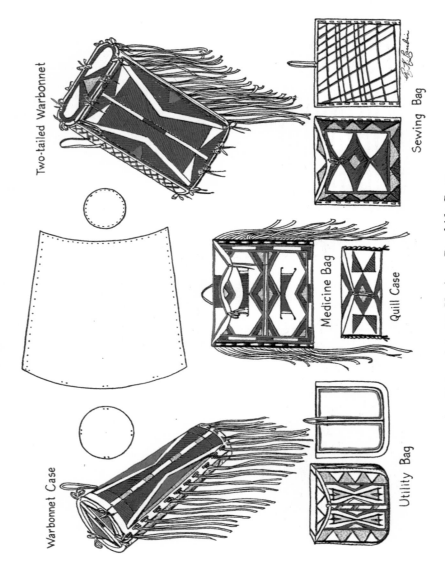

Two-tailed Warbonnet

Sewing Bag

Medicine Bag

Quill Case

Warbonnet Case

Utility Bag

Color plate 17. Various Rawhide Bags.

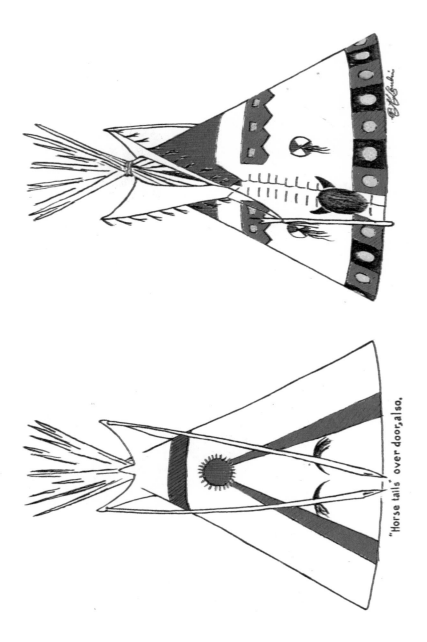

"Horse tails" over door, also,

Color plate 18. *Tipi Designs with Horsetails and Buffalo Head.*

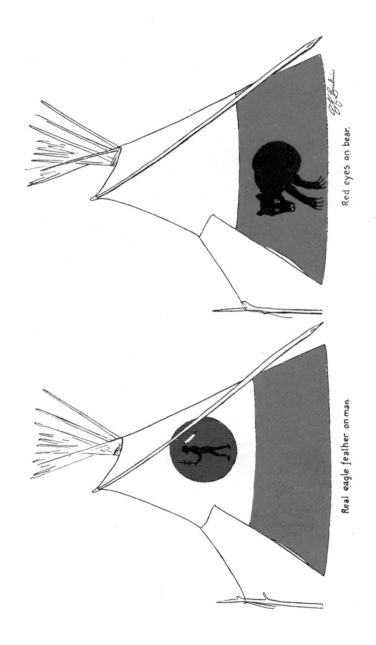

Real eagle feather on man.

Red eyes on bear.

Color plate 19. Tipi Designs with Eagle Feather and Black Bear.

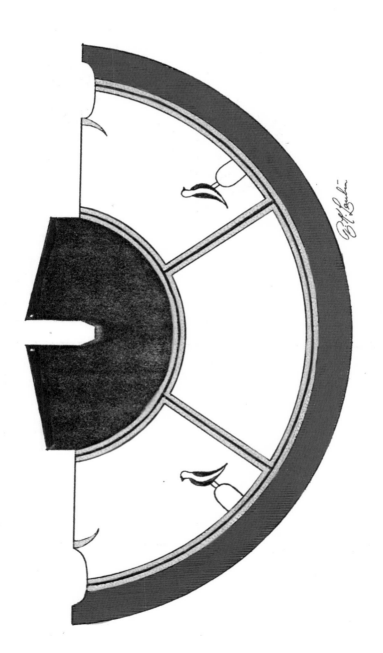

Color plate 20. Symmetrical Crow Tipi Design.

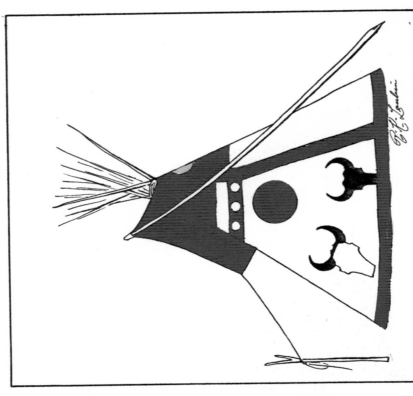

Color plate 22. Assiniboine Design with Buffalo Skulls.

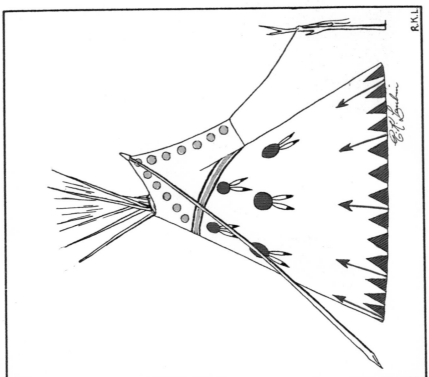

Color plate 21. Assiniboine Tipi Design with Lances and Shields.

for these sizes. Bradley said a six-skin lodge was ten feet in diameter, whereas Edwin Thompson Denig, writing of the Assiniboin, said the average lodge was of twelve skins and was about thirty-one feet in circumference,[5] which would be about ten feet in diameter. Bradley said a twelve-skin lodge was about fifteen feet in diameter and would shelter eight or nine persons. Denig said a sixteen-skin lodge would take care of about ten people. Denig also mentioned Sioux lodges of thirty-six skins, made in two sections.

Captain Clark, of the Lewis and Clark expedition, writing on the homeward journey, reported seeing a lodge belonging to a Cheyenne chief made of twenty buffalo skins and said it was the largest he had so far seen, although several others near it were of about the same size. He said they were new and *very white*. He reported this in August 1806.

Many people have written us who wanted to make an "authentic" hide tipi for display purposes. We have not offered them much encouragement for several reasons. Chief of these is that, even if they can get buffalo hides, we do not know a single Indian woman who would tan them today. Few have even seen a real hide tipi. But we have examined some in museums and we did ask lots of questions of the old people who are now gone. One Bull and Scarlet Whirlwind had a little hunting tipi of buffalo skins which had been in the family many years—the first one we ever had a chance to see and handle. Clark Wissler, former Curator of Anthropology at the American Museum of Natural History in New York, took us into the "poison room" where we had an opportunity to look over and study several old hide tipis stored there. Also we examined and measured the hide tipi in the Museum of the State of North Dakota.

All the hide tipis we have examined had the hair side of the hides on the outside of the cover, flesh side inside. On well-tanned Indian hides, however, it is sometimes difficult to tell which side is which, for they always removed the grain in scraping off the hair.

If tanned hides could be obtained, even imitation Indian tan, who is going to sew them up? If you could get Indian women to sew them together they would want to use thread nowadays instead of sinew. To our notion, a hide tipi, made of commercially tanned hides, either cattle or buffalo, and sewed on a machine with thread, would be less authentic than a canvas tipi, which the Indians de-

[5]Edwin Thompson Denig, *Indian Tribes of the Upper Missouri.*

veloped for themselves and preferred over hide when they could get it. Under average usage one of canvas will probably outlast one of hides.

One organization even went so far as to make a tipi of commercially tanned buffalo skins with the hair left on, the hair side being placed on the inside of the tipi. They had never seen a picture of a hide tipi with hair on, so decided it went on the inside! What a dark, gloomy lodge this must be! A tipi made like this would be so bulky it would be almost impossible to handle or to pack on a horse, or even a travois, for traveling. There is no doubt that the hair would add insulation, but if it were on the outside it would also aid in shedding water. Indians did make door covers of hide with the hair left on for just this reason. The only people we ever heard of who made a skin dwelling similar to a tipi with the hair left on were some in Siberia, and they had the hair on the outside, where it belonged. The Mongols, who used the yurt, the only other primitive dwelling comparable to a tipi for comfort and convenience, made it of fur felt.

We have seen buffalo hide tipis on exhibition in the American Museum of Natural History in New York, at the Southwest Museum in Pasadena, and at Pipestone National Monument in Minnesota. The finest one is in the National Museum in Washington, D.C. At the Cowboy Hall of Fame in Oklahoma City there is a display showing an Indian family erecting a tipi on the prairie. The Cowboy Hall of Fame made room for the tips of the poles by cutting a hole in the ceiling!

We know that there are now more tipi displays to be seen in museums across the country, for several people connected with museums have written to us for information. When we first wrote the tipi book we decided not to go into detail on hide tipis because we thought there would be little interest in them. But since then we have had so many inquiries that we are including more information in this edition and hope it will be helpful not only to museum directors but to other interested people.

A canvas tipi was handled in much the same way as a hide tipi. It was made as a community project. The long strips of canvas were sewn entirely by hand, but with greater ease than the skins, and with needle and thread instead of with awl and sinew. No one showed the Indian women how to lay out the canvas as they made the change from buffalo hides, but they did a far better job of it than have the white tipi enthusiasts who have tried to improve upon their methods. The actual pattern, of course, was copied directly from the skin tipi, and it, in turn had been the result of many years of trial and experiment until it became the excellent dwelling that it was.

Canvas was used to some extent even before the near extinction of the buffalo, because of its light weight. Whereas a skin tipi eighteen feet in diameter weighs a trifle over one hundred pounds, a canvas tipi of the same size weighs about fifty-five. At the same time much less work is involved. Actually, even more buffalo skins may have been needed to buy the canvas for a tipi than to make one of the skins themselves because buffalo hides were a standard medium of exchange and the traders demanded exorbitant prices for their goods. A commodity as much in demand as canvas brought a great price in hides. But the hides were accepted raw, eliminating the drudgery of tanning, patching, and sewing them together which was necessary for a skin tipi cover.

TRIBAL TYPES

Since this book was first published, much interest in the tipi has been aroused across the country, and a number of tent manufacturers are now claiming to make authentic Indian tipis, or tipis based on the patterns contained herein. We know of one company, at least, that states it has *improved* the Sioux pattern by omitting the gores and substituting the Crow type of ears, or smoke flaps, and throat.

One of our objectives in writing the book was to make available accurate information on tribal types of tipis and to correct the many wrong ideas concerning the structure of tipis. For many years pseudo-Indian styles of tipis were foisted upon the public, and now some manufacturers are back doing the same old thing. It does not seem logical that non-Indians, who have never really had to live in tipis, can do much improving on a dwelling that was used for hundreds of years by a very practical-minded people.

The above-mentioned "improved Sioux tipi," for example, is not improved at all. The Sioux and Crow styles were developed to fit entirely different pole arrangements. Furthermore, the Crows *do* use gores, but theirs run the entire length of the smoke flaps. To omit the gores completely and cut a larger opening around the tie-flap may fit the poles all right, but the resulting flaps would be very ugly in appearance and more rain would come in around the poles. Also, this manufacturer merely sews triangles across the tips of the flaps, instead of using the Sioux pockets, again adding ugliness. Why do people always have to change things that are already practical, beautiful, and well-established?

Anyone who has studied the various tribal types of tipis can tell at a glance whether one is a three-pole or a four-pole type. No one would confuse Blackfoot, Crow, or Sioux tipis, even a long way off, if he had ever paid much attention to them, but he might confuse Sioux, Cheyenne, and Arapaho until he got close enough to study them in detail, for differences in them are slight. Three-pole tipi poles have a peculiar twisted appearance at the throat—looking into the smoke hole from the front—spreading like a fan. From the side the door pole sticks out lower in the back than any of the other poles. The four-pole tipi has an entirely different appearance, from both the side and the front. It tends to group the poles on the sides and looks somewhat square at the top; from the side you can see two apexes, not one, as in the three-pole type, and two low poles at the rear instead of one.

In the early days it was an advantage to be able to recognize these differences, for on approaching a strange camp, one could tell at a glance whether it was friendly or hostile. During the late Indian wars, Crows were friendly to the white people, Blackfeet at least not openly hostile. They were four-pole people. The heaviest fighting was against the Sioux, Cheyennes, Arapahoes, Kiowas, and Comanches, all three-pole tribes except the Comanches, who used a four-pole base, though a very peculiar one that actually looks like three poles.

From studying a number of old photographs, we were convinced that the Comanches were three-pole people, but Comanches themselves have informed us that they used four poles. When their method was demonstrated to us, we could easily understand why we had been confused, for they set the two forward quadripod poles on each side of the door, to serve as door poles, and spread the two rear poles as for a three-pole tipi. The remaining poles were spiraled in and bound around with the anchor rope, as for a three-pole tent, and as they also used pockets for the smoke-flap poles, from the front their tipi looks like a three-pole tipi. The side view is the giveaway. There you can see the two low poles at the back, as in any other four-pole tent.

The Comanche tipi is not nearly as neat as either the standard three-pole or the Crow four-pole lodge. How they ever came to use it, when surrounded by three-pole people, is hard to understand unless they borrowed it from Ute or Shoshoni relatives. And the Utes were known as the "bad lodges" by other tribes.

It is easy to see why we were puzzled, while in Oklahoma, to learn that the Comanches use a four-pole foundation. The mystery was explained when, on a later visit, we had an opportunity to see a group of Comanche tipis. From the front they looked like Assiniboine tipis, that is, the poles were spiraled in the reverse of Sioux and Cheyenne tipis. But, as has been indicated, a look at the sides and rear showed the two poles at the back instead of one, one being the distinctive identification of the three-pole type lodge. The two quadripod poles at the rear were spaced far enough apart for the lifting pole and two other poles to go between. The frames average fifteen poles, plus the two smoke-ear poles. Three were laid in the front crotch, starting on the left side (facing the door), then three more on the right side. Two poles were laid in the south crotch, one on either side of the foundation pole, and two in the north crotch in the same manner. A rope was wrapped around all but the lifting pole, further giving the illusion from the front that the tipis were three-pole. This was the first time we had ever seen a rope around a four-pole frame, and the only time we had ever seen such a frame, although we have heard that the northern use a similar one.

The structure is less bulky than the Blackfoot frame, but that is about all you can say for it. It is not nearly as compact as the usual three-pole method. Also, not all the tipis we examined were exactly the same, so that a good deal of individual choice was evident. The type we have described seemed to us to be the most prevalent and also the most compact.

We were still puzzled about the early photographs, but inquiry revealed that this four-pole arrangement is a fairly new development among the Comanches. The people we talked with said it was recent and told us that they adopted it because four poles made a sturdier frame than the three, which they had formerly used. This, of course, is untrue structurally. Our informants did not know where the idea came from, but we think their northern relatives paid them a visit and sold them a bill of goods.

As has been pointed out, Alice Fletcher, in her study of the

Omahas,[6] stated that they used the four-pole structure, but the photographs illustrating her article show, without any doubt, the three-pole type. Being so closely related to the Sioux proper, they could rather be expected to be "three-pole people."

A Shoshoni tipi we saw in Idaho and an Assiniboine lodge set up by visitors at Crow Fair, in Montana, led us to believe that these tribes were also users of the three-pole tipi. Both of these tipis had the poles laid in reverse position to that used by Sioux and Cheyennes. The tripod was tied in reverse, too, and the door pole was placed to the north instead of the south. Otherwise, the poles would not have rested solidly in the front fork of the tripod. Kiowas have also told us that they placed their door pole to the north. Later we learned the Shoshonis are actually a four-pole people and what fooled us was that the tipi we saw at Fort Hall in Idaho was a Peyote tipi. It may be that this accounts for setting up on a three-pole base, for the Peyote worshippers recognize a Trinity in their religion. At Fort Washakie we camped with the Shoshonis and found their tipis set up on a four-pole base, similar to the setup of their relatives, the Comanche, but in our opinion much neater and better. We wonder now if the Comanche tipis we saw in Oklahoma were not set up by young people, amateurs who were not quite sure of themselves. From the front Shoshoni tipis do look like Sioux or Cheyenne tipis, and those we saw at Fort Washakie did not have the poles reversed, like the one at Fort Hall.

THE SHOSHONI TIPI

Figure 29 shows the Shoshoni way of measuring the four main poles, and their positions for tying. The tie rope is wrapped around, as indicated, several turns, and tied in two half hitches. There is no reason why the Sioux tie would not be excellent for this type of construction. Some pictures show frames of only fifteen poles but even a small tipi at Fort Washakie had eighteen poles in the frame and none of them had a guy rope out behind, although photographs of old Chief Washakie's tipi do show an outside guy rope.

In raising the quadripod you pull the *under* door pole, RD, and the left rear, or back pole, RB, to the *right*, thus locking the

[6]"The Omaha Tribe," Bureau of American Ethnology, *Twenty-seventh Annual Report*, 1905–1906.

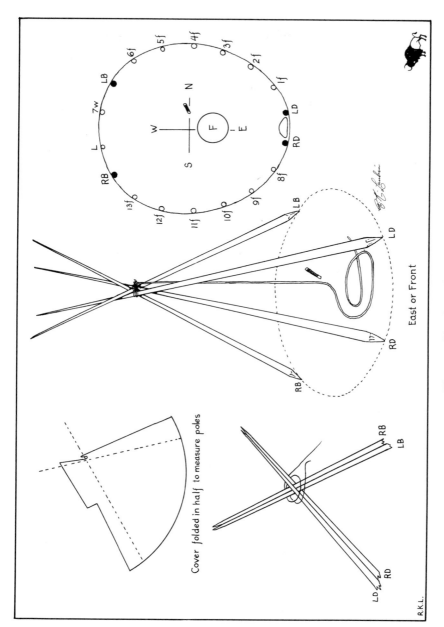

Cover folded in half to measure poles

East or Front

Fig. 29. Shoshoni Setup.

R.K.L.

foundation poles in the special manner necessary to accommodate the other poles in Shoshoni fashion. The drawing shows how they appear from the front, after being spread in proper position.

Poles 1, 2, 3, 4, 5, and 6 all go in the front crotch. Pole 7 goes in the west, poles 8, 9, 10, 11, 12, and 13 go in the front crotch on top of 1, 2, 3, 4, 5, and 6, and the lifting pole goes in the obvious opening at the rear.

When the poles are all in place the rope is wrapped around, sunwise, as for a Sioux tipi, and secured to a large stake behind the fireplace. Or two crossed stakes can be used, as for other tribes.

Except for the Peyote devotees, the Shoshonis, like the Crows, use their tipis for show only, at the time of tribal fairs, and do not like to get their tops smoked up. When we camped with them we had the same experience we had had earlier with the Crows—we were the only ones to have a fire in our tipi. We were besieged by many visitors who had never seen a fire in a tipi before.

Some of the younger people, with the new interest in things Indian, are now using tipis in the summer and enjoying the fire, but the older people still want all white tipis at fair time. So some of our young Shoshoni friends now have two tipis—one to live in and one for fairs and celebrations!

A few Shoshonis know how to set up a tipi in their own tribal style, but even they have had no actual experience living in a tipi nor any knowledge of how a tipi was furnished and used. One of their oldest men, in his nineties, said the lining was placed behind the poles, next to the outside cover! We found out that he had been born in a wall tent—a white man's tent—and had never lived in a tipi.

It seems to us that the four-pole people were mainly those who live in the Northwest, in or close to the mountains, which would be one explanation why they retained this method. The winds in those regions are not quite so strong as farther out on the open prairies. The Blackfeet, the Crows, and, as is to be expected, their cousins the Hidatsas, or Gros Ventres of the Village, the Sarsis, close to the Blackfeet, the Flatheads, Kutenais, and Nez Percés were all four-pole people. The Atsenas, or Gros Ventres of the Prairie, long allied with the Blackfeet, used three poles. This is still logical, since they are relatives of the Arapahoes, who used three.

As soon as the prairie people obtained horses, they began to make larger tipis, and after they began to use canvas, they could make them larger yet. Also, by this time, they had wagons, which enabled them to carry more luggage and equipment. The Crows and Blackfeet still have quite a number of canvas tipis which they set up for special occasions, and their average size is about twenty feet in diameter. We have seen one as large as twenty-eight feet across and several twenty-three and twenty-four feet. McClintock says the Blackfeet occasionally had lodges forty-feet in diameter, and Grinnell even speaks of two tipis connected by a corridor of canvas supported on a ridge pole, which in turn was fastened to a tipi frame at each end.

Extremely large covers, when made of buffalo hides, were sometimes laced or actually buttoned up the back as well as the front because they were too heavy to handle in one piece. This meant that two lifting poles were used. These large tipis some-times required two fires to heat them in winter.

THE CHEYENNE TIPI

Because we were adopted by a Sioux family and most of our Indian articles are Sioux, we were at first interested in having an all-Sioux tipi. But we wanted a "medicine tipi," a painted one, and at that time the best designs we could find were Cheyenne. Also, when we started to furnish our lodge, we could find no Sioux backrests. We were even told by a museum curator that the Sioux never had them, or any fancy tipi equipment, though we knew this was not so, for old-timers had described them to us. During the last period of their wars with the white soldiers the Sioux were forced to discard much of their equipment, and some of the most beautiful things were the first to be lost. Furthermore, once they came in to the reservation, discouraged and heartbroken, they sold many of their fanciest articles to the soldiers and neighboring whites, realizing that the old days were gone and being told that such things only represented savagery anyway.

Although the Cheyennes had also been at war, they were more isolated from the settlers. At any rate, they held on to more of the old things, and we were able to get a pair of Cheyenne backrests. Old Sioux pronounced them exactly like their own and showed us how they were placed in the tipi.

By making the smoke flaps a little narrower and adding to the bottom of them the little Cheyenne-style extensions we mentioned

A Cheyenne-Arapaho camp scene showing a large number of canvas tipis, includig two large painted tipis. Photograph taken by J. A. Shuck, in the vicinity of Fort Reno and Darlington Indian Agency, Oklahoma Territory, circa 1890. Credit: Western History Collections, University of Oklahoma Library.

in the discussion of the Sioux tipi, we now had a Cheyenne tipi. For many years the two tribes were friends and allies, and they had many things in common, although their languages are entirely different, as are many of their customs and rituals. To this day a number of Northern Cheyenne families live on the Pine Ridge Sioux reservation in South Dakota.

If a purely Cheyenne tipi is desired, use a strip of 29-inch material, instead of 36-inch, for the upper strip in laying out the cover (Fig. 1). But radius point x remains the same as for the Sioux pattern. This will give the narrower, longer-appearing smoke flaps typical of the Cheyenne tipi. Of course, the entire cover can be made of 29-inch material, or of almost any width material, but using the widest available eliminates much sewing. In tying the tripod, Cheyennes wrap the rope vertically around the crossing, instead of

A Cheyenne-Arapaho camp near Fort Reno and Darlington Indian Agency, Oklahoma Territory, circa 1890. Photograph by J. A. Shuck. Credit: Western History Collections, University of Oklahoma Library.

horizontally, as the Sioux do. But we still think that the Sioux method is better—less likely to slip.

While we were camping with the Crows one time, a group of Cheyennes came to visit us. Most of them were old men who knew no English, so I said to one of the young fellows with them, "Tell them this is a Cheyenne tipi." He spoke to them, and they began to laugh.

"Why are they laughing"? I inquired.

"They know that already," the young one replied.

THE CROW TIPI

As we have already mentioned, the Crows are four-pole people. The four-pole tipi is different in many ways from the three-pole.

Three-pole tipis usually have more tilted cones, making them steeper up the back, although this is not always the case, for some present-day Crow tipis are almost perpendicular at the back. But certainly the four-pole type does not need to be as tilted, because it is impossible to place so large a proportion of the poles to the front as in the three-pole type. It has been said that the four-pole people use more poles than the three-pole people do. This is true of the Blackfeet, but not of the Crows.

All four-pole tipis do have the smoke flaps set farther apart, in order to encircle the larger mass of poles at the top that is characteristic of this type. This makes a smoke hole that is larger at the top and lower around the poles. Consequently, the smoke hole does not extend as far down the front of the tipi and the smoke flaps are much shorter. These short smoke flaps are another means of identifying a four-pole lodge from a distance. See Figs. 30 and 31.

Another peculiar thing—most four-pole people seem to insert the smoke flap poles through holes or eyelets in the corners of the flaps, whereas the three-pole people always use pockets. The only exceptions are the Comanches, Shoshonis, and certain extreme northwestern mountain tribes, who are not typical tipi dwellers anyway. There you occasionally may find a four-pole lodge with pockets, or a three-pole one with smoke-flap holes. Old photographs of Kutenai tipis bear this out. As a result of inserting the smoke poles through holes in the smoke flaps, they can be as long as any others. Those for the three-pole must be cut off to the right length. A little cross stick is tied to the smoke pole of the four-pole tipi where it is secured to the flap to prevent its going through too far.

The cover for a four-pole tipi is cut quite differently from that for a three-pole one. Old Crow tipi covers have a break in the outline, as shown in the drawing (Fig. 32). Because of the stretch of the cloth and the cut of the smoke flaps, the break in the curve of the pattern is not noticeable in the erected tipi. Recent Crow tipis show no break in the curve, but, apparently as a result of the older pattern, the old-style Crow tipi ground plan is more nearly elliptical than a Sioux or Cheyenne tipi, which is egg-shaped.

Although Fig. 32 shows the radius to be used in laying out the main part of the Crow cover, it will be better not to cut out the bottom, but to pitch the tipi first and after it is properly erected, mark the bottom for cutting while it is still up, the way the Indians did.

To pitch the Crow tipi, first measure four stout poles by laying

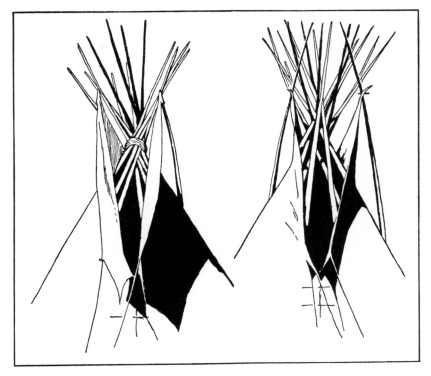

Fig. 30. Comparison of Three-pole Tipi (Cheyenne, left) with Four-pole Tipi (Crow, Right).

them on the outspread cover in the same relative positions they will occupy when the lodge is erected (Fig. 33). Lay the two front poles on the ground first and cross the two rear poles on top of them. The Crows use a special tie, also shown in Fig. 33. Make the first tie with a long (6 to 8 feet) buckskin or rawhide thong. Then repeat the tie with a soft cotton rope. You can use cotton rope for both, but the leather thong is better. Such a thong is nearly an inch wide. After tying the poles with this Crow tie, attach a heavy anchor rope and hoist the "quadripod" into place, in the same manner used for the tripod in the Cheyenne and Sioux tipis. For raising extremely heavy poles, Crow women have been known to attach the anchor rope to a horse to pull them into position.

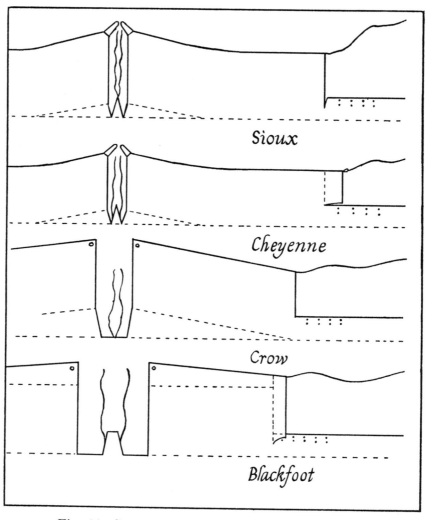

Sioux

Cheyenne

Crow

Blackfoot

Fig. 31. Comparison of Tribal Smoke-flap Styles.

Considering that your assistant is pulling on the anchor rope and you are raising the quadripod by walking up under it, when you have it nearly erect, spread it by pulling the right-hand rear pole *toward* you, then the right-hand front pole *toward* you, and you will have it locked. The anchor rope is pegged directly to the ground, usually around crossed stakes. It does not go around the other poles, which is one reason the four-pole tipi is not as sturdy as the three-pole. But because of the way the four-pole frame is stacked, it would be impractical to wind the rope around it.

The way the poles for the frame are laid in is almost the reverse of the way the Sioux do it. Lay the first pole in from the rear, but in the *south* crotch. Then lay in the other poles, alternating from opposite sides, according to the drawing in Fig. 33. This helps to keep the frame in balance and to nest the poles as compactly as possible. As you can see from the drawing, the front foundation poles are to the northeast and southeast, the rear foundation pole northwest and southwest.

Pole number 8 is the north *door pole*, number 9 the south *door pole*. The lifting pole, of course, goes to the rear and is *the only one in the west crotch*. There are only 16 poles in the average Crow tipi, 14 for the frame and 2 for the smoke flaps. Occasionally, 2 or even 4 more are used for a big lodge, and they also go in the front crotch. Their positions on the ground, however, are on the sides. Only 2 poles go between the quadripod poles in the front and rear.

The Crows tie the cover to the four foundation poles at their butts before pegging the tipi down. Sometimes they attach tie thongs to the cover for this; at other times they merely lash the cover to the poles with an extra piece of cord. Sometimes one, two, or even four guy ropes are attached to the lifting pole before the cover is raised. When only one guy, which is usual, is attached, it is pegged down behind the tipi. When more are used, they are spaced more or less evenly around the tipi. Outside guys are not needed on the three-pole tipi because a tripod is more rigid than a quadripod and all the poles are bound together with the anchor rope.

We have never seen a Crow woman set the four foundation poles in the ground, but we have seen them set the other poles, using a crowbar, as we explained in connection with pitching the Sioux tipi. In raising the Crow cover, one woman pulls forward on a guy rope, while another walks up under the pole and cover

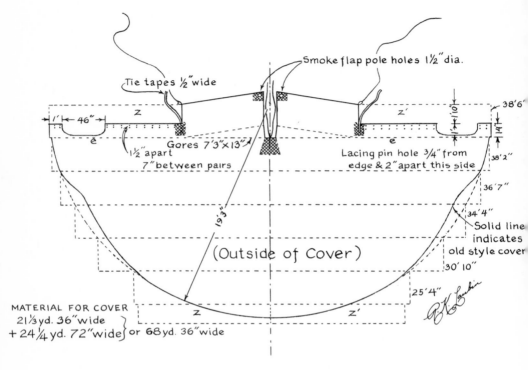

Smoke flap pole holes 1½" dia.

Tie tapes ½" wide

z   z'

38'6"

1' 46"

e   e

Gores 7'3"×13"
1½" apart
7" between pairs

Lacing pin hole ¾" from
edge & 2" apart this side

38'2"

36'7"

34'4"
Solid line
indicates
old style cover

(Outside of Cover)

30'10"

25'4"

MATERIAL FOR COVER
21⅓ yd. 36" wide
+ 24¼ yd. 72" wide } or 68 yd. 36" wide

z   z'

Fig. 32. The Crow Tipi.

until it can be balanced straight up and dropped into place.

Today one seldom sees a painted Crow tipi. The Crows take pride in keeping their tipis perfectly white and consequently do not even build fires in them. Their tipis are usually exceedingly well pitched and appear quite tall and stately. Sometimes the pattern of the cover is changed to make them taller than ever. They do this by tapering the upper, straight edge of the cover as it is spread on the ground. In other words, the pattern appears as a segment of a circle instead of nearly a half-circle.

Sometimes the Crow tipi poles are so long and extend so far above the top of the tipi that the structure looks almost like a huge hourglass. The appearance is further enhanced by long stream-

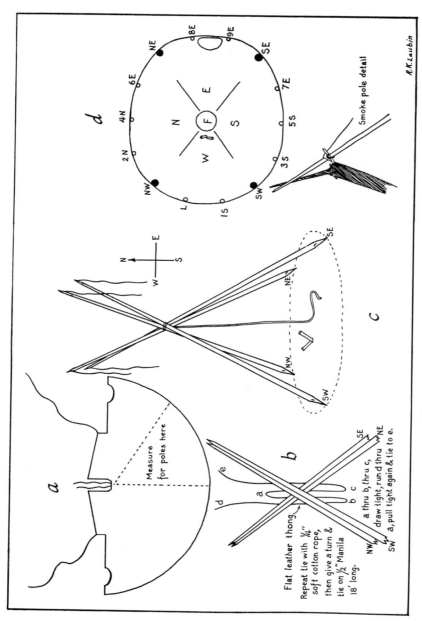

Fig. 33. Erecting the Crow Tipi.

ers hanging from the tips of the long poles. The best streamers are long thongs of white buckskin, five or six feet long, but less well-to-do families use long strips of white cloth. These long streamers blowing in the breeze from the top of almost every tipi are an outstanding characteristic of a Crow camp. Occasionally such streamers were seen in earlier times on Atsena, Cheyenne, and Kiowa tipis, but were not nearly so common as among the Crows. Our Cheyenne medicine tipi is supposed to have red streamers as part of its "medicine."

We have been told that the streamers were originally the thongs used for fastening the poles to the pack saddle when moving camp, but the only purpose of their present extreme length is beauty alone. The tall white cone, the neat cut of the smoke flaps, and the long poles with streamers flying make the Crow tipi perhaps the most graceful and beautiful of all Indian lodges.

THE BLACKFOOT TIPI

The Blackfeet and their relatives, the Piegan and the Blood Indians, still have many beautiful painted "medicine" tipis, and in this respect they have the most colorful lodges to be seen today. But their smoke flaps are even shorter than the Crow and appear rather dumpy-looking. (See pattern in Fig. 34.)

We had supposed that the Blackfeet and the Crows, both being four-pole people, set their poles up in the same way, but a trip to Browning, Montana, showed us that they do not. Of the two, we think the Crow is better, in both appearance and sturdiness, but for the latter quality, neither is as good as the Sioux and Cheyenne.

For the Blackfoot structure, lay the two rear quadripod poles on the ground first, then the front ones on top. Wrap a soft rope, about 1/4-inch cotton, 6 to 8 feet long, vertically around the crossing, pulling as tightly as possible and tying it fast in a square knot. Tie another piece about the same length, but of 3/8-inch Manila, on top of the first tie, in the same way, and make it as tight as possible. Then tie a long anchor rope around this completed tie, as the Crows do. This tie is simpler than the real Crow tie, but may be used just as well for tying the poles for a Crow tipi. In fact, we have seen Crow women use this tie and recently saw a Blackfoot woman use the Crow tie.

McClintock shows a photograph of Blackfoot women tying a

quadripod just as the Crows do,[7] but in this case they must have reversed the procedure of erecting the frame, for we cannot understand how the poles would fit otherwise. At least we are describing the method we have seen in recent use among the Blackfeet.

The quadripod is hoisted in the same way as any other, but it is spread in the opposite direction to that of the Crows, because it is laid out opposite (Fig. 35). That is, the *left rear* pole is pulled toward you, then the *left* front toward you, locking the quadripod. (Remember that in hoisting any tripod or quadripod, the "door" is to your left as you walk up under it.) Next the poles are laid in, beginning on the south side, the butt of number 1 to the left of the southeast quadripod pole, the tip in the south crotch.

The Blackfeet used many more poles than the Crows in the tipis we observed, but contrary to a popular notion, the Blackfeet do not use longer poles than the Crows. All that we saw were far shorter. The frames contained from twenty to twenty-two poles. Numbers 1 (already mentioned) 2, 3, 4, 5, and 6 all go in the south crotch. Numbers 7, 8, and 9 all go in the front, or east crotch; 10, 11, and 12 in the north crotch. The drawing (Fig. 35) shows the positions. Numbers 13 and 14 go in the west crotch. Number 15 is the left door pole, and 16 the right door pole. The lifting pole goes between 13 and 14 in the rear, or west crotch.

Mrs. Yellow Owl put the poles we have numbered as 7, 8, and 9 (the ones that go in the east crotch) in first, but this means that the poles on the south side must be put *under* them, and with big, heavy poles, this is more work. It is easier to start laying the poles as described above.

We saw Mrs. Yellow Owl set up the quadripod by spreading it the same as the Crows do, although she had tied it as just described. She pulled the right rear and right front poles toward her, which naturally had the effect of reversing the lock. Actually the quadripod is not nearly as securely locked in this way. Then she laid the poles in as we have already described, but beginning in the north crotch, placing only the two door poles in the front, or east, crotch. This had the effect of bunching most of the poles too far to the rear, and put a terrific strain on the canvas cover.

Mrs. Yellow Owl had the reputation of being expert at pitching tipis, but hers was the only one set up this way. She may have just made a mistake in spreading the quadripod and the rest of the pro-

---

[7]Walter McClintock, *The Blackfoot Tipi.*

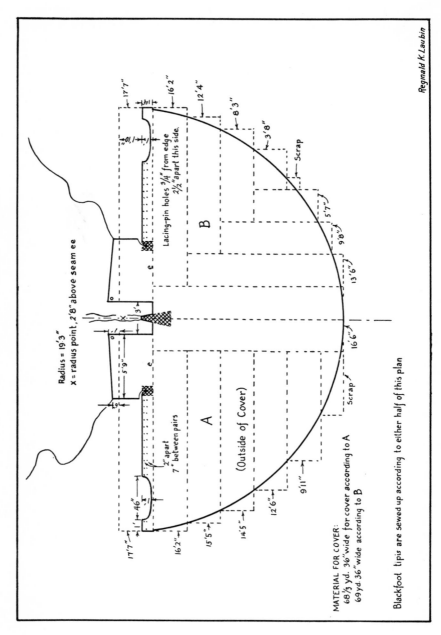

Radius = 19' 3"
x = radius point, 2' 8" above seam ee

Lacing-pin holes ¾" from edge
2½" apart this side.

17' 7"

16' 2"

12' 4"

8' 3"

3' 8"

Scrap

5' 7"

9' 8"

13' 6"

16' 6"

B

(Outside of Cover)

A

2" apart
7" between pairs

Scrap

9' 11"

12' 6"

14' 5"

15' 5"

16' 2"

17' 2"

4' 6"

1' 10"

3' 1"

5' 9"

1' 9"

e

e

o

o

x

MATERIAL FOR COVER:
68⅔ yd. 36" wide for cover according to A
69 yd. 36" wide according to B

Blackfoot tipis are sewed up according to either half of this plan

Regnald K. Laubin

Fig. 34. Pattern for Blackfoot Tipi.

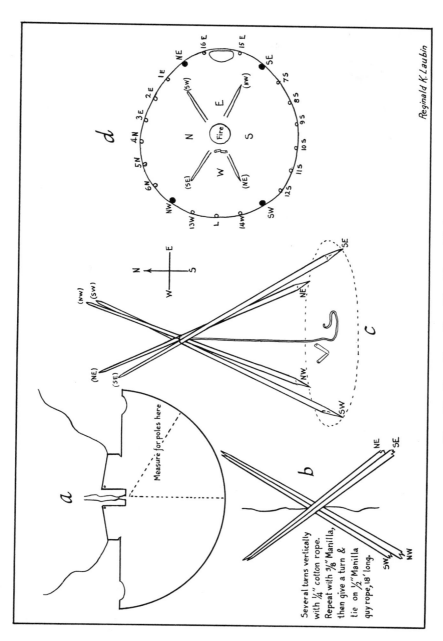

Fig. 35. Erecting the Blackfoot Tipi.

Reginald K. Laubin

cedure followed through naturally. Actually, the Blackfeet do not seem to be nearly so fussy in setting up their tipis as are the Crows, Sioux, and Cheyennes, and their tipis show it in their structure. Except for their paintings, Blackfoot tipis are not nearly so attractive as are those of other tribes.

Some of the Blackfoot tipis we saw had hemmed bottoms and sewed-on peg loops. These tipis were made of 29-inch canvas, and peg loops were sewn at each seam and between seams, making a large number of pegs necessary. In our diagram of both Crow and Blackfoot tipi covers, we have followed the same plan of using 36-inch and 72-inch material as suggested for the Sioux, thereby saving a great deal of sewing.

Regardless of the huge smoke vent and the great bundle of poles at the top, the large number of poles and pegs do enable the Blackfeet to set up tight lodges. In making their tipi, instead of laying all the canvas strips horizontally, they laid two strips vertically down the center, then laid strips horizontally on each side to complete the cover pattern. One cover, from the Bloods in Canada, was made by laying two strips vertically, then alternating a horizontal with a vertical strip, each succeeding strip consequently becoming shorter as the curve filled out.

Many Blackfeet still have some beautiful tipi furnishings and some of their lodges, set up for a fair or other celebration, are most attractive inside. We feel that the Blackfoot tipi on display in the Southwest Museum in Los Angeles is disappointing and gives anything but a true idea of an old-time Blackfoot home. The poles are crooked, broken off, unpeeled, and the butts are not even pointed. Any Indian woman who was such a careless housekeeper would have had a very poor reputation among her people. That tipi is also badly furnished. It has only one backrest, and even that is set up against a tripod of rough-looking sticks. All the Blackfoot tripods we have seen, even at this late date, are beautifully carved and painted.

The Blackfoot tipi in the American Museum of Natural History in New York is also disappointing. It is set up on only eleven poles. In addition, it is presented as it would appear at night, which gives visitors to the museum in broad daylight a faulty impression. As a consequence, they think that the old-time lodges were dark and gloomy. Actually skin tipis were bright and cheerful, and it is lighter in a canvas tipi than it is in most houses.

The Blackfeet ordinarily do not bother with cords to the lower corners of the smoke flaps, and the cords on the few tipis that do have them are merely tied to a couple of the pegs at the bottom of the tipi. They do not set up a pole in front of the door as most other tribes do.

THE YAKIMA TIPI

It might be expected that the Yakima Indians of Washington would use the four-pole method of erecting a tipi, since we have reliable information that their neighbors, the Nez Percés[8] and Umatillas, the Confederated Salish (including the Flatheads), the Kutenais, and Coeur d'Alènes all use the four-pole method.

But the Yakimas actually use a three-pole base, although it is quite different from that of the Sioux and Cheyennes. In fact, it even looks like a four-pole base. The Yakimas set the tripod in reverse position to that of the usual three-pole type. That is, two legs of the tripod are set toward the door, or east, and one to the rear. This means that the two forward poles are longer than the rear pole. The tripod is also tied in a peculiar way (Fig. 36). The poles are measured as for any other tipi, except that two long ones and one short one are marked. After they are marked, the two long ones are laid on the ground with butts toward the door and the short rear pole is laid in between them, with its butt to the west. The measured markings are made to coincide and the poles are tied by placing a clove hitch around each one as they lie side by side. The loose ends are brought underneath and tied in a square knot. A heavy rope is then passed around and tied, to be used as an anchor rope, as for other tipis.

The tripod is raised by hoisting the three poles perpendicularly, and either one of the front poles can cross on top, because the tripod, tied in this way can be locked in either position simply by spreading the two front poles. Mr. Yallup, our informant, demonstrated with a model using only twelve poles but said that, depending upon the size of the tipi, more poles were used. The method

[8]We have never heard anyone in the Northwest say *"Nez Percé."* Everyone says "Nez Pers," with a strong z and no final *e* — even the Indians themselves pronounce it this way. But the name is French and the formal French pronunciation is "Nez Percé," with the accent.

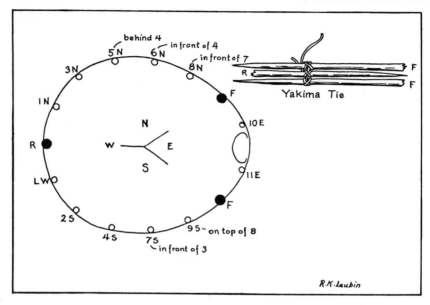

Fig. 36. Foundation Plan of Yakima Tipi.

we now describe for placing the poles proved to be a sensible and practical one for construction of a tipi well braced against the wind, using fifteen poles in the frame and two more for smoke flaps—our usual set.

Lay the poles, beginning at the rear, as for a four-pole lodge, number 1 pole next to the rear tripod pole and on the north side. Skip a space for the lifting pole and lay number 2 on the south side, number 3 is north, 4 south, 5 north, and 6 *north*, in front of 4. Number 7 is south, in front of 3; 8 north, in front of 7; 9 south, on top of 8; 10 is in the east crotch, north of the door; and 11 east, south of the door (Fig. 28). Place the lifting pole to the west, in the obvious opening, without a rope around the poles, so that, as previously stated, the general appearance of the finished frame is much like that of a Crow tipi. This is one type of tipi that could fool an observer, but the Yakimas do use the smoke-flap pockets, typical of three-pole tipis.

Recent information we have received tells us that the Mescalero Apaches use this same type of tripod and doubtless the same setup, as it would be difficult to place the poles efficiently in any other way. How this method jumped from the state of Washington to the Apache country in the Southwest is difficult to explain.

THE CREE TIPI

Our neighbors, the Craigheads, have a little Cree tipi that is quite interesting. Although only about a 12 footer, it is quite squatty and offers a lot of room for such a small structure. We call it "the big little tipi." It is made of 36 inch light weight duck, probably 8 ounce, and Fig. 37 will give some idea of the way it is laid out. It is all sewed by hand, and is one of the few real Indian tipis we have seen with a hem around the bottom and sewed-on peg loops. These loops are made of folded canvas strips. It is almost certain the tipi was sewed together and pitched; then the bottom was trimmed and hemmed, for it is evident that it is not cut on a true arc. Seams are made by laying two selvage edges together on the wrong side, folding them both over about a quarter of an inch, and then using a running stitch through all four thicknesses.

The tie flap is a separate piece, 8 inches long, 7 inches wide, and tapered to 2 inches at the tip, hemmed on three sides and added to the cover. Tie thongs of smoked buckskin are attached. Over the tie flap and extending down the back is another piece, 21 inches long and 12 inches wide, added on the *outside* as reinforcement. So the complete tie flap is of two thicknesses. It is decorated with a strip of red flannel appliqué, as indicated in Fig. 37. Another strip of red flannel decorates the upper edge of the smoke flaps.

The smoke flap pockets are rather different, too, as you can see. They look better than the triangular pieces sometimes used, especially on commercially made tipis, but are not as attractive as the extended little narrow pockets we see on Sioux and Cheyenne tipis.

The Sioux three-pole method of pitching the tipi can be used for the Cree tipi, but some old photographs show the poles laid in reverse, which means tying the tripod reverse, too.

Notice that the lacing pin holes are in pairs on one side of the

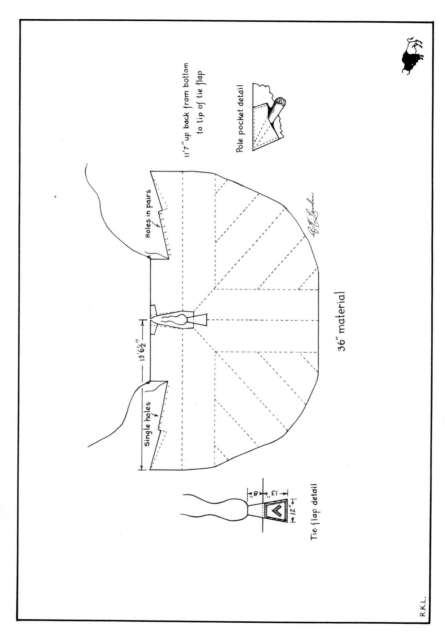

Holes in pairs

11'7" up back from bottom
to tip of tie flap

Single holes

13'6½"

36" material

Pole pocket detail

Tie flap detail

13"
8"
12"

Fig. 37. Cree Tipi ("Big Little Tipi").

R.K.L.

tipi and are single on the other side. We have an old Crow tipi with lacing pin holes the same way.

OLD PHOTOGRAPHS

Old photographs in the Bureau of American Ethnology, dating from 1868 to the early 1900's, show interesting details of some of the tipis we have been talking about. Photographs of Umatilla tipis show flap pockets, fourteen to sixteen lacing pins, and few ground pegs. They appear to have been set up in the manner of the Yakima tipi, the last poles going in at the door. The Umatillas also made an odd lodge, in tipi style, but much like an Iroquois long house. In other words, it looked like a number of tipis, close together in a row, all connected by one covering. Some of these were covered with mats, had no smoke flaps, and seem to have been much like the bark wigwams of the Woodlands.

A photograph of an old Yakima hide tipi shows only eight poles in the frame. Kiowa-Apache pictures show a three-pole foundation, with fifteen poles in the frame, fourteen lacing pins, and flap pockets. One photograph shows a tipi with two covers, one draped over the other.

Photographs of Shoshoni tipis appear to be of Sioux type construction, but with shorter smoke flaps, much wider at their upper edges. As with Comanche tipis, side views sometimes show the two low rear poles, a giveaway for the four-pole type, and some have guy ropes attached to the lifting pole, as on other four-pole type tipis.

Pictures of Ute tipis are not clear, but the lodges look squat and poorly pitched. Some show streamers from the top, so at least these Indians had some feeling for beauty. Comanche tipis, photographed by Soule from 1868 to 1872, look like three-pole, or Sioux, with pocket flaps and fifteen lacing pins, but those pictured from the side show the two low poles projecting from behind. One photograph shows a "lining" outside, on the south side. It possibly went all the way around. A photograph of old Nez Percé hide tipis shows a four-pole foundation, smoke poles through "slits in the ears," and many lacing pins, but few ground pegs. These tipis were quite tall, with short flaps and short streamers. An old Nez Percé lady told us they used "either three or four" poles. Kiowa tipis look much like

Sioux. They, too, have no extensions at the bases of the smoke flaps.

CHILDREN'S TIPIS

The small lodge for hunting has already been mentioned. Little girls had still smaller play tipis which they made under their mothers' directions, and in which they "played house." They even made little tipis for their favorite dogs. Children also made tiny tipis and villages from the larger leaves of the cottonwood, pinning them together with splinters or thorns. Following the Custer battle, the paper money found on the soldiers was turned over to the youngsters, who made play tipis of it.

It might be interesting to make a small tipi for your children and set aside a corner of the yard for an Indian reservation. A pattern for such a small tipi has been included in Fig. 38. For a little one like this you need only eleven poles, nine in the frame and two for the smoke flaps. The poles need be only eleven or twelve feet long, and will be so small where they cross that you need pay little attention to the way they are placed in the frame.

I made my first tipi when I was about ten years old. Since I had no idea what a tipi was really like, mother cut it out in long triangular pieces, as if she were making a shirt, and it had no smoke flaps. When we tried to make a little fire in it we found it smoked something awful. Then from Ernest Thompson Seton's book, *Two Little Savages*, I got some idea of how a tipi should be made and we added the smoke flaps.

This little tipi was pitched in our back yard and stood there way into the winter. I remember on one occasion we had an ice storm and it became almost solid. When some companions and I made a fire inside it became so hot we could hardly stand it. After all, it was only about eight feet in diameter, but we thought it quite large.

When it was too cold to use the tipi any longer, I took it down and pitched it in the attic, "staking" it to the wooden floor with long nails. My brothers and I played in it all the rest of the winter. We put an electric light bulb in the center, with red crepe paper over it, for a fire. It is a wonder it did not start a real one!

Spring arrived, and as the weather warmed and became more pleasant, the tipi was taken down, rolled up, and placed on the

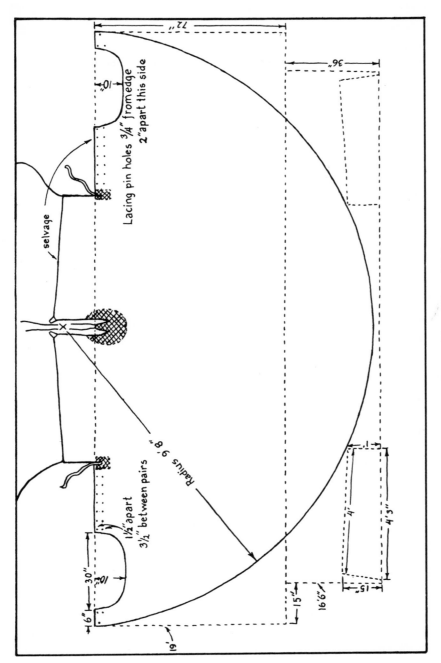

Lacing pin holes ¾" from edge 2" apart this side

selvage

72"

10"

36"

Radius 9'8"

1½" apart
3½" between pairs

30"

10"

6"

19'

15"

16'6"

4'

1"

4'3"

15"

Fig. 38. A Play Sioux Tipi.

back porch, awaiting the day when I would come home from school
and set it up in the yard again.

Then one day a rag man called at the house and asked if we
had any old rags or papers to sell. Mother assured him that we
did not, and he asked, "What's that bundle of rags here?"

"Don't you dare touch that! That's my son's tent," she answered.

But when I came home the tipi was gone. It was one of the
unhappiest days of my life, but I sold newspapers and did all sorts
of chores to help earn money enough to buy more canvas and make
a new tipi. This one we made entirely according to Seton's directions, and we thought it was a beauty, even if it was round instead
of egg-shaped, and a true cone instead of straighter up the back,
as I later learned a real Indian tipi should be. I still have a picture
of it but it is so old and faded that it would never reproduce. I have
lived in a tipi at least part of every year since.

One time Gladys and I met a new friend who lived in New York
City and had pitched a tipi on the top of the Times Square Hotel!
He said he had quite a time getting the poles up on the roof in the
freight elevator, for they were about eighteen feet long, but he
managed to do it. This must be the record of all records for tipi
living!

When I was about 12 years old my friend Dan and I rolled up
my little tipi and took turns carrying it on our backs for about two
and a half miles to a quiet woodland spot along a creek. (We thought
it was five miles, but years later clocked it with a car and found
it just half of that.) With our blankets and grub we shared a sizeable
load. It was no great task to find poles for such a small tipi and we
soon cut enough dead ones to have it up in good order. We made
beds, of a sort, of grass and leaves and spread out our blankets
on each side of the fireplace, for which we dug a small hole, for
there were no rocks or stones around. By this time it was dark.
We crawled in and were soon sound asleep.

About midnight we were suddenly almost bounced out of bed
by a terrifying clap of thunder and within a few minutes were in
a violent cloudburst, with the smoke flaps wide open! Since the
tipi was mine and I knew more about handling it, I was elected
to go out and close them. It was blacker than pitch, except when
a startling flash of lightning made everything bright as day for
an instant. I stripped off what little clothing I had been sleeping
in and hustled out into the cold, pouring rain, felt my way around

the little tipi until I found the smoke poles, and stumbled around until I finally got the flaps closed. It probably took only a few minutes, but it seemed an hour, and then I could not find the door to get back in.

I went around and around, getting wetter and colder and more frightened by the second, when, bang!, came another ear-splitting thunder clap and flash of brilliant lightning, and there was the door right in front of me! In my excitement I had been feeling above the door all the time. We did not even have a door cover and for once I was glad of it, for I popped through that little doorway and inside almost as quick as the lightning flash. Inside it was almost as wet as outside, but our beds were only wet in spots and the blankets felt mighty good. We lay there, two thoroughly scared kids, talking to each other, sometimes shouting to be heard above the thunder. Then all at once the storm was over. The rain stopped, the wind died down, and it was quiet and peaceful again, the only sound being the dripping of the water from the trees. But it was still dark, as black as black can be.

We decided we should have a fire, so I had to go out and open up the flaps again. We had been smart enough to have a few shavings and some kindling by our wood pile inside the door, and fortunately had placed it far enough to one side that it was still dry. We had no flashlight. Dan was supposed to have the matches but could not find them in his coat pocket. In the dark we discovered the fire hole was full of water; so we tried to lay our fire to one side of it. We were using our coats as pillows and decided we must have gotten them mixed.

I started to feel in my pockets. No matches in the first one. I put my hand in the other pocket and right into a mess of wet, gooey, broken egg! Then we knew we had switched coats, for we had raided the hen house before we left and the two eggs we had found there had been placed in Dan's pocket. Scrambled in the eggs were the matches. How we ever got a fire going we will never know, but it was about the most welcome one we have ever seen. Soon it was blazing merrily, bright and cheery, warming our hearts as well as the rest of us. The fright and discomfort of the storm were all but forgotten in the joy of being in a real tipi and having weathered our trials so successfully.

We turned in to get some more sleep but it was soon dawn and sleep was impossible with a bright new world to see. We went out to take a look around and discovered that our tiny creek, which ordinarily was only about ankle deep, was almost to the top of its banks. At the bend below our camp it was calm enough that we went in for a morning dip, and found the water over our heads! This was a delightful surprise to have an unexpected swimming hole which lasted all morning, and more than made up for all we had gone through the night before.

CHIEF'S TIPI

A chief's tipi was not necessarily the finest one in camp, although it was usually one of the largest because of the amount of entertaining he was called upon to do. It might even be one of the poorest, for the chief was regarded as the father of his people and so was always being called upon to assist others in many ways. He constantly gave away his possessions, kept open house for visitors at all hours, and entertained his own tribesmen and delegations from other tribes. He was expected to be kindhearted and generous and to share his food with anyone in need.

In most tribes a chief's lodge was distinguished from all the others by fastening a horse's tail or a large imitation scalp to the top of the lifting pole. The lifting pole was often the longest pole in the structure, so that the emblem hung far above the entrance. We have one of these emblems from the Oglalas which is made of a small shield of raw buffalo hide on which the hair remains and to which is attached a long black horsetail. The shield is painted red on the flesh side and the exposed skin of the tail is yellow. The entire ornament is more than four feet long, but hanging high in the air it merely looks like a very large scalp, appearing not nearly so long as it really is.

Because of his many duties and all the entertaining he was expected to do, an important chief often had more than one wife. Sitting Bull had two wives who were extremely jealous of each other. Both insisted on sleeping with him at the same time. He had to sleep flat on his back, one woman holding him by one arm and one leg, the other holding him the same way on the other side, so that it was impossible for him to face either of them. He complained that he awoke in the mornings so stiff and lame that he could hardly walk. Had he had as much experience in the matrimonial customs of his people as he had in their customs governing war and religion, he would have married sisters. The elder of two sisters was automatically head of the tipi, and little bickering was expected to result from such a union. But even so, a man who could afford two wives often found it better if he could also afford two tipis, one for each wife, for then harmony reigned with surety.

WARRIOR SOCIETY TIPIS

All the tribes of the Plains had fraternal organizations, usually known as warrior societies. Nearly every man of any reputation belonged to at least one of these societies. Among the Sioux, for instance, the Chief's Society, Strong Hearts, Owl, Lance Owners, and Foxes are a few of the better-known ones. Some societies were chosen to act as camp policemen. They were supposed to see that the orders of the council were carried out, to supervise the march when moving camp and see that none lagged behind, and to see that each tipi was in its proper place when camp was established. Their most important function, however, was to supervise the tribal buffalo hunts and prevent any overeager hunter from getting away before all were supposed to go.

Each warrior society usually had its own big tipi, where meetings, feasts, dances, and rituals were held. These were usually large painted lodges that occupied prominent places within the inner circle of the camp. When a meeting was held, backrests, linings, and other furnishings were sometimes commandeered from prominent families, as well as the food for the feast. These families were supposed to be highly honored to receive such recognition, and their prestige increased immeasurably.

THE COUNCIL LODGE

Often a very large tipi was set aside as a council lodge. Such a tipi might be as large as 30 or more feet in diameter. A council lodge was rarely furnished, being left bare except, sometimes, for a sacred altar prepared by a holy man. Each member brought his own robe to sit on, and sometimes backrests were furnished for distinguished leaders, especially if they were old men.

Catlin and Maximilian recorded seeing skin tipis over one hundred years ago as large as fifty feet across, but no one else seems to have seen such huge ones. What they saw may have been still a different type of council lodge, specially constructed to take care of a big crowd. It was made by combining two or more large tipis and really was a great open shade. Tripods were pitched, as usual, but with the rear legs overlapping. Poles were added only to the rear sides and to the two ends. The covers were hoisted and spread fanlike, corners overlapping. The finished structure was a huge arc of a circle, or sometimes a half-circle, open to the east but shaded from the sun on the south and west.

Or they may have seen something like the two connected tipis Grinnell described.[9] Such a big intertribal council lodge was erected at the All-American Indian Days, in Sheridan, Wyoming, in August, 1955.

BURIAL LODGE

When death overtook an important individual, he was sometimes left in a burial tipi. The body was dressed in full regalia and placed on a bed, usually in a fully furnished tipi. His medicine bundle was often tied to a lodge pole overhead. Such a tipi was usually pitched in a sheltered place in a thicket near a stream. The poles were planted in the ground and the smoke flaps closed tight. The door was lashed fast and blocked with poles and brush, the bottom securely fastened all the way around to keep animals and enemies out.

The entire camp was moved after such a burial, and the mourners, in addition to cutting their hair and gashing themselves, sometimes cut off several feet from the bottom of their lodges, reducing them to a small size, causing great inconvenience and discomfort. Sometimes they also cut off their horses' manes and tails and they themselves walked barefoot. Often they pitched their own camp at a distance from the main camp, exposing themselves to danger from attack by enemies. At such a time they entrusted their own medicine bundles to friends or relatives until the period of mourning was over.

Just before Custer attacked the great Sioux camp on the Little Big Horn, one of these burial lodges was discovered. His Arikaree scouts burned it to show their contempt, and while it was burning, some of the dead warrior's relatives, who had returned to make

[9]See page 124, above.

sure that the body was undisturbed, discovered this vandalism and rode back to camp to give the alarm. This family was among the first to know that soldiers were near. After the fighting, the Sioux left several warriors, who had been killed in the battle, in a large burial lodge west of the river. Terry's and Gibbon's troops discovered this lodge and stripped the bodies for souvenirs.

MEMORIAL TIPIS

About 1936, we saw a large tipi, owned by the local American Legion post, pitched on the Standing Rock reservation during the Fourth of July celebrations. The post name and number were painted on it in big letters and the names of all the Indian boys who had served in World War I were listed down the back of it. On the sides were painted horses and riders—war records of other days.

MEDICINE TIPIS

Symbolism is nearly as old as man himself, and the Indian had no monopoly of it. Some of us, not realizing that we still use a great deal of symbolism ourselves even today, think the Indians were rather crude or ignorant because they used symbolism in nearly everything.

Indians used symbolism throughout their entire lives. It showed up in practically everything they did. Even the home was symbolic —a church, a place of worship—as well as a mere place to eat and sleep. The floor of the tipi represented the earth—the Mother. The lodge-cover was the sky above—the Father. The poles linked mankind with the heavens. The little altar behind the fireplace showed the relationship of man to the spiritual forces surrounding him.

To the Cheyennes the two door poles (the one on the south being a tripod pole), plus the other two tripod poles, represent the four directions, and the lifting pole at the rear is the one that "holds up the sky."

The Indian usually placed his altar in the west, where the sun set, thus keeping the fire alive all through the night in the place where the sun disappeared.

The painted, or "medicine," tipis were owned by only a few

Fig. 39. This is the most elaborate tipi design we have ever seen. It is on a model in the American Museum of Natural History in New York. The buffalo, elk, antelope, and bear are painted quite naturalistically. Note that the circles and some of the stripes are different colors on opposite sides. Indians are fond of informal designs, designs that are not the same on both sides, in either shape or color.

Red →

← Red

Red →

← Yellow tips

distinguished families, except among the Kiowas, where every fourth tipi was painted. Some such Kiowa tipis, however, were merely heraldic, painted with the warlike exploits of their owners. The medicine designs usually originated in dreams, some a long time ago, and were handed down from generation to generation. Such designs could be purchased in proper ceremonies and the "medicine" and rituals "passed" from one owner to another.

The Blackfeet, who had as many, if not more, painted tipis than almost any other tribe, averaged about one painted lodge to ten plain ones. McClintock said that in a camp of 350 lodges there were 35 painted tipis.[10]

Among the Blackfeet certainly, and among other tribes generally, each painted tipi was associated with a ritual, including songs and taboos, sometimes dances, and usually had medicine bundles containing various ceremonial objects associated with them. Sometimes a medicine bundle was hung above the door, especially if the tribe was on the move and making only short stops. Others were hung from the lifting pole on the outside of the cover, just below the tie flap. Some were hung on a medicine rack behind the tipi with other objects of ceremonial importance—war bonnet cases, shields, and lances.

The medicine tipis, with their designs and ceremonies, were supposed to protect the owners and their families from misfortune and sickness and to insure success in hunting and war. Some were even believed to bring good fortune to the tribe generally. No two medicine tipis could ever be painted alike, or be associated with the same rituals. When such a tipi wore out, a new one was made in exact duplication, but the old one was always destroyed—never cut up to make moccasins and clothing, as were worn-out ordinary lodges. The Blackfeet destroyed a worn-out medicine tipi by spreading it out on the surface of a lake, so that it would sink.

Just as the proper observance of the customs and rituals governing a medicine tipi could bring success and good fortune to its owners, so any infraction of these rules could bring misfortune or even death. Therefore, the ownership of such a tipi was a great responsibility as well as an honor, and a medicine tipi distinguished a family of worth and character.

When a medicine tipi was passed from one person to another,

[10]*The Old North Trail*, 217.

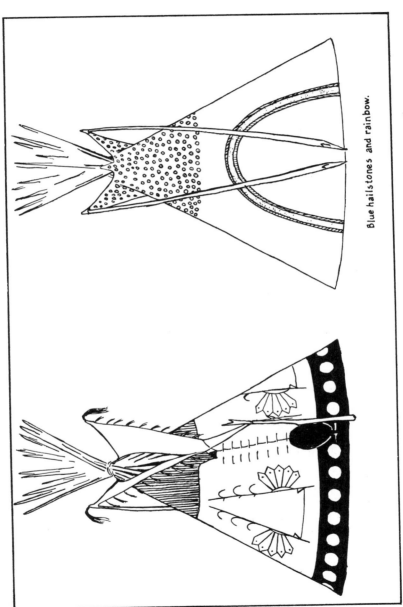

Blue hailstones and rainbow.

Fig. 40. The pipes on the tipi at the left are ceremonial wands, or calumets, used in the Hunkayapi, or adoption ceremony. The tipi owner evidently belonged to this society. Such pipes were not smoked, but were used in a graceful dance.

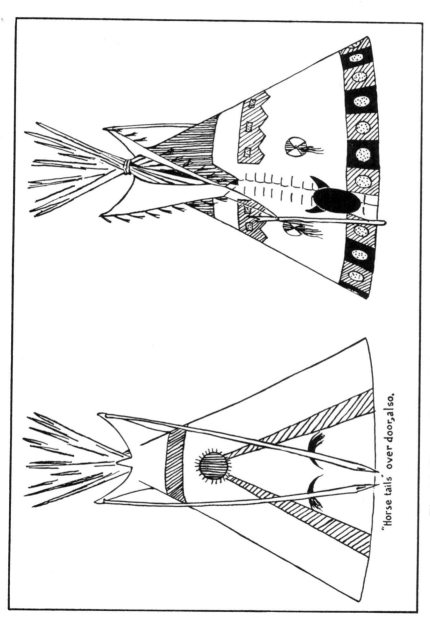

"Horse tails" over door, also.

Fig. 41. Horsetails on the tipi on the left are also connected with an adoption ceremony, one more simple than that using the wands. (See color plate following page 206.)

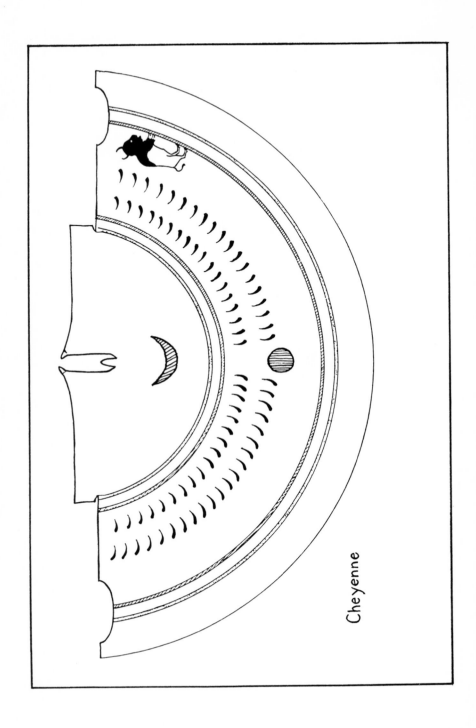

Cheyenne

the one receiving it had to make a vow to accept all the duties and responsibilities associated with it, to observe the ceremonies and taboos, and also make a substantial gift of horses and other presents to the former owner and prepared a feast for him and his relatives.

On these ceremonial tipis, the border designs at the base, generally speaking, represent the earth and things pertaining to the earth. The designs at the top refer to the sky and the spirit world. In between is the life of man. Actual life experiences, such as battles and hunts, were sometimes painted on this in-between section, as well as symbolic paintings representing religious and visionary experiences. To the Indian, things of the spirit world and of his mind and imagination were just as real as the tangible things of the material world.

Most of the designs we see in books and pictures are Blackfoot, for they have kept many of their painted lodges up to the present day. Walter McClintock, in *The Old North Trail* and in his booklets for the Southwest Museum,[11] did a great deal of writing about the paintings and ceremonials of these people. Sioux and Cheyenne designs have been much harder to find. Some Cheyenne and Kiowa designs are to be found in the Chicago Museum of Natural History and in the National Museum in Washington, D.C. We made quite a search to find the designs we are presenting. We made sketches in our notebooks over the years, but have lost track of some of the origins. Some are to be found in the *Eleventh Annual Report of the Bureau of American Ethnology*. Several were sketched in the American Museum of Natural History in New York.

[11]In *Publications of the Southwest Museum* (Los Angeles).

Fig. 42. It is easy enough to recognize the moon in the crescent at the top. The circle is the sun. Perhaps the black marks are rain, signifying that honors fell like rain upon the owner. This owner may have had a name like Reginald's—One Bull or Lone Bull, or something of the kind. But this Cheyenne painted his emblem at the left of the door.

The buffalo was the symbol of generosity, abundance, and industry. The buffalo gave the Indians everything, from food, clothing, and shelter to the fuel for their fires. The Buffalo Spirit was the protector of maidens and of the aged, the comrade of the Sun himself, who was the highest manifestation of the Great Mystery.

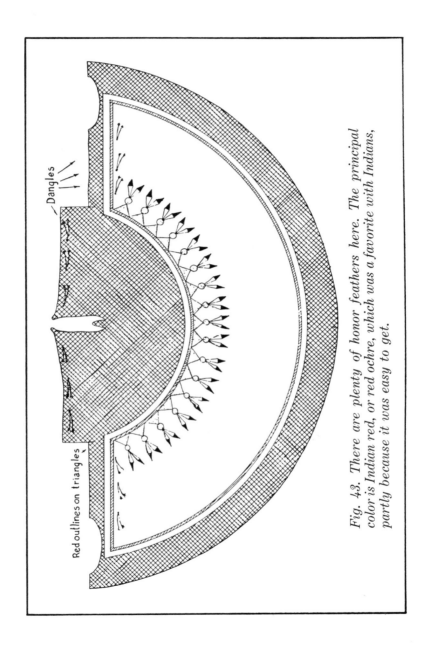

Dangles

Red outlines on triangles

Fig. 43. There are plenty of honor feathers here. The principal color is Indian red, or red ochre, which was a favorite with Indians, partly because it was easy to get.

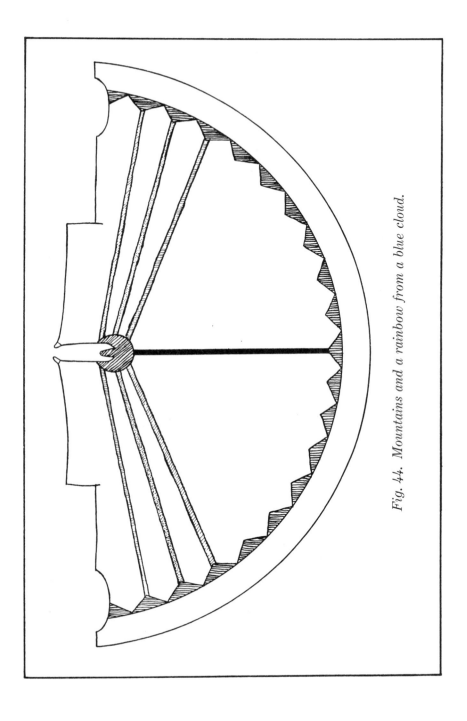

Fig. 44. Mountains and a rainbow from a blue cloud.

Fig. 45. This is a bear medicine tipi. The red spot is the bear's den. Claws and tracks are on the trail at the bottom. The zigzags are lightning and storm, followed by the rainbow. The bear was the patron of wisdom, magic, and medicine. The Indians knew the bear kept well by eating certain herbs and roots. They followed him and watched him and learned much of their medicine from him. The Bear Spirit might be invisible, or he might appear as a huge bear or as an old man. Both the bear and the buffalo were patrons of courage, and Indians regarded it as high an honor to "count coup" on a grizzly as on an enemy. Big medicine, this tipi!

No horse on opposite side

Fig. 46. This tipi belonged to Black Elk, a famous Oglala medicine man, and a friend of ours. His medicine dream is well described in Black Elk Speaks, *by John Neihardt, and the religious beliefs of his people in* The Sacred Pipe, *by Joseph Epes Brown.*

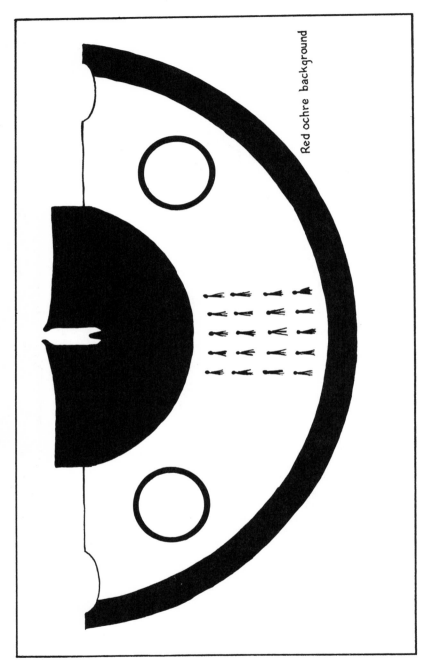

Red ochre background

Fig. 47. Hoops are symbolic, representing the unity of the tribe, the world, complete, and perfect life, return of the seasons, the sun, moon, and so on. On the back are painted scalps, representing honors in war. This is a very simple but effective design.

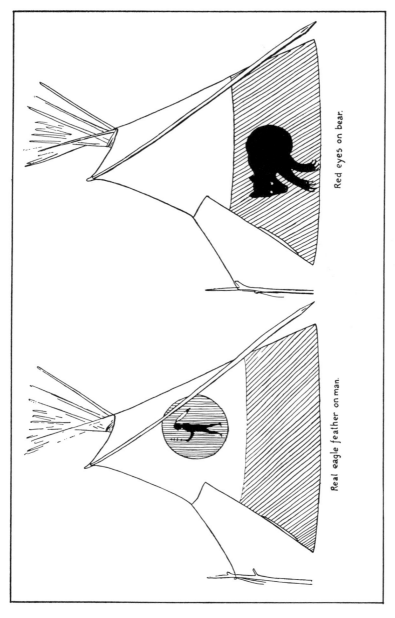

Real eagle feather on man.

Red eyes on bear.

Fig. 48. The owner of the tipi at the left belonged to a special dancing fraternity, members of which carried dew-claw rattles. A real eagle feather was attached to the painted figure, which represents the owner himself. (See color plate following page 206.)

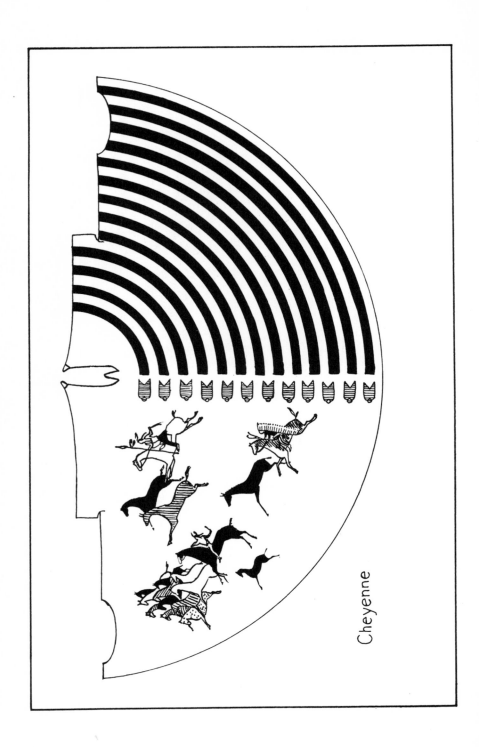

Cheyenne

In addition to the designs we reproduce here, we have seen an all red tipi and an all yellow one, with no other design but the color. Most of the designs presented are Sioux except for those indicated to be of other tribes. We were unable to get full interpretations of some of them. The designs range from the extremely simple to very elaborate, so there should be a choice for almost every taste and ability.

A number of rainbows are represented, and one has hailstones, which must have belonged to a Thunder Dreamer. Only one who understood Thunder Medicine, *heyoka*, would have dared use such a design, and it may have protected him from sudden storms.

SYMBOLISM OF SIOUX AND CHEYENNE TIPI DESIGNS

Indians used colors symbolically, but it is not possible to say a certain color always represented a certain thing. For instance, in one Sioux ceremony red is the east, black the south, yellow the west, and blue the north. In others black is west, and in some red is west. Sometimes white is used for north. Sometimes red and sometimes yellow represent the sun. The red is the morning sun, yellow the setting sun. But in any one ceremony the colors are constant. Since most ceremonies originated in visions or dreams, the symbolism could be very different.

Our own painted tipi, as before mentioned, has a Cheyenne medicine design. From what I have been able to learn, it formerly belonged to a warrior society known as the Red Shield Lodge. The red top, in this case, represents the west, where the Thunder lives.

Fig. 49. This is the most striking and fantastic design of all and must have made a person blink on seeing it in an old Cheyenne camp. The black stripes may represent the thirteen moons of the year, or they may be war trails. A war record and buffalo tracks are on the other side. Some tipis have war records all over the outside, just as they are often found on the linings inside. One of the Kiowa tipis had a design quite similar to this one, except that it had fifteen black stripes, outlined with white on a yellow background.

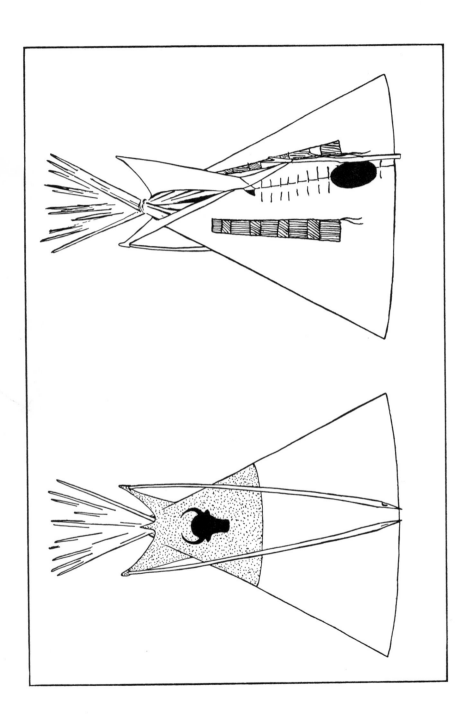

Below is a trail, representing eternal life and continuous time, the moons going all around.

A trail from each of the four quarters ascends from the earth to the sky. On this trail are dragonflies, bearing messages to the Thunder. The black band at the bottom of the tipi represents the earth. Above it are the puff balls that grow on the prairie and the red road, the good road of life. The puff balls are sometimes called "dusty stars," for they appeared so quickly and grew so fast they were thought to be stars fallen from the sky. When crushed or stepped on after becoming dry they emitted a puff of powder, like a yellowish or brownish dust.

Up the back is a direct path—the warpath, lined with scalps, signifying victory and honors—but it leads directly to the Shadow Land. Here also is the red shield, emblem of the society. On either side are a bay and a blue horse. They may symbolize the horses captured by the members.

On the right of the door I painted a buffalo to represent my own name. I took this buffalo from another Cheyenne tipi, so that the entire painting would be in keeping and in key. Sitting Bull had a picture of a buffalo in a sitting position on the right of the door of his tipi. Since I was adopted into Sitting Bull's family, I used the emblem of my name in a similar position.

When I was painting the dragonflies on our tipi, a real dragonfly alighted on one of the painted ones. Indians would say this was big medicine. Certain it is that bad weather almost always changes to good when we put up our tipi, and we have had terrific winds and storms on many occasions immediately after taking it down.

Figures 39-50 and 52-54 reproduce Sioux and Cheyenne tipi designs and explain the symbolism connected with them.

Some women decorated unpainted tipis with triple dangles made of thongs wrapped with colored cornhusks, from which hung

---

Fig. 50. At the left is a very simple design, yellow top with a black buffalo head. The tipi on the right was taken from an old photograph whose color values looked like red and green. In a case such as this, it should be permissible for one to make his own choice of colors, and if he likes other colors better, to use them. Such a design may not be "medicine" at all, but just decoration, such as any family was entitled to have.

pairs of rattling pendants of dew claws, dyed wool, and strips of buffalo or horse hair. These dangles were spaced down the front of the smoke flaps and along the lacing pins, and usually one large beaded rosette was placed at the tie flap behind and four smaller ones spaced around the tipi about shoulder height. These rosettes were called "stars," but the four smaller ones also represent the four directions on the outside of the tipi just as the four poles do on the inside. The rosettes were sewed on with proper ceremony, the large one at the tie flap representing the sun, being sewed on first. One of the smaller rosettes representing the South, really on the southeast, was next, then the West, North, and East were sewed on. If a mistake were made in the sewing, four old men who had counted coup in battle were called. The faulty rosette was removed; one of the men took the sewer's awl and counted coup on the place where it had been; he then returned the awl, and the rosette was resewn. After the tipi was pitched, buffalo tails were hung to each "star," also with much ceremony. In recent years the tails have been replaced with strips of buffalo hide from the mane or forelegs, these being easier to get than separate tails. No man was permitted to touch the "stars" until after they had been sewn in place.

Figure 51 shows how these dangles are made. Usually eight are fastened to each smoke flap and seven along the lacing pins. Cheyennes fasten those on the smoke flaps near the seam, so they do not rattle quite as much in the wind as the ones the Sioux used, which were hung near the outer edge. The Sioux dangles were often quilled. The Cheyenne dangles are made on a foundation of harness leather, and sometimes the toe section of the hoof is used as the rattle rather than a dew claw. The dangles can be wrapped with raffia, and it would be easier to do than with corn husk.

The hoof or dew claw can be softened in boiling water and carved easily with a knife. Holes can be drilled, or they can be burned with a red hot nail. Either way smells bad, but the burning is worse. Slip a dew claw (or toe) on the long, or lower end of one of the buckskin thongs, push it up out of the way, then catch a short piece of the harness leather, to form the loop, to the thong, wrap with the corn husk (or raffia), bring both ends of the loop together and sew, also catching a tuft of dyed wool or yarn. The goat hair, wool, or yarn can be dyed any color but are usually red or yellow. Push the dew claw down over the loop, run the two upper ends

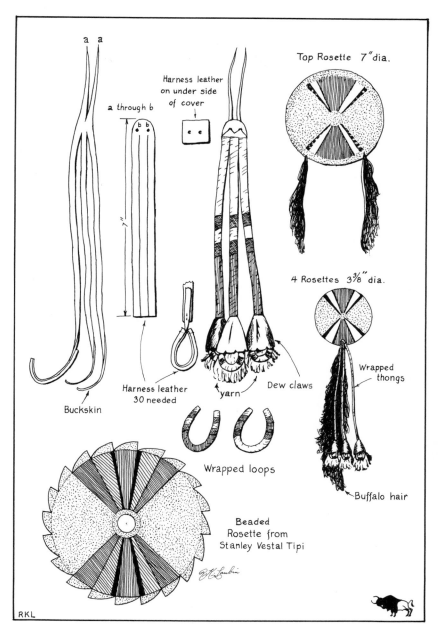

a a

a through b

Harness leather
on under side
of cover

Top Rosette 7″dia.

7″

4 Rosettes 3⅜″ dia.

Buckskin

Harness leather
30 needed

yarn

Dew claws

Wrapped
thongs

Wrapped loops

Buffalo hair

Beaded
Rosette from
Stanley Vestal Tipi

RKL

Fig. 51. Cheyenne Tipi Decorations.

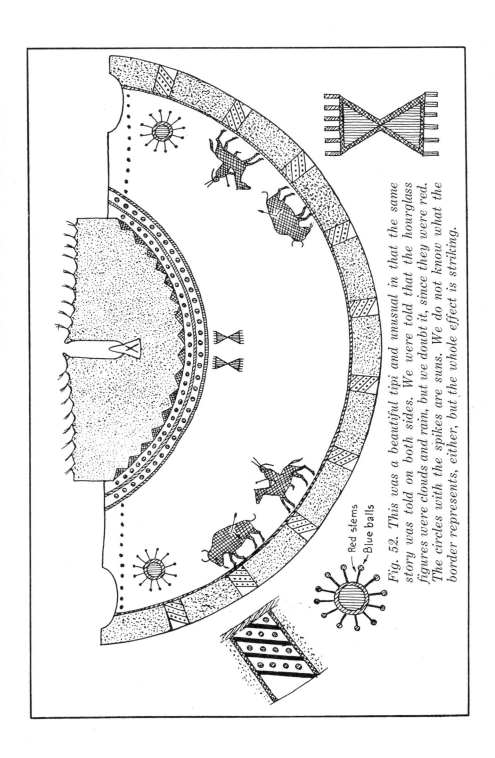

Red stems
Blue balls

Fig. 52. This was a beautiful tipi and unusual in that the same story was told on both sides. We were told that the hourglass figures were clouds and rain, but we doubt it, since they were red. The circles with the spikes are suns. We do not know what the border represents, either, but the whole effect is striking.

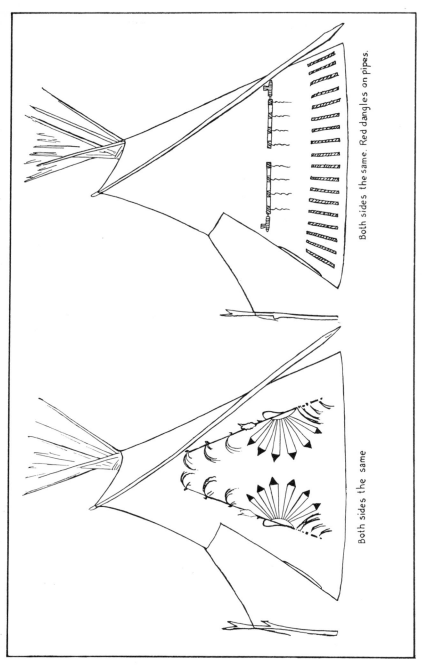

Both sides the same. Red dangles on pipes.

Both sides the same

Fig. 53. The Hunkayapi pipes again on the tipi at the left, and smoking pipes on that at the right. They show that the owner has "carried the pipe," meaning that he has been the leader of war parties.

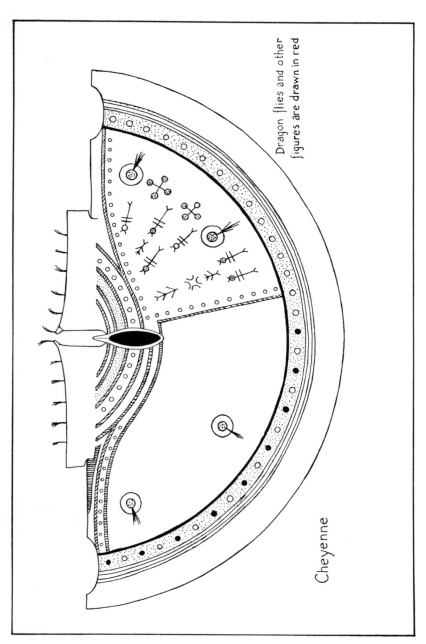

Dragon flies and other figures are drawn in red

Cheyenne

Fig. 54. Another of the odd, lop-sided designs, of which the Cheyennes are particularly fond, but common to many tribes. This is big medicine. Anyone can see that the four world quarters and dragonflies are represented.

of the buckskin through the holes in the harness leather foundation, and wrap the main section with the dyed corn husk.

When finished, each dangle really has three parts and each of these is on a double layer of harness leather and buckskin. The two thongs at the top of each dangle go through the canvas and through a little square of harness leather on the under side, where they are tied in a square knot. The leather keeps the canvas from tearing through.

While on the subject of tipi dangles and decorations, perhaps you would like to know that Indians also had door knockers which were quite ornamental. One

Fig. 55. Tipi Door Knocker.

in the Museum of the American Indian in New York is made of a buffalo leg and hoof, but I made a nice one from an elk leg (Fig. 55). The skin on the leg, from hock to hoof, is split down the back and the hoof carefully removed from the bone. The two toes are split apart and the front of the skin also split part way; so the two halves of the hoof act like clappers. To this, at the top, is hung a large bunch of red-dyed horse hair and a bunch of buffalo hoof tips, each strung on a thong and the entire cluster of thongs fastened together to make one unit of rattles. Again, dew claws can be used as well as hoof tips.

This door knocker was hung to one side of the door and used just as we use door knockers today. When wishing to enter a neighbor's tipi, this knocker was shaken instead of scratching on the tipi cover or shaking the door.

Sometimes a series of narrow horizontal stripes of beadwork a yard wide extended down the back of the tent from top to bottom. It looked like a beaded ladder and was said to represent many trails in this life, and trails from the four directions to the Above Persons and the Spirit World. Such decorations were very handsome, as well as protective and symbolic. The dew claws rattling together in the wind reproduced the actual sound made by the clicking hoofs against dew claws of walking buffalo, and were supposed to bring buffalo to the lodge.

The Cheyennes are particularly fond of this kind of tipi decoration, especially in Oklahoma. Only certain qualified women had the right to make such decorations.

The Sioux sometimes painted pictures of their exploits in war on such a tipi, but it seems that the Cheyennes did not, reserving them for a painted tipi.[12]

Rarely, tipi covers were painted on the inside. One such Sioux hide tipi, a small one only about eight feet across, had a vertical pipe with four feathered wings and a red Catlinite bowl painted up the back, and a buffalo below the bowl. To one side, among the other figures, was the story of the White Buffalo Maiden who brought the sacred pipe to the Sioux, the most sacred story in all Sioux religious lore.[13]

This tipi, kept in the Berlin Museum, unfortunately was destroyed in World War II. However, its design was reproduced in color, and interpreted by the late Frederick Weygold.[14]

Such a tipi was rare, and only those admitted to it could see the paintings.

The famous Oglala chief, Red Cloud, is said to have had a tipi which was painted blue at the top for the sky, with a green border at the bottom for the earth, and four rainbows on the sides. He also had a buffalo painted on the door, which meant that no one would ever go away hungry.

Concerning the decorated tipis of the Blackfeet, Walter McClintock has this to say: "A decorated tipi was in itself an announcement that within rested a sacred bundle whose owner possessed the ritual associated with it. Both men and women made vows to these tipis in time of danger and in behalf of the sick. The design and ritual of the decorated tipis, and all that went with them, came originally through dreams and belonged exclusively to their founders, who might transfer to others, but no one could copy them. Only among the Blackfeet was there a definite association by which the

---

[12]See Francis Densmore, "Teton Sioux Music," Bureau of American Ethnology, *Bulletin 61*, Plate 72 opposite p. 448.
  [13]See *ibid.*, 63.
  [14]See *Globus*, Vol. LXXIII, No. 1 (January 1, 1903).

decoration of the tipi became an integral part of the ritual. But the esthetic value of the decorations was secondary.

"In these pictures and decorations we have a fine series of examples of Blackfoot religious art — in fact, almost the entire range of such art. The specific symbols were usually of three classes — the mythical originator and his wife, their home, and their trails. They were depicted in pairs, male and female; for large animals, a single pair; for small ones, four or more. In most cases the animal figures were highly realistic and usually were painted in black. Their vital organs and lifeline were represented in color — red, yellow, green.

"Most of the painted tipis had a darkened area at the top to represent the night sky, with white discs for constellations (the Great Bear and the Pleiades), a similar border at the bottom with one or two rows of star-signs (fallen stars), and a row of projections for hills or mountains. In the rear and at the top was a cross, said by some to represent a moth, or the sleep-bringer, by others the morning star.

"Sacred objects were commonly represented by certain conventional symbols: red, yellow, and blue bands for red cloud, yellow cloud, and the blue sky; black for the night. Male animals were mostly on the south side, female on the north. The thunderbird stood for lightning; colored bands for the rainbow, symbolic of a clearing storm. Of all animals, the buffalo was believed to have the greatest power, but that of the deer and elk was also great. The eagle and raven were especially strong helpers, and the underwater animals also were powerful. But of all the animals, the most sacred was the beaver, to which the otter was supposed to be related. The mink was another powerful aquatic animal, and the weasel was related to it."[15]

Occasionally the sacred bundle that accompanied the tipi was fastened to a pole on the outside. We have seen the medicine bundle of a Crow Indian family fastened to the lifting pole just below the tie flap, raised with the cover when it was put into place.

PAINTING THE TIPI

Painting a tipi was usually man's work, and certain individuals specialized in it. The owner of a tipi to be painted announced a

[15]*Painted Tipis and Picture-writing of the Blackfoot Indians.*

Fig. 56. Crow Tipi Design with Pipe.

feast and invited his friends and one or more of these specialists. Afterwards, following songs and prayers, all helped him paint his tipi under their direction. Straight willow sticks were used for rulers in laying out the designs and in making straight lines. Then the patterns were traced on with a bone stylus or a small stick, and a thin glue, made from hide scrapings, was rubbed in with the same tool. Brushes, or perhaps they might better be called pens, for ap-

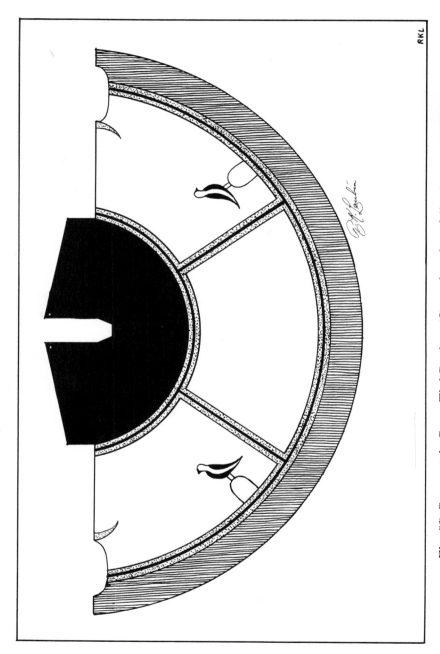

RKL

Fig. 57. Symmetric Crow Tipi Design. (See color plate following page 206.)

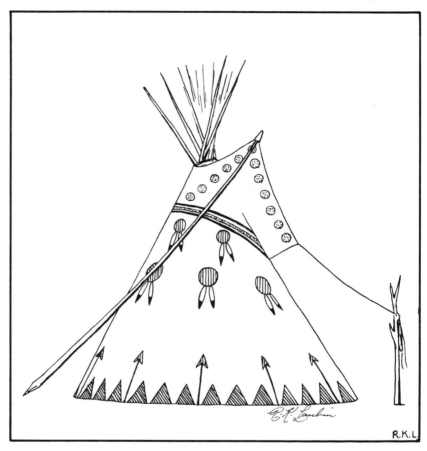

Fig. 58. Assiniboine Tipi Design. (See color plate following page 206.)

plying the color were made from porous bone, and on large areas the paint was rubbed on with the hands.

If you wish to paint a tipi, spread it out on the flattest place available and stake it out as tightly as possible, a stake at every peg loop and one at the tie flap, so that it will not shrink when water and paint are applied. The easiest way to paint it is with ordinary house paint or enamel, but mixing powdered paints is cheaper and more Indian.

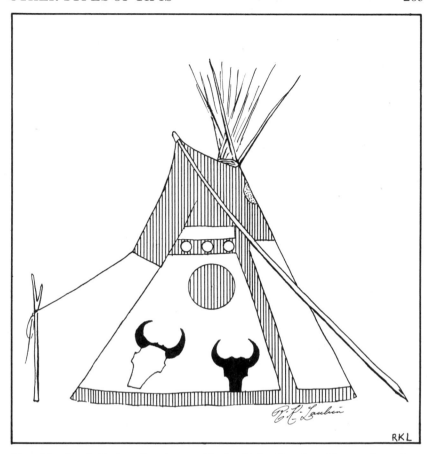

Fig. 59. Assiniboine Design with Buffalo Heads. (See color plate following page 206.)

If the canvas has been treated with a wax waterproofing,[16] the paint can be applied directly to it. Otherwise, it is best to wet the canvas first. Use a pail of water and a sponge. Go over a small area at a time with a spongeful of water, so that the canvas is wet but not puddled.

[16]As mentioned previously, we do not recommend wax waterproofing for the cover.

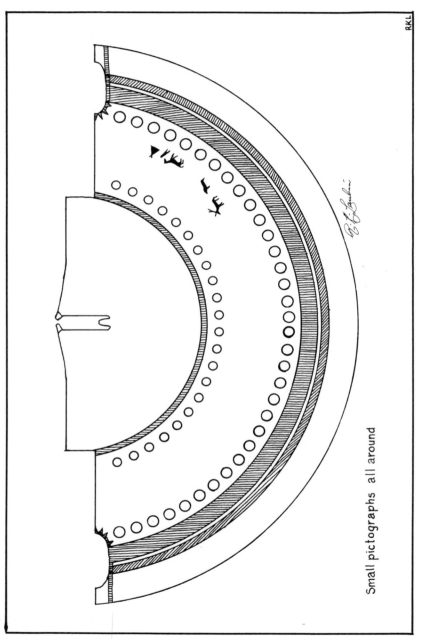

Small pictographs all around

Fig. 60. Assiniboine Design with small Pictographs.

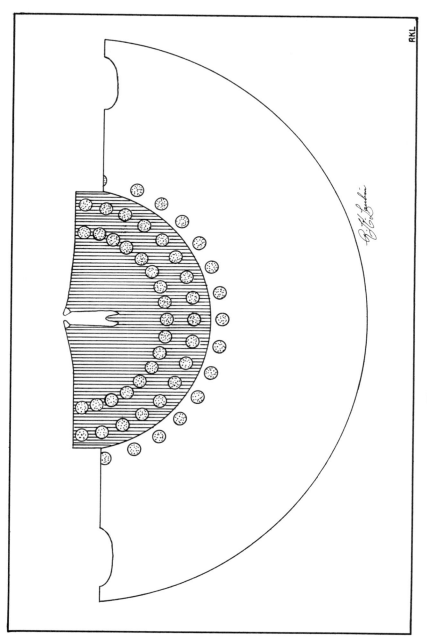

Fig. 61. Assiniboine Design.

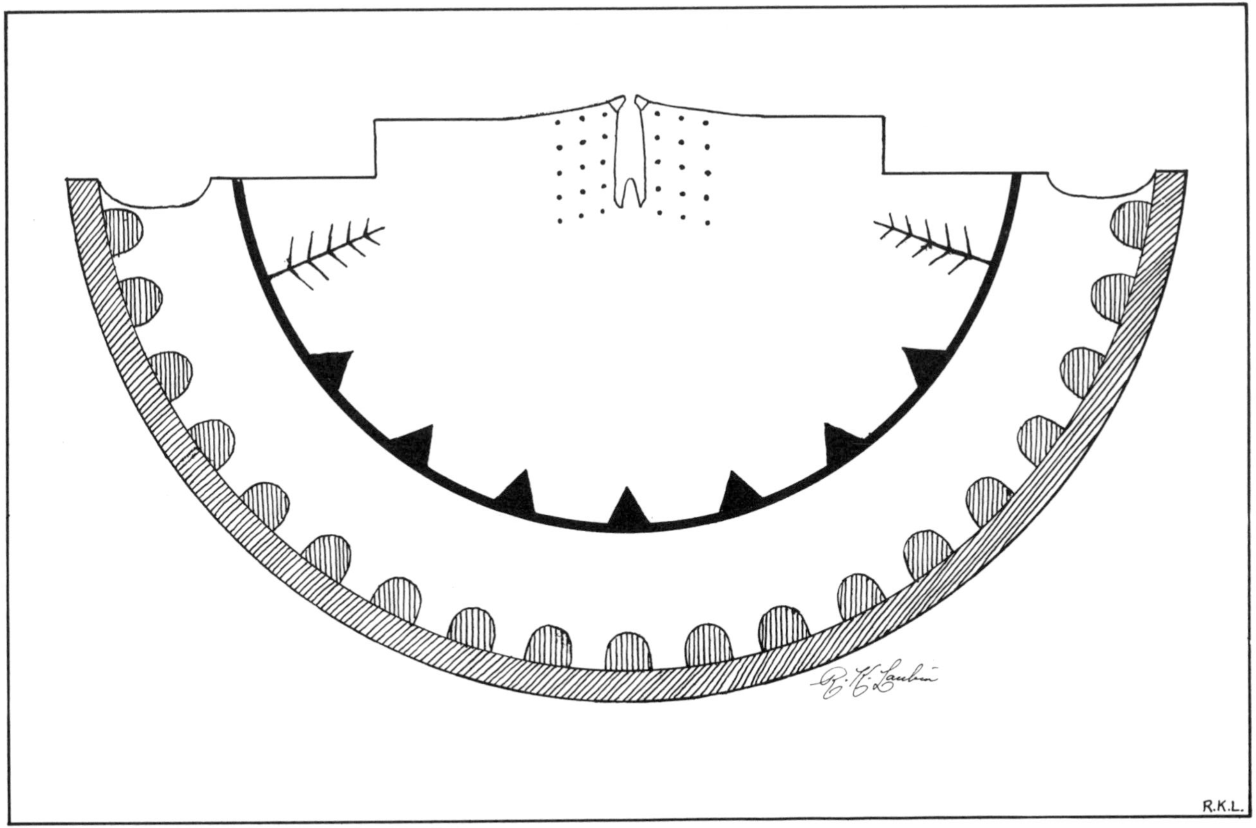

Fig. 62. Assiniboine Design.

We have been told that for painting tipis Indians mixed their paints, which were mostly obtained from colored earths, with tallow, to which had been added some melted resin, but for modern painting it is much easier to use commercial powdered pigments, mixing them with linseed oil and a little Japan dryer, and thinning, if necessary, with turpentine. Or use the ready-mixed paint. Either way, apply the paint to the wet canvas, a small area at a time, then wet more canvas as the work progresses. Wetting the canvas prevents excessive use of paint. Too much paint is not only expensive but makes the cover stiff and heavy.

Some designs, like animal figures and repeated motifs, can be cut out of cardboard or heavy wrapping paper, and traced with chalk or charcoal, then filled in with the proper colors.

Draw the curved border lines with a piece of charcoal on a rope (thin cord has too much stretch), using the same radius point used in making the tipi for the lower border, but for painting the top, set the radius point one foot closer in if you want the design to look parallel to the ground when viewing it from the side.

When dedicating a newly-painted tipi, after the paint had dried the Cheyennes spread the cover out on a clean piece of ground where everyone could walk on it. A camp crier announced that all should do so, as this was believed to bring good fortune to everyone who did so and to prevent calamity and disease.

Two Blackfoot Indian women and small child with a horse-drawn travois. Credit: Western History Collections, University of Oklahoma Library.

8.   TRANSPORTATION

OUR EARLIEST records show the Indians transporting their tents and luggage on drags harnessed to dogs. The same method was employed after they obtained horses, but then they were able to use much larger tents and their general living standards were improved because they were able to carry so much more equipment. Eventually they obtained wagons, and although a wagon could not be taken over as rough terrain as was formerly covered by dogs or horses and drags, such travel was no longer necessary because the buffalo were gone and many of the old trails fenced up. Today tipi poles are carried on automobiles or trucks, or even shipped by rail. The methods used in each case show the good sense and ingenuity of the tribesmen.

The big disadvantage in transporting the tipi is the poles, since at least seventeen are needed, each weighing from fifteen to twenty pounds. They create quite a transportation problem, but the Indians did not seem to find it too difficult when they were living their wild, free life on the Plains. By the early 1800's they had plenty of horses and one horse could drag eight to ten poles. An Indian camp, with men, women, and children and all their household effects, could travel faster and farther in one day than could the best-equipped army of the period.

It is almost incredible how rapidly a great camp could be either pitched or "struck." Catlin, describing the sudden breaking of a large camp of Sioux, wrote: "At the time announced, the lodge of the chief is seen flapping in the wind, a part of the poles having been taken out from under it. This is the signal, and in one minute 600 lodges (on a level and beautiful prairie), which before had been strained and fixed, were seen waving and flapping in the wind, and in one minute more all were flat on the ground. Their horses and dogs, of which they have a vast number, had all been secured upon the spot in readiness, and each one was speedily loaded with the burden allotted it, and made ready to fall into the grand procession."[1]

[1]George Catlin, *Letters and Notes.* . . .

Early paintings and sketches show that the heavy ends of the poles were dragged on the ground, but they lack sufficient detail to be entirely clear. Old-timers have also told us that the butts of the poles dragged on the ground. It is certain that the "pony drags," or travois, were made in this way, and the same principal would apply to a travois and to loose poles.

The poles were kept from slipping in various ways. Sometimes a clove hitch was tied around each one, the poles being kept together in bunches of four to six, the hitches coming where they were to fasten to the saddle. The usual Indian pack saddle had a horn both fore and aft and was kept in place with breast collar and breeching, just as ordinary pack saddles are. One bundle of poles was hung on one side of the horse, another bundle on the opposite side. Poles and cover were transported in different ways, depending, apparently to some extent, on choice, and also on expediency.

We were told that when extremely long poles were carried, one bundle was hung from the fore saddle horn, the tip ends of the poles crossing the horse's withers. Another bunch crossed the withers from the opposite side, also being hung from the fore horn. A long thong was tied around the tips of the poles in one bundle, then across to the other bundle and around its tips, thus keeping the poles from spreading as they were dragged along. When the poles were very long, the cover was usually carried on a separate travois.

Luther Standing Bear, in his book, *My People the Sioux*, mentions little holes burned in the poles, saying that all tipi poles had holes in them for fastening them to the horses. He does not say just where the holes were located, but, according to accounts we have had from informants, these holes must have been where the poles fastened to the saddle, which would be just above their crossing in the tipi frame. If below that crossing, holes would weaken the poles.

John C. Ewers, in his work, *The Horse in Blackfoot Culture*, has an illustration of the Blackfoot method of attaching poles to the horse. The tipi cover was folded so that it projected far over the sides of the horse and the poles were fastened to it, thus holding them away from the horse's head and hindquarters, so that they did not come into contact with him. The cover itself was first lashed to the pack saddle. The poles were each perforated by a half-inch hole, made by burning them with a hot iron rod, near their small

Blackfoot travois with children seated on travois. Credit: Western History Collections, University of Oklahoma Library.

ends. Six poles were carried on each side. A long, flat thong or strap was passed through the hole in each pole, then completely around the bunch of six, up over the tipi cover on the horse's back, and through and around the bundle of six poles on the other side. If the poles were exceptionally heavy, four or five could be fastened to each side in the same way, instead of six. The opposite ends of the strap were then brought underneath and fastened beneath the horse's belly, like a cinch.[2]

[2]J. C. Ewers, "The Horse in Blackfoot Indian Culture," Smithsonian Institution, Bureau of American Ethnology, *Bulletin 159*.

Blackfoot dog travois. Credit: Western History Collections, University of Oklahoma Library.

Gilbert Wilson, writing of the Hidatsas, describes a similar method of fastening the poles to the saddle.[3] It sounds like the simplest and most efficient way. Other tribes, including the Sioux, used this same method, according to information we have gathered.

The remaining poles in the set were fastened to another horse in the same fashion, using robes and the lining to make up a pack to take the place of the tipi cover.

Thomas Yallup, a Yakima friend, told us that he remembers his family's packing their tipi on horseback when he was a small boy. He states that two poles were selected as "main poles" for each horse. One of these poles was fastened to each side of the horse, and to it the other poles were attached. On each main pole, at the place where it was to be fastened, toward its upper, or small, end, a lump of pine pitch was formed all around it. While the pitch was still soft, a heavy, wet rawhide strap, about one inch wide, was wrapped around the pitch. It shrank and dried, as did the pitch, becoming hard and immovable. The rawhide strap formed a large loop, large enough to hold one or two other poles above the main

<hr>

[3]G. L. Wilson, *The Hidatsa Indians.*

Blackfoot travois arriving at a dance. Note backrests. Credit: Western History Collections, University of Oklahoma Library.

pole. The poles were then tied fast to the main pole, and the rawhide loop was tied to the saddle horn with a rope. Other poles were sometimes tied below the main pole, if they were not too long or heavy.

The poles were slung low enough so that they were also fastened to the breast strap of the saddle. In this way the horse had the entire load on his shoulders only when standing. When moving, much of the pull was also on the breast strap. We were not told just how the poles were fastened to the breast strap. The poles ordinarily did not project beyond the horse's shoulders. Mr. Yallup remembered positively that the butts of the poles were dragged on the ground. He gave us the impression that the poles he was talking about were for a rather small tipi. They were tied in two

Camp on Crow Indian Reservation in Montana. Lodge poles tied to burro. Backrests on top of load. Credit: Western History Collections, University of Oklahoma Library.

places farther back from the main tie to keep them in a bunch, so that they would not spread out as they were being dragged.

We wanted to know if longer poles were crossed over the horse's withers, as we had been told by informants of other tribes. Mr. Yallup answered that they were.

On our visit to Sweden, we went to the National Museum in Stockholm, where a comprehensive exhibition of Lapp life was displayed. The Lapps live in conical tents, supported by poles, similar to a tipi, but rather more like a wigwam, having no smoke flaps and being much smaller than a tipi. Their poles are dragged by reindeer. These poles were drilled with small holes near the butts and laced to a wide leather strap attached to the cinch and the pack saddle. The poles were fastened side by side, one above the other, the small ends dragging on the ground. Old Coyote, a

Crow Indian who was with us, declared that his grandfather told him that that was exactly how his people used to drag their poles.

Perhaps under different conditions the poles were transported in different ways. By using the method described above, the Indians could travel a narrower trail, but it is certain that the small ends of the poles would wear off much faster than the butts and would be more likely to break when caught on sagebrush or other obstacles. Also, we doubt that the long poles the Crows prefer today could be moved in this fashion. Old Coyote's statement that poles were so carried is the only personal account we have had, but he has been very much interested in the lore of his people. All other Indians have told us the poles were carried with the butts on the ground.

One other mention of carrying poles with the small ends on the ground is made in the account of Mrs. Nathan D. White, when writing of her experiences as a captive of Chief Little Crow's band of Mdewakanton Sioux after the Minnesota outbreak of 1862.[4] She wrote: "Their manner of moving was very ingenious. Every tepee has six poles, about 15 feet long, which were fastened by strips of rawhide placed around the pony's neck and breast, three poles on each side of the pony, with the small ends on the ground. A stick was tied to the poles behind the pony to keep them together and spread in the shape of a V; and on the stick and poles bundles of various kinds, kettles, and even papooses were fastened when occasion required. It is astonishing to see the amount of service these natives will get out of one tepee and an Indian pony . . . The tepees were of uniform size, about 12 feet in diameter on the ground, with a door about three feet high, that is, merely a parting of the tent cloth or hides, of which latter the tepees were usually made."

Although this is a very interesting account and one might say, "She was there," there are a number of flaws in the story. She, like so many early observers, may not have been a very careful one. She had no interest or desire in becoming an Indian. Generally she despised her captors and refused even to try to learn their ways, or abide by their rules of etiquette. The Indians laughed at her when she went in and out of a tipi. They said she went in "just like a frog."

They must have been some tipis! Mrs. White said the tipis were of uniform size, all small ones, with only about six poles each

[4]Minnesota Historical Society *Collections*, Vol. IX, 172–73.

of about 15 feet in length. A tipi would hardly be serviceable with only six poles in the frame and that leaves none for smoke-ear poles. One horse could easily carry seven such small poles on one side, or one horse could carry three on a side and another four on a side, since the ear poles can be even lighter. This would be a little more like it. Even a frame of nine poles and two for ears would work on a small tipi, but not six! Such small poles could be carried in the way she says, but it just is not possible to put heavy weights on the small ends of such poles without breaking them.

These Indians, for the most part, were already living in houses at the time of the trouble with the Minnesota settlers. The only tipis they had were probably little hunting tipis left over from earlier times, or still used for hunting expeditions. It is interesting that she says there were some of cloth, even at this early period, twenty years before the buffalo were almost exterminated.

Most of the Sioux in Minnesota never did live in tipis all year around. They lived in wigwams, similar to those of the Chippewa, before adopting houses. But their little hunting tipis came in handy when they were forced to abandon their homes. They probably had the butts of the poles pointed, as was the usual Indian custom, and Mrs. White may have mistaken these for the small ends. Also, she wrote her reminiscences many years after the actual event and may not have remembered such details too clearly.

As many as five horses were sometimes required to move a large tipi and all its furnishings, although three were sufficient to move the average lodge. As we have seen, two horses were needed to carry the poles, cover, and lining. Three horses might be needed to carry a set of extra-heavy poles for a big lodge. This third horse might also carry some of the camp gear on his back, but generally the household furnishings and utensils were carried on a drag, or travois.

The travois was made of two poles, shorter than the average tipi poles, crossed on the horse's withers. Behind, out of range of his hoofs, was attached either a rectangular platform or a netted oval hoop, on which goods were piled and lashed. Such travois were dragged by dogs long before the days of horses, and dogs were still used right up to the end of the buffalo days. Of course, dogs could not carry the heavy loads that horses could, but they proved their worth as pack animals whenever camp was moved.

The spring of the poles and the jogging of the horse over the rough ground made the travois a jouncy sort of carriage. Some-

Horse travois, Northern Cheyenne. Photograph by Charles Barthelmess. Credit: Western History Collections, University of Oklahoma Library.

times old people, wounded warriors, or small children rode on a travois, but at such times it usually had a dome-shaped structure of willow shoots built over it to afford some protection in case it turned over. It looked a bit like a moving sweat lodge. It might also be sheltered from sun and weather with a covering, or partial covering, of canvas or hide. Puppies and other pets were often carried on such a travois, too. On the march, water bags made of buffalo paunches were hung from the travois platforms. Such a bag would hold from six to eight quarts of water, and the average family had four such bags.

On the pack saddle of the horse pulling a travois were hung the parfleches containing dried meat and clothing; also the beaded buckskin saddle bags. The parfleches served in the same capacity as panniers on the white man's pack saddle. Since many of the travois horses were ridden, their total load was considerable. The woman riding such a horse tied her fancy saddle bags behind her and often hung her husband's fringed cylindrical war bonnet case from the front horn. The backrests, instead of being rolled up and packed in compact bundles, were often laid flat on the travois plat-form, their fancy ends hanging down, so that horse and rider pre-sented quite a gay appearance. (See page 279.)

Following the first edition of this book, Flying Cloud wrote, "I have seen the travois in use as late as 1907. In the Cannon Ball District old Clown Woman, *Heyo-ka-win*, used a dog travois as late as 1912."

"When Plains Indians (particularly the Sioux) broke camp their equipment was divided into 5 groups to be carried on travois; one had just two cedar poles between which the tipi covering was car-ried; next travois carried tipi poles, (7 or 8 on either side) 14 to 16 poles; next travois carried wearing apparel and battle equip-ment; next travois carried large stone bone-crushers (to extract marrow) and last but not least, the dog travois, which carried tipi pins, dolls and playthings. Also the dog travois carried small chil-dren; all those able to walk, walked. This information was related to me by my own mother and grandmother. The Sioux bored holes near the small end (of the tipi poles) and ran a parfleche thong thru; some cut grooves and tied thongs. In all cases of horse travois, a saddle was used."

"Our tipi is always open to welcome you. Ho-hecetu! It is well!"

But traveling was not always so gay. McClintock says: "I passed a travois bearing three aged squaws. They were berating their horse, a rawboned old cripple, trying to urge him from a slow walk, so that they could keep up with the procession. One was vigorously beating him with a stick, but it was in vain, for he hobbled placidly along, with eyes closed and head hanging down, unmindful both of the stick and their execrations."[5]

Even more common than the true travois was an improvised one made by lashing a platform across the bundles of tipi poles behind a horse. It is astonishing how much of a load a horse could carry in this way, but some consideration had to be given the poles, as well as the horse, for too big a load would permanently warp them and they could no longer be used in the frame of the tipi.

When not in use, travois were stored in various ways. Some-times they were merely leaned against the sides of the tipis, but it was necessary to keep them raised off of the ground to keep dogs from chewing on their rawhide lashings. The usual way to

[5]*The Old North Trail,* 197.

store one was to prop it up with a long pole, for then it had several uses. With an old robe or piece of canvas covering it, it made a sun shade which could easily be turned with the movement of the sun. It also served as a drying rack for meat. Sometimes a travois was leaned against the back of the tipi and the medicine bundle and other sacred paraphernalia were hung from it during the day, instead of a medicine rack. A travois might also be used as a ladder when pinning up the front of the tipi, or when taking the tipi down, by leaning it against the front and climbing upon the struts of the platform. Sometimes three or four travois were stacked together, like stacked rifles.

When it was necessary to cross a deep river, the horses were unpacked and crude rafts were made of the poles. On top of these the travois were tied, so that their loads were kept safe and dry. The hide tipi cover itself was spread out, furnishings and baggage, even children, were piled on it, and the edges were pulled up around this load and drawn up by running a rope through the peg holes in the cover all around the bottom, like a draw-string purse. The whole thing was then pushed out into the water and pulled across the river with ropes, men pulling in front, women pushing behind. Horses also helped ferry these loads across.

A large Indian camp on the move, warriors riding well in advance, singing their war songs, horses dragging the long tipi poles, boys dashing back and forth on their ponies, showing off, dogs barking, and bells jingling, must have been a sight to remember.

The evening before a village was to move, a herald rode through the camp, crying, "The grass is short, wood is scarce, the water is getting stale, and the game has moved away. Tomorrow we go on to other hunting grounds."

The head chief's lodge was the first to come down and all the others followed. If there was no hurry, the chiefs and head men usually walked at the head of the column. This was especially true when starting off on a buffalo hunt, before the herd was located. This seems to have been a ceremonial requirement dating back to the days before horses were common. The leaders halted at intervals to allow the main caravan to catch up. Under more pressing circumstances everyone rode, chiefs and leaders in advance, scouts sometimes as far as three miles ahead. Members of warrior societies rode on the flanks and brought up the rear on a well-organized march. When such precautions were neglected, raids by waiting enemy war parties often inflicted heavy casualties.

The caravan usually got under way early in the morning, for on moving day the camp was astir at dawn. A halt was made for a noonday lunch which usually consisted of pemmican and other dried foods and water, either from a stream or spring. If no fresh water was available, the supply in the paunches was used.

The chief's emblem, tied to the lifting pole of his tipi, was often raised on a tripod when the caravan halted. If it projected only a short way beyond the tripod, it indicated that the remainder of the march would be short. If it projected far out beyond the tripod, it meant that there was still a long march ahead. The men sat and smoked and everyone enjoyed this brief rest before moving on again.

The new camp site was usually decided upon well in advance. When it was reached, the leaders halted, the tribal elders dismounted, sat in a circle, and smoked again. The chief's emblem now was placed standing nearly erect and indicated the center of the new camp circle.

Before the coming of the automobile, Indians went the next step on the road to modernity by obtaining wagons. The first wagons, issued by the government, did not make a very good impression, for they were narrow gauge and too light for the rugged work the Indians expected of them. But after the buffalo were gone and the old roving days were over, what little moving had to be done was done with wagons. The Southern Plains tribes used to sling their poles, butts forward, on the left side of a wagon, outside of and lashed to vertical stakes five or six feet tall, resting in the rings on the stanchions. This left the bed free for baggage and riders, and the poles could be unloaded quickly without disturbing the load in the wagon bed. The poles were lashed to the left side because the Indian custom was to climb on the wagon as they mounted a horse, on the off, or right, side.

We have seen Sioux wagons with the poles bundled together along the center of the wagon bed and hanging far out behind. Camp equipment was piled on top of the poles, and on top of all sat the entire family, the man of the household usually sitting alone on the driver's seat.

In like manner, poles may be carried on a truck, either lashed on the side, stowed in the bed, or, if too long, tied on top of the cab and stretching across to rest on the tail gate, butt ends on the cab.

Poles may also be sent as freight on the railroad to the station nearest your camp site, but you still need some other mode of transportation for the final lap of the journey from station to camp. A set of seventeen poles twenty-five feet long weighs about three hundred pounds. They should be divided into bundles of four poles each, one bundle having the two smoke poles and three others, but weighing about the same as other bundles of four. The bundles should be lashed with stout wire at the tips, near the butts, and every four or five feet in between. The bundles are then shipped in a lot on a flat car or in a boxcar.

Talk about unique methods of transportation! It would be hard to beat a story the Crows tell about Old Man Coyote. One day he came upon a very pretty woman, who was all alone in front of her tipi. He wanted to know where her man was, and she told him she had none and lived all alone.

"What a pity," said Old Man Coyote, "for such a beautiful woman to live alone. I would like to have you for my woman."

"But I like to travel a lot," the woman said.

"Oh, so do I," replied Old Man Coyote, "so we should make a fine pair."

"All right," she answered, "then we'll start right now," and she began to take the tipi down, although it was already sunset. She laid all the poles side by side on the ground, tied them together with a rope, so it looked like a long raft, and piled the tipi cover and all her goods on top.

"What a peculiar way you have of packing your tipi," Old Man Coyote remarked. "How can dogs and horses carry a thing like that?"

"Hop on and you'll see," said the woman. "Put your arms around me and hold on tight."

So Old Man Coyote jumped on and had hardly time enough to sit down when the whole thing took off like a flash and they were immediately high up in the air. They flew over mountains, streams and villages, but could hardly see them because it was so dark. They traveled all night, but at the first sign of light the woman brought her flying raft back to earth and then Old Man Coyote had to help her set up the tipi. She slept all day and just when Old Man Coyote thought it time for her to wake up and get him a good meal, his new wife started to take the tipi down again and packed it up as before. Again they traveled all night long. This went on for several days, Old Man Coyote becoming so tired and hungry he

The Modern Travois. Photograph by Gladys Laubin.

hardly knew what to do. He finally realized he had married a ghost woman; so on one of the days while she was sleeping he sneaked out of the "flying tipi" and ran away.

Nowadays, unless one wishes to travel by truck, the problem of traveling with a tipi would seem to be complicated. No longer can you strike out across country in whatever direction you please. Modern highways enable us to travel farther in one hour than could be done in "the good old days" in more than a day. But otherwise our scope of travel is more limited.

It would be natural to think of jointed poles to facilitate tipi transportation. We carried such poles all over Europe, North Africa, and Israel with our Indian dance troupe. The tipi was used only as a stage setting, but those jointed poles were the bane of our existence. The poles were sawed off square at the center and trimmed to fit iron tubes, which slipped over each end of the joint. Sometimes the tubes would slip while we were trying to adjust a pole. The thing would become unjointed and the entire pole fall out of place, sometimes narrowly missing hitting one of us on the head. These poles were only twenty feet long, but even at that length none of us felt that they would be strong enough to stand any rough weather. Furthermore, as we mentioned earlier, they would be a lightning hazard, so, as far as we are concerned, jointed poles are out. We finally had to abandon the poles in Spain because they were too long for the little plane in which we were then traveling. Were we ever glad! Except for the largest stages, such as the one in the Theatre des Champs-Elysees in Paris, we seldom had room enough to pitch the tipi anyway.

There is a much easier way to take care of modern tipi travel. Several years ago, with the help of a Sioux friend who was a blacksmith, we made racks of half-inch iron pipe which can quickly be attached to the front and rear bumpers of our car. Our twenty-five-foot poles are carried on top of the car, supported in front and in the rear on these racks. With our little trailer hooked on, the poles come just over the end of it. We can travel quickly and safely and hardly know the poles are there. We call this arrangement our "modern travois." It may be a queer-looking outfit, but it certainly does the trick. We have carried the tipi, all its furnishings, and the poles all the way from Montana to Connecticut. You should see the Indians look at us as we drive by on our way across the reservation!

To make the rack, we used about twenty-nine feet of half-inch galvanized iron pipe, four elbows, eight T-joints, and two unions, plus twelve feet of 3/8-inch iron rod, for braces, and a pair of flat hinges. The unions make it possible to disconnect the rack so that when not in use it makes only a small bundle of short iron pipes, plus the two six-foot braces. Fig. 63 shows how we made the rack and the way it works when in use.

The biggest bother with this contraption is that you will be pestered with questions every time you stop. You can answer, as we do, "It's a raft to cross the Missouri River."

In the years since we first designed the pole rack, car designs and bumper patterns have changed considerably. The basic plan for the pole rack is still sound, and by changing the bumper attachments can still be used on most modern cars. A simple sketch may explain this (Fig. 64).

Also, if you have a top rack on your car, such as a ski rack, and plan the height of the pole rack right, so that the poles also lay snugly across the top rack, you can tie the poles down to it and dispense with the rod braces to the front of the car.

We heard recently of another way to carry poles on top of a car, with claims that it is quicker and more efficient than the way we have described. Although our way was the first, anyone is at liberty to try any method he may choose if he thinks it may be

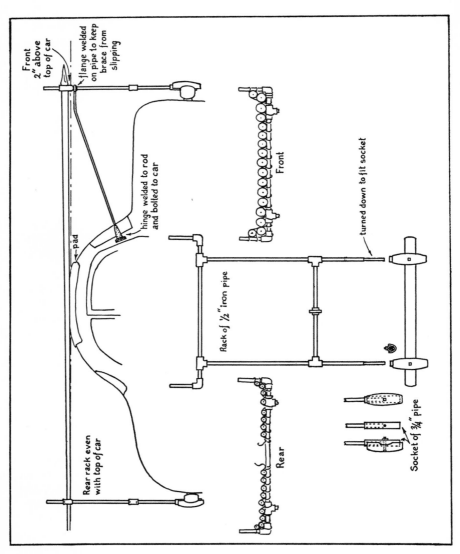

Fig. 63. Pole Rack.

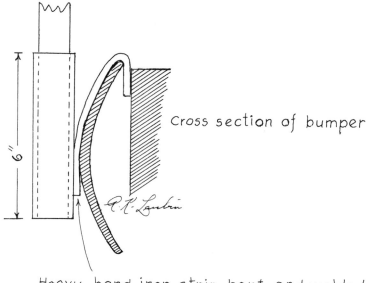

Cross section of bumper

Heavy band iron strip bent and welded
to 3/4" pipe for sockets to hook over bumpers

Fig. 64. Bumper Socket for Pole Rack.

better and believes it to be safe and secure. The new way is to place the poles in one bundle on top of the car with the tips forward, instead of the butts. Cradles are attached fore and aft on top of the car and the poles laid across them, one at a time, as they are taken from the tipi frame; then they are bound together into one large bundle with the use of heavy straps. This is supposed to be quicker than laying them side by side on the racks, as we have described, mainly because it eliminates lashing the poles to the racks. However, anyone familiar with ropes, lashing, and knots would hardly find it so. I can lash my poles to the racks in only a few minutes and when I am through I know they will not slip or shift.

In an article suggesting this new way it was pointed out that the poles, taken from the tipi frame one at a time and placed in the bundle in their proper sequence, were all ready for re-assembling at the next camping place. What would prevent anyone placing the poles in the same order when laid out flat on the racks? In fact, that is exactly what we recommend. To our way of thinking it is even easier to make the proper selection when all are laid out flat and all visible at once. So we are convinced that our well tried and tested way is still best under most circumstances.

The new way may work well enough on a van or station wagon with their larger tops, but we do not think it would be as good on a regular car for several reasons. Without a rack on the rear bumper it would seem that the average car is too short to give adequate support to a set of long poles. (The new way does use a simple rack on the front bumper.) The only advantage we can see in having the tips of the poles forward would be to eliminate rear overhang. But would it be any better to have a long overhang in front? In experimenting with the racks years ago it seemed to us the poles packed easier and rode steadier with the butts to the front. Another reason for laying the poles out flat, side by side, is that you do not have to climb on top of the car to take care of them. Still another reason is, it would seem that the load is better distributed and would not be as top-heavy. Again, if you do not mind extra weight on top of the car, you can pile the tipi, lining, and other gear on top of the "raft." And the "raft" makes a wonderful sun shade on bright, hot days!

9. CAMP CIRCLES

IN WINTER, when a large segment of a tribe camped together, tipis were pitched along some sheltered valley or river bottom by bands and families, each lodge where it seemed most convenient. Such a camp might extend for miles along a stream.

Occasionally, when feed for the horses gave out or firewood became scarce, a camp was moved in the winter, but usually only a short distance away, for moving camp in severe winter weather was far from pleasant.

But in summer, when all the bands of the tribe were together and no shelter was needed, they camped on the open prairie in a great circle, with an opening or entrance, some twenty yards across, on one side—the camp circle. In recent times the combined tribes of the Sioux Nation, the Seven Council Fires, have never been together all at once. Rarely even did all seven divisions of the Teton, or Lakota, camp together, for such great numbers of people all in one camp made the problems of food, water, wood, and grass enormous.

But it was common for one division, like the Oglalas or the Hunkpapas, or the Minikonjus, to stay together throughout much of the year. Smaller tribes, like the Cheyennes, Arapahoes, Kiowas, or Crows, used to stay together, but in historic times even some of these were divided. There were Northern and Southern Cheyennes, Northern and Southern Arapahos, Mountain and River Crows. There were usually small parties visiting back and forth, but the entire tribes never got together again after the initial division.

A tribe did make a special effort to unite at the time of the Sun Dance, usually held during early summer, and for the great spring and fall buffalo hunts. Great camps usually pitched in a circle at this time. Even smaller divisions of the tribe, traveling as individual units, camped in circles, each band and each family knowing exactly its particular location within the circle. The only exception to this camping in a circle seems to have been the Comanches. That tribe seems to have made no circle camp.

Indians have been called nomads, but the word *nomad* implies no conception of property or national boundaries. So the Indians were not nomads in the true sense of the word, for they had very definite tribal areas with well-defined boundaries. It was sometimes necessary, in following game, to cross into country belonging to another tribe, but such an act led to intertribal wars and was understood to mean trouble, even when conditions forced it upon them.

The camp circle was so well organized, the boundaries so well established, and the habits and movements of the tribe so well known, that war or hunting parties could be away for weeks, or even months at a time, and yet know exactly where to go to find their people on their return.

On our first visit to the Crows, in Montana, to attend their tribal fair, we were sent to see Mrs. Goes Ahead, wife of the famous scout for Custer. She showed us where to camp, next to her, and told us, "This is your place forever." From then on, we always had our own place in the Crow camp circle.

The Crows tell one story, however, about a warrior who returned after a long absence. He had no difficulty in finding the camp of his people, but it was getting dark when he returned and he did have trouble locating his own lodge. He thought he knew right where to find it, so he entered and sat down by the fire. As he started to remove his moccasins, he said, "Old woman, I had a hard time finding the lodge tonight." "Old woman," far from being a term of derision or contempt, was a term of endearment, for age was revered and the term implied long and happy association.

But the man heard an unfamiliar young woman's voice say, "Mother, who is that strange man in the lodge?"

The warrior, realizing then that he had made a mistake, made a dive for the door, but it was cut lower than his own and he hit his head against the tipi just over the doorway and was flung back, off balance, and landed in a kettle of soup which sat beside the fire.

With a yelp of pain he made another charge at the door, this time ducking low enough to clear the entrance, but he stumbled over the picket rope of the war horse tied outside the door and landed astride the animal, which was lying down. The horse, startled by such an unceremonious mounting, jumped to his feet and bucked the man off, pitching him right back into the lodge and into the kettle of soup again!

Generally the camp circle opened to the east, just as the individual lodges did, for east is the direction where the sun returns, bringing life and power. Some camp circles were made up of smaller circles of lodges, each small circle being a clan, or gens, or some other subdivision of the tribe. Usually the camp circle, however, was one large complete circle, the tipis being arranged in proper order, band by band, and family by family, about its circumference. The painted tipis were placed within the main circle, in a smaller circle of their own, but here, too, each lodge had its own place. Soldier societies, dancing fraternities, and other ritualistic organizations also had their lodges pitched within the main circle. And, of course, the chief's lodge and the council lodge were there.

The main pony herd grazed outside the camp and was usually watched by boys, but favorite war horses and buffalo runners were kept inside the camp circle, the really choice ones picketed near the lodges of their owners. Sometimes an owner went to bed with the picket rope tied around one foot, so that no clever enemy could sneak into the camp and stealthily remove his property.

In the Blackfoot camp there were three lodges of camp policemen pitched near the center of the circle. In the largest lodge were stored weapons and dress clothes, and since there was usually little policing to do in an Indian camp, these warriors spent most of their time, both day and night, in feasting and dancing.

When it was necessary to erect one of the large council lodges, the tipis which were to be used in its construction were chosen and it was pitched near the center of the camp.

When an entire tribe was gathered for the Sun Dance, the ceremonial dancing lodge was of utmost importance; therefore it was built near the center of the circle. At such times the circle was extremely huge, sometimes a good half-mile in diameter and each subdivision of the tribe was camped in its respective location. The ceremonial tipis of the participants were pitched near the dancing lodge.

On the occasion of the Sun Dance, many tribes faced the individual tipis toward the center, instead of east as was customary. Recent Cheyenne and Arapaho Sun Dance camps have been pitched with the tipis facing the central Sun Dance lodge, and old photographs of Sioux and Arapaho Sun Dance camps show the tipis facing the center. Thus they all drew power from the ceremonial lodge.

On several occasions we have seen Sioux camps where the few tipis used and all the other tents faced the center of the circle. But the Sun Dance was held during the summer, when no fires were necessary in the tipis, and today the Sioux seldom make fires in

296

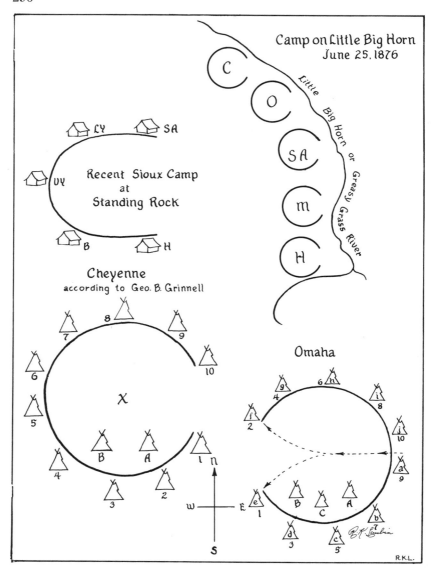

Fig. 65. Camp Circles.

CAMP ON LITTLE BIG HORN
C — Cheyenne
O — Oglala
SA — Sans Arc
M — Minikonju
H — Hunkpapa

RECENT SIOUX CAMP AT STANDING ROCK
SA — Sans Arc
LY — Lower Yanktonai
UY — Upper Yanktonai
B — Blackfoot Sioux
H — Hunkpapa

CHEYENNE
according to George B. Grinnell *(The Cheyenne Indians)*
A — Sacred Arrows
B — Sacred Hat
X — Dance lodge or council lodge,
   not a usual part of the circle

1. I vis tsi nih pah (Closed Aorta)
2. Suh tai (People left behind)
3. Wuh ta piu (Eaters — Sioux)
4. Hev a tan iu (Hair-rope people)
5. Ho iv i ma nah (Scabby)
6. Is si o me tan e (Hill people)
7. Hof no wa (Poor people)
8. Ohk to o na (Protruding lower jaws)
9. Mah sih ko ta (Reclining with knees drawn up)
10. Omis sis (Eaters)

OMAHA
A — War tipi
B — White buffalo skin
C — Sacred pole tipi
a, b, c, d, e, f, g, h, i, j, order of clans
in the camp circle
1, 2, 3, 4, 5, 6, 7, 8, 9, 10, order of pitching
camp when heading west

their tipis. Old Sioux told us emphatically that, except for the Sun Dance, it was the custom to face tipis east.

In some ceremonies, as the one for the Sacred Buffalo Calf Pipe of the Sioux, the ceremonial tipi faced west. But it would be nearly impossible to make the fire draw on most days if the tipi faced that direction.

At the other extreme, the Crows, who almost never build fires in their tipis nowadays, still face them east if possible. The only exceptions are a few faced south to avoid dust from the road beside which they are pitched on the tribal fair grounds. The Blackfeet keep their tipis facing east, even in the Sun Dance circle.

As recently as 1934, the encampment for the Sioux tribal fair at Standing Rock kept a semblance of the old camp circle. There was only one tipi in evidence, the rest all being wall tents, but they were arranged as in early days. The sketch of camp circles in Fig. 65 shows the arrangement. The Sans Arcs were visitors from a neighboring reservation. The Hunkpapas always camped at the opening of the circle, for that is what the name implies—"those who camp at the head of the circle." Red Tomahawk told us that formerly the Hunkpapas split their camp, half being on the north side of the entrance to the circle, half on the south side. They were the toughest warriors in the tribe and in the distant past were chosen to guard the camp entrance.

The great camp on the Little Big Horn at the time of Custer's defeat was said to have contained more than two thousand lodges. It consisted of five large camp circles strung along the river, each opening east towards the river. The Cheyennes, under Two Moons, were farthest downstream. Next came the Oglalas, under Crazy Horse, then the Sans Arcs under Spotted Eagle, the Minikonjus under One Horn and Makes Room, and the upper camp, guarding the entrance to the great flat and the back trail over which the soldiers had to come, was that of the Hunkpapas, fiercest warriors of all, under Sitting Bull and Four Horns. This is the division into which we were adopted.

According to James Owen Dorsey, the Poncas camped in three concentric circles and the Omahas in two similar circles. Consequently they were called by the Lakota, *Oyate Yamni* and *Oyate nonpa*, the "Three people" and the "Two People." In more recent times these two tribes have camped in a large horseshoe with clans in regular places. For that matter, the so-called camp circle of any tribe was often more of a horseshoe. The Poncas and Omahas originally used the earth lodge as their permanent home, and there was no particular formation in a village of earth lodges. Each lodge was built wherever the head of the family desired. But the women selected the tipi sites according to the tribal arrangement.

When only a division of these tribes was on the move, there was no systematic order of camping, except that each family camped near its kindred.

When the entire Omaha tribe was out on a hunt and stopped to make camp, the leaders of the caravan crossed the imaginary circle which the encampment was to occupy and families paired off as they came along, moving to the right or left, according to their proper places in the camp circle. The leaders of the caravan formed the opening to the circle, or we might say the points of the "C," on each side. If an enemy attack was likely, the lodges were pitched close together, and in this case the entire horse herd was kept inside the circle. But in following the hunt, with meat to dry and skins to tan, more room was left between lodges.

On the return trip to the home country the camping order was reversed, and the former leaders became the rear guard of the movement. Thus the opening of the circle was always in the direction of the line of march. But the tipis themselves faced east.

Just before making camp, a crier announced the location. The Omahas had three sacred tents which were always pitched in the same relative positions, that is, on the south side if moving east or west. One was the war tipi, another the tipi containing the Sacred Pole, perhaps the most sacred object of the Omahas.[1]

The Cheyennes had two special tipis, one containing the tribal Medicine Arrows, the other the Sacred Hat. These two tipis were pitched close together, a few rods within the entrance of the circle and a little to the south. The Medicine Arrows are still with the Southern Cheyennes in Oklahoma, but the Sacred Hat is with their northern relatives on the Tongue River reservation in Montana.

The movies have yet to make a really good Indian picture, showing the old Plains Indian life. Whoever their technical directors are, they have some very odd ideas of what an old-time Indian camp looked like. We visited a movie set supposedly portraying such a camp. After careful examination of the grounds, we failed

[1] J. O. Dorsey, "Omaha Sociology," Bureau of American Ethnology, *Third Annual Report*, 1881–82. Also, Alice Fletcher, "The Omaha Tribe," Bureau of American Ethnology, *Twenty-seventh Annual Report*, 1905–1906.

to find one single thing that was right. The tipis were dark and drab-looking, with smoke flaps that looked like the ears of African elephants flapping as they charged. To represent the seams where the hides were sewed together they had painted on stitches at least two inches long. Actually, a real hide tipi was sewed as neatly as a pair of moccasins.

The tipis otherwise were wrong in shape and were set up with the poles all fastened to iron rings; doors were on upside down; a deer, supposedly just ready for butchering, was hanging upside down. A huge fire ring was in the center of the camp, with an arrangement that looked like a well-sweep erected over it. A director's idea of a way to torture prisoners, no doubt. Rawhides were staked to the ground with strings attached to the pegs, and, funniest of all, dried meat was hanging on strings, so that it waved and spun in the breeze like pinwheels.

The Indians themselves were dressed in dark brown leather, with modern bows, arrows, and quivers. If old-timers could come to life to see such a sight, they would die again from laughing.

What a thrill it would be to see a village represented as it really was, with handsome tipis, beautiful costumes, painted ponies, the sounds and sights, yes, even the smells of an old-time Indian camp. For smells were an integral part of Indian life. They were not all of meat drying and hides curing. Campfire smoke, kinnikinnik, sweet-grass incense, sage, and subtle perfumes, of which Indians were fond, were ever present. Such smells, coupled with the sounds of horses, dogs, bells, high-pitched chants, and booming drums, made lasting impressions upon all fortunate enough to have experienced them.

10. MODERN INDIAN CAMPS

IN 1937, WE went to Bull Head, South Dakota, Sitting Bull's old home, to attend the "doings" on the Fourth of July. Our brightly painted tipi immediately became the center of attraction. One middle-aged woman seated herself near the door and looked around for several minutes without saying a word. Finally she asked, "What kind of tent you got?"

"Why! This tipi is fixed up like an old-time Lakota lodge!" we answered.

But she said, "Oh no! Our people never have anythings like this. This nice tent, but must be some other kind of peoples."

We told our visitor about having just been with One Bull and Scarlet Whirlwind and that they had approved of everything as being "the real Lakota," but she was still unconvinced. So many years had passed since the Lakotas had had such things and the only tipis she had ever seen had been mere empty shells.

Just then two old men, Makes Trouble and Red Fish, came in. We offered them seats in the rear of the lodge, in the place of honor, against the two backrests. A younger man, Elk Nation, followed them to act as interpreter.

The old men sat for some time, looking at the parfleches, boxes, and beaded bags, shield, medicine bags, and articles hanging from the poles. They talked together softly for some little time, and I finally asked them, "Did you ever use painted linings like this in the old days?"

"*He´chetu!*" replied Red Fish. "Certainly! We had things just like this."

Makes Trouble added, "I used to have a painted lining in my tipi and *three* backrests like this. Everything you have is all right. *Li´la washté!* Very good!"

"How long ago was that?" I asked.

Makes Trouble thought awhile, then replied, "Fifty-seven winters ago."

Then I asked the woman, who was watching and listening all this time, "How old are you?"

301

Crow Camp. Photograph by Gladys Laubin.

"Fifty-one," she answered.

For a long time we had heard about the great tipi encampment the Crow Indians set up each year for their tribal fair, and we decided to go to Montana and see it for ourselves. It really was a sight to behold! The camp was on the Little Big Horn River, not far from the Custer battlefield. There were 116 tipis in the huge camp circle. A small number compared to that other great camp under Sitting Bull, but even a dozen tipis are something to see in this day of square houses. The old Indians say there is no power in a square house, that they lost all their power when they gave up the round house to live in a square house.

Each year Crow Fair dwindled a little more. Fewer tipis were pitched. About 1954, there were only forty tipis. Old ways were dying out almost as fast as the old people themselves took the Spirit Trail. Even in 1938 the Crow tipis were the only things that looked old-time.

When the Crows camp today, they bring their best parlor rugs to put on the floor, their innerspring mattresses, their kerosene refrigerators, and their kitchen ranges. Here and there throughout the Crow camp you may find nice tipi equipment. One family may have the backrests, another a fine lining, occasionally there will be a few pieces of parfleche, beadwork, horse trappings, and so on, but none of the lodges are complete in themselves, and the tipi that wins the prize for the best in camp is not the one that looks most like early days, but the whitest one, containing, not tipi furnishings, but the biggest exhibition of beadwork!

But within the last few years a great revival of interest among the Indians in their own heritage has taken place, which is encouraging, to say the least. But it is rather ironical, now that the old ways have nearly disappeared and the old folk who knew about them are gone, that the younger Indians want to know about their own history and culture. Crow Fair has been rejuvenated, at least to the extent that once more they are pitching a great tipi camp, and the parades and dances are being revived. Recently, as many as 300 tipis have been seen, and beadwork and horse trappings that have been under cover for nearly twenty years were brought out into the open again. The activities cannot compare, of course, to those of years ago, when the old people were still alive and in charge. Nevertheless, it is a fine show and people not fortunate enough to have seen it in the past can at least enjoy the thrill of seeing Indians in action once more.

In all that great camp on our first visit to Crow Fair, we were the only ones to have a tipi completely furnished as in the past, and to have a fire inside. We were the only ones at every fair we later attended to have a fire in a tipi. We can hardly blame the Crows if they do not want to cut a hole in their best rug to fit around a fireplace, but we do not quite agree with them that a pure white tipi, uncolored by smoke, is the most beautiful. Perhaps we are just not civilized yet, for we think a tipi looks more picturesque when it is smoked up a bit.

Not long after our lodge was pitched the first time at Crow Fair, Robert Yellowtail, who was then superintendent of the reservation, came around to see it. Until then it had looked as if it would rain any minute. Yellowtail said, "You've got a medicine tipi there. Now it will rain for sure."

"No," we told him. "On the contrary, it will now clear up. This tipi makes clear weather."

And, sure enough, we had hardly put our lodge in order when the weather began to clear, and we had not a drop of rain all during the fair. Believe it or not, when the fair was over and we took the tipi down, we had no more than packed it when the wind began to

Laubins' Tipi in Crow Camp. Photograph by Gladys Laubin.

blow and soon approached hurricane velocity. It took the roof off of one of the local buildings, knocked over several big trees, and scattered branches everywhere.

We had a similar experience when we went to visit the Blackfeet in Browning, Montana, but the most impressive experience of all was at All American Indian Days in Sheridan, Wyoming. There we were told by the Camp Marshal to set our tipi up facing the grandstand, which meant that it had to face west. We pointed out to him that ours was a medicine tipi and should always face east. "It's easier to turn the tipi around than the grandstand," he replied, so we said, "Okay, but don't blame us if we get a big storm."

Flat as the camp ground looked, we were surprised to find the spot allotted to us was just a few inches higher than the sites where other nearby tipis were pitched. We had no more than finished erecting it when the sky began to get black and we could hear thunder rolling in the distance. Everyone knew we were going to get a bad storm, and everyone was out with shovels trenching tipis, or scurrying around trying to make other preparations to meet it. The little rise on which our tipi was located was so slight that we trenched it too. Some of the Indians dug their trenches

quite far, a foot or more, away from the tipis and placed the dirt
from the trench against the tipi wall. Perhaps they thought this
would drain the water off of the cover and into the trench, but it
did not look good to us. They may have gotten the idea from stories
of sealing the tipis with earth in the winter before the heavy snows
came. Anyway, this dirt around the bottom soon became mud, and
the trenches were so far away that all the water that ran down the
cover came in underneath instead of running into the trench.

The thunder was growling right over our heads and lightning
was flashing in terrifying bolts everywhere. For a few minutes
the wind raged, then down came the rain. You never saw so much
water come down at once! Like pouring it from buckets! In a matter
of minutes we were surrounded by a lake of water and had to take
our moccasins off and roll up our trousers to go outside to help our
friends who were still trying to draw water away from their camps
by more trenching.

We never did get over our tipi being the only one that remained dry during the entire deluge. Nary a drop of water entered
our lodge, and none of our rare and beautiful articles was wet in
the least. But our poor neighbors! Their tipis were afloat. They
lost precious beadwork, buffalo robes and buckskins, and their
bedding and rugs were completely soaked. So you can hardly blame
us if we believe we really do have a medicine tipi!

We went to Sheridan that time on an invitation to bring our
tipi, with the poles and all the furnishings, to help the Indians re-
vive an interest in the early days and to encourage them to furnish
their tipis in similar fashion. Of the forty or more tipis there, representing Indians of many tribes, ours was the only one completely
furnished as in the olden time—painted lining, four willow backrests, parfleches, rawhide boxes, beaded saddle bags (both men's
and women's), along with quilled and beaded pouches and bags
hanging from the top of the lining, buffalo robes, and other furs.
We were given the first prize for the most beautiful tipi. We returned the prize money to the committee to be applied to their
many worthwhile projects but we were delighted to retain the
honor.

One day Max Big Man, who might be called the historian of the
Crows, announced to the gathering: "You come here each year to
set up this camp and reproduce old days. You think you are Indians,
but if you want to see some real Indians, you go visit those two
white people in their lodge. They have the only old-time lodge,
like early days."

Mr. Yellowtail used to bring visitors, both red and white, to see our lodge. He told them: "I want you to see this tipi. This is a pre-Columbian lodge." It is hardly that, but it is like those of buffalo days.

The first time we camped with the Crows quite a group gathered to watch us pitch our tipi. We heard one Indian remark in an aside, "Enemy tipi." Even the young people standing around, who would not know how to begin putting up a tipi, could see that we were doing it differently from the way their own folk did.

On another occasion, when we were digging the little fire pit for our tipi, some visiting Shoshoni children watched us.

"What are you doing there?" they asked.

"Digging the hole for the fire."

"Fire!" exclaimed one of the little girls. "You'll burn it up!"

"Oh no!" we assured her. "You just have to be careful and not make it too big."

"Then you'll smoke yourself out," she said.

We told her, "Your ancestors had fires in their tipis long before we came along and they seemed to do all right. We'll have a fire tonight and you come over and see what it is like, see how your people lived in the long ago."

That evening not only the little Shoshoni girls, but their parents, as well as Crow and Cheyenne families, came over. The night was chilly, and since ours was the only fire in the entire camp, it drew Indians like moths to a candle. We had thirty guests that night. They just about filled our lodge! That is one time we wished we had a thirty-footer, but it probably would have been crowded, too.

That same night one of the Crow tipis burned down because someone placed a coal-oil lamp too near the canvas. And another burned that same week-end from a gasoline lantern. "Too bad, such kind of civilization!" one old Indian remarked.

We had a "full house" every night of the fair. Ute, Yakima, Assiniboine, Cree, Gros Ventre, Mandan, Chippewa, Arapaho, and even Kiowa and Apache Indians from Oklahoma were represented in our guest book. It is filled with such names as Strawberry Sings Pretty, Bull-over-the-Hill, Medicine Crow, Holds-the-Enemy, Stands-in-Timber, Tall Bull, Real Bird, Bird-in-the-Ground. Some of our visitors wrote something like this: "We like you because you are like us. You do not high-hat us like some people do." Another wrote, "Thank you for having a time with us."

11. VISITORS

WE SPENT OUR HONEYMOON as guests in a huge tipi on the Ten Sleep Ranch in Colorado. It was a twenty-four foot tipi, but seemed even more immense because there was nothing in it but a "bed" that went all the way around it from door to door. Flat boards about six inches wide were placed on edge on the ground and held in position with stakes around the wall of the tipi, another row of boards about six feet from them made an inner circle. The space between the two circles of boards was filled with soft pine needles, the sweet fragrance constantly permeating the interior of the tipi. It was the only time we ever slept in a round bed.

One day we came home to find four half-grown heifers in the tipi, seeking shelter in its shade! We had quite a hassle trying to chase the villains out. They would go round and round but refused to go out the door. Eventually we got rid of them and we were relieved to find that the only damage was the eating of a tube of toothpaste and a tube of glue. This experience taught us never to leave camp without closing the door flap and tying it down, and we have been partial to small doors ever since.

We have many four-legged visitors, as well as two-legged ones. Cats, mice, chipmunks, squirrels, pack rats, California ground squirrels or chislers, camp robbers (Canada jays), chipping sparrows, and bluebirds, even bears have come to see us.

One afternoon Gladys caught me in front of the tipi yelling at a magpie, "Hey! You! Come back here with that!" She said, "For heaven's sake, what's the matter with you?" I told her, "I was inside the tipi, painting the new lining, when that sassy magpie flew right down the smoke hole and flew away with my pencil. Then he took my brush, then all of my crayons, and now my eraser." A few days later we found he had returned while we were away and dropped everything he had stolen beside the fireplace!

One night we were awakened by a lot of noise in our "grub box," accompanied by loud sniffing. I turned the flashlight on a big skunk! Up went his tail and out went the light! We lay there as quiet as mice (although mice sometimes make a great deal of noise).

We could tell just where our hyacinth squirrel was by the difference in the sound of the various places he was investigating. Finally he walked up along our bed and practically sniffed in our faces.

After what seemed eternity he went towards the door, and Gladys whispered to me, "Shall I get up and let him out?"

"No!" I almost yelled. The trouble was that he had climbed up over the little enclosure below the doorway and now could not find his way over it again. But I figured he would have to find out for himself, because so long as we did not frighten him he seemed to be peaceable enough.·In fact, he was so peaceful that we finally went to sleep on our guest and never did know how or when he got out.

Another time we took our cat with us. Some time about the middle of the night she came in with a great meowing to show us a mouse she had caught. We patted her and said, "Nice kitty," which seemed to be what she wanted, and we went off to sleep again. Soon she was back with more fuss and another mouse. After this had happened three times, we finally decided too much was plenty and tied Igomo (Lakota for cat) to a piece of rope inside the tipi so that she could not go mousing again that night. That's what we thought! Hardly had we fallen asleep again when she started her noise all over again, and we found she had another mouse, caught right inside the tipi and while she was tied to a rope at that!

The next night Igomo made more fuss than ever, and we wondered what in the world she had this time. She came prancing in with a piece of frankfurter some picnicker had discarded that afternoon!

The flying squirrels gave us a time for several nights. They jumped out of a big pine tree in back of the tipi and "flew" right down on the tipi cover and slid halfway around it. They made an awful racket and it took us several nights to discover what it was. It seemed that every night, around two o'clock, they all got together and said, "Now fellows, let's all go over to the Laubins' and raise cain!"

Then came the moles. In the late fall they were evidently looking for warm winter quarters, for suddenly they chose the tipi for their activities. We have been told they can't see, so we do not know why they cannot do their tunneling in the daytime as well as at night. But they always wait until we are sound asleep. Then suddenly we wake up with a lump as big as a fist in the middle of our backs and have to tear the bed apart and level off a mole burrow.

Nevertheless, we would not trade our beds of buffalo robes for the best inner-spring jelly-bed in town. Our biggest difficulty when traveling is finding a bed hard enough to make us feel at home. Our hard beds have not frightened away friends who have wanted to try a night in the tipi. We always try to make them as comfortable as possible by piling up all our extra robes and skins into a nice thick pallet for them to spread their bed rolls on. We even let them sleep in the rear of the tipi, in the *chaktu*, or place of honor, as the Indians used to honor their guests.

In the summer we have seen a mother antelope hide her little one, hardly bigger than a mosquito, in the sage brush not far from the tipi. It stayed out of sight all day, but when the mother returned in the evening it came bounding out from nowhere and ran to greet her.

One night a big bull moose woke us up pawing and grunting out in the back of the tipi, and night after night hundreds of elk go through the little draw out in front, heading for the refuge at the south end of the valley. We hear the bulls bugling all around us, but the cows lead the herds into the refuge in the fall, making a soft mewing sound almost like kittens. The bulls are in the lead in the spring when they head for the mountains again.

One of the greatest thrills is to hear geese honking and then to see a great flock fly above the smoke hole directly overhead.

It is an eery night when a great horned owl sits on the end of one of the long poles projecting above the tipi, hooting to his mate over in the river bottom, who softly returns his call. Indians probably would not like this, as most of them have a superstitious dread of owls. They can fly without the slightest sound, and are thought by some to be departed spirits. Only a person with strong medicine power can use owl feathers or have anything to do with owls. After an experience like this most families would break camp and move to a different location.

Sometimes the coyotes come so close to our camp that we can hear them catch their breath before they howl. But make one move towards a gun, no matter how silently, and there is no coyote. He vanishes like a shadow. Otherwise he may stay and serenade us for an hour or more.

Because the coyotes come so near, we have to watch Igomo Inonpa (Igomo the Second) closely, but he seems to enjoy the tipi as much as our old Igomo did. He likes to watch us prepare the meals and is always on hand when they are ready. Sometimes he scampers up the lacing pins on the outside and peeks down at us through the smoke hole. Sometimes he curls up asleep against a backrest, or finds a still more cozy spot behind it.

We like the coyotes, and we like the bears, too, in their place. But it was almost the last straw when we came home one evening and discovered bear tracks all over the outside of the tipi. Even so, we were lucky they were outside and not inside, for bears do not seem to understand doors. They often go right through the side or back, whichever is handiest, and we did not want to find a bear on our buffalo-skin bed!

Eventually the time comes when we must break camp and take up a pleasant and more serious way of life. But we are always anxious to get back in the tipi again. Once the bug bites you, the disease is incurable. Every once in a while we meet someone almost as smitten as ourselves. We knew a retired army officer who looked forward all during his army career to the time when he could retire and take his family to live in a tipi. At least we did not have to wait until we retired.

And once you have tried tipi life, you may be equally enthusiastic about it. We like camping generally, but we would never be happy for long in any other kind of a tent. We just could not stand being without the comfort, color, and beauty of the tipi.

Visitors exclaim over the beautiful light in the tipi. During the day it is cheerful and mellow. It is like living in a big lampshade. Even on dark, gloomy days it is brighter than most houses. But especially are the nights wonderful. To lie there by the fire, listening to its merry crackling, watching the shadows flickering on the wall, the the final dusky glow, with a few stars peeping down at you through the poles in the smoke hole, is beyond words to describe. No other kind of ceiling, from log cabin to mansion, is half so interesting. And some nights the moon climbs right up over the poles and looks in. Outside a coyote howls or a great horned owl hoots in the distance.

One evening I was leaning against my backrest, enjoying a bright little fire, when Gladys spoke up. She said, "If there is any such a place as Heaven, I hope it is a big tipi, with you sitting there and a big pile of firewood by the door."

One lady when she first saw the interior of our tipi, exclaimed, "I do believe that is the most attractive and comfortable-looking place I have ever seen in all my life!"

And that is just the way we feel.

Chief Wades-in-the-Water and his wife, Julia, visit the Laubins in their tipi. Photograph by Crandall.

TIPI LETTERS

QUESTIONS AND ANSWERS

WE ARE OFTEN asked, "What can I do to help Indians?"

We believe that the best thing anyone can do is join one of the organizations working for Indian benefit. Here are two of the best:

National Congress of American Indians
1430 K Street, N.W.
Washington, D.C.   20005

Association on American Indian Affairs, Inc.
432 Park Avenue South
New York, N.Y.   10016

We belong to both but, if we had to choose only one, we would choose the first, NCAI. It was established some thirty years ago, represents 100 different Indian tribes, and has been working effectively to bring about legislation and programs to help Indians help themselves. It is an all-Indian organization but welcomes non-Indians as auxiliary members. Auxiliary members have no vote but their dues contribute to the many worthwhile projects of the organization.

The Association on American Indian Affairs, largely a non-Indian organization, was founded many years ago, and continues to do much, including provision of legal service, for Indians. The association now has Indian representation on its board of directors. It is tax-exempt.

From a young lady in California—No doubt many persons have expressed their appreciation to you for writing the book *The Indian Tipi,* but I am not going to let that stop me from thanking you also. . . . I am very happy with my tipi. I took it to Canada last summer. It is absolutely lovely. Everybody that saw it liked it.

313

I believe that we are affected by our living structures. I am sure that the tipi had as much to do with shaping and sustaining Indian culture and consciousness as the culture did in shaping the tipi. If people live in tipis then I feel there is some hope for American culture as it is today. Tipis are a consciousness in themselves and demand inner changes if one is to have rapport with them. Well, at least that is how I feel about it. Thank you so much for what you have done to keep alive many of the good traditions of Indian life. My deepest thanks.

Answer—It is heartening to hear you say that if people live in tipis, then one can feel there is hope for American present-day culture. The tipi does demand an inner change, in thought and attitude, if one is to enjoy living in one. No wonder the Indians loved the circle and had so many meanings for it.

We know some young people who have earned degrees in various branches of education but who feel that their most important contribution at present is to plant trees in depleted forests of Idaho, Wyoming, Colorado and Utah. They chose the tipi for living quarters, not only because it is more practical and comfortable in all seasons than any other kind of tent, but also because of its beauty and simplicity.

About a School for Indian Living—My wife and I have considered for a long time the idea of tipi life. But beginning such a life contains certain problems for a person who has only dreamed of such a life. What we would like to know is if there is a school in North America from which we could learn everything necessary to construct a tipi, possibly even to construct our own tipi while learning at the school.

If you know of no such school we were hoping you would be interested in starting one. If you are we would consider it a pleasure to be your pupils and would try our best to gather other pupils for this school.

Answer—We were happy to receive your letter inquiring about a school for tipi living, and that you and your wife were considering tipi life. But to go back to living that way does entail many problems. It would be as difficult now for the average Indian to go back to living in a tipi as it was for his ancestors to give it up in the first place and try to live within our civilization. Although their life was much simpler materially, it was every bit as complicated psychologically, socially, spiritually and ethically, and such attitudes were an important part of Indian life. They found it as difficult to jump from a stone age into a machine age as we would find it to return to those early buffalo days. For those who have had other camping and woodcraft experience the tipi is supreme, but for those without such training it would take some adjusting. For those of us who have made the change, even occasionally or for a little while, the reward has been great satisfaction and peace.

We feel highly complimented that you would like us to start a school to instruct in tipi living. Several others have also made the suggestion. We know of no such school, but at this time there is no way we could attempt to handle one ourselves. We are busy with our writing and with our concerts of Indian dances, so for the time being the best school is just putting the information in the tipi book into actual practice. It could be a lot of fun.

To Spend a Year in the Wilderness—Having spoken to you on the phone we are now writing with some questions which we feel that only experience can answer.

We are a family of four; we intend to spend at least a year in the mountains at 4500-6000 feet. We are making a tipi according to the patterns in your book. We spent the summer and fall of last year in a para-tipi at the 4000 foot level, north Sierras, and when we were snowed in, we were taught the inherent value of a dwelling made to live in.

The area in which we camped was primarily cedar, conifer, and several species of oak. Therefore I ask the advisability of a small wood stove to enable us to burn "poppers" for heat, saving the hardwood for open fire cooking, etc. Also, I estimate about 5 cords of wood for the winter. Would that give me enough reserve (based on an anticipated 2-3 feet of snow)?

How long do you think it will take the dew cloth to rot at the bottom during a year of continuous exposure, if we put a waterproof sheet under as well as over where it turns under the ground cloth?

Do you still think pentachloraphenol an adequate treatment for the poles? I am also going to treat the pegs, is the reason for asking.

Can a fire be going when the ozan is in use? If we must resort to a stove, could we use it with the smoke flaps closed or would a pipe long enough to carry the smoke to the crossing of the poles be too close to the fabric?

We intend to use about ten-mil poly sheet for a ground cloth, over which two layers of carpet type rugging, with a layer of foam between, and foam insulite pads for our beds. Do you think that this would be adequate?

We are looking forward to this experience. God bless you for having made your knowledge of the tipi available in such a pleasing fashion.

Answer—The answers to most of your questions you will find in this edition of *The Indian Tipi* under *Winter Camping* and *Living In the Tipi*. I still think pentachloraphenol is the best preservative, at least for the butts of the poles.

You can get the little sheet iron stoves from Herter's, Inc., Waseca, Minn. 56043. They have all sorts of outdoor equipment. We would never enjoy the tipi without the open fire. Otherwise, you might as well use any old kind of tent.

Foam insulite should make a comfortable foundation for beds and for sitting, adding insulation at the same time.

We have camped at 27 below zero with nothing but the open fire, but it is sometimes difficult to find enough good wood that doesn't throw sparks. The book gives some information on woods to burn. We burn about six cords of wood here over the winter, but our winters are about eight months long and it sometimes goes to 45 below. Of course we burn this in our house, and it is pine, which is pretty poor stuff for a tipi, for it smokes and sparks both.

After all, Indians did not go into the mountains for the winter. They went the other way, out on the plains to a sheltered river bottom, or to a nice valley at the foot of the mountains. But if there is any tent suitable for winter camping, anyplace, the tipi is it.

The ozan does not come out far enough into the tipi to affect the drawing of the fire. In fact, some tipis, we have been told, put an ozan on both sides and the back, but this still leaves an adequate opening for the smoke to go out.

More on Spending a Year in the Wilderness—May your blessings be as abundant as ours! At last we have our floor—270 square feet of rug and felt pad, from a house that was under renovation. We've also decided to use the foam only where we're sleeping and sitting.

Please don't feel as though we are pressing you—it's just that we've no one to share this with who will understand and no one who knows how to answer our questions.

We are having a time trying to find out how to keep canned foods in weather below freezing. No one has any idea except my mother-in-law, who says to use straw. This I can see, but the techniques of such storage seem to be lost in the mists of antiquity. Any information will be of inestimable value.

One thing I don't understand is how to set the smoke flaps so as to have a fire during rain.

Would you mind sending me a string measurement, such as you suggest, for spacing the tripod poles properly on the ground?

A few people here who frankly thought we were crazy, after having read your book are almost as excited as we are in our preparations.

Answer—We are glad to hear that your plans for spending a year in the wilderness are progressing so nicely. We have heard that people used to bury cabbage, carrots, and all sorts of vegetables by digging out the surface of the ground a foot or so, then placing the vegetables on the freshly exposed earth, covering them thickly with straw and then throwing the dirt back on top of it all. Whether this would work on canned goods we don't know. It no doubt would be all right if the weather didn't get too cold. There are many canned foods that will not be palatable after freezing. We have used frozen evaporated milk. It breaks down in freezing, so looks strange, but tastes all right. There are warnings on some brands of dog food not to freeze them.

People around here in Jackson's Hole are still using dug-out cellars. They are dug out in the side of a hill, and of course the really good ones are lined with logs. We know some people who used to keep their vegetables from freezing by putting them in the bed with them!

Of course the Indians got around this problem by using dried foods, although they didn't have dried milk, which is available today. You can also get all kinds of dried fruits and vegetables, which are put up for outfitters like Herter's, and the tipi book

tells how to make jerky and other dried foods. I would not depend
upon modern *store-bought* jerky as a food supply, for it is full of
preservatives, additives, salt and even artificial smoke!

It looks as if you have quite a variety of foods but the Indians
would have more protein, with lots of dried meat, pemmican, dried
berries, etc. Indians on the coasts and around the Great Lakes
stored plenty of dried fish, too. You can also get whole-ground
corn meal, which would keep well in cold weather. In fact, it should
be refrigerated. And you might enjoy some wild, or herb tea.
Several varieties of mint are found in most parts of the country.
Comfrey, Camomile, alfalfa are also tasty and the children would
enjoy them as well as the grown-ups.

To keep things safe from rodents, mice, squirrels, etc., you
should have some large cans, such as bakers get lard in.

You asked about smoke flaps in a rain. Just keep them down
wind, as at any other time. Unless you have a real gullywasher
there won't be enough rain come in to bother you.

As to your inquiry about spacing the tripod poles on the ground
you will also find this under Pitching the Tipi.

Tipi Wrinkles—I doubt if you remember me from a letter I wrote
you about two and a half years ago. It may refresh your memory
if I tell you that I was building a Sioux tipi at that time and I enclosed a strand of thread in my letter and asked you if it was strong
enough for button-hole stitching around the lacing pin holes. You
were right, my thread was perfect for the job. I thoroughly enjoyed
your return letter. I still have it and keep it in the front cover of
my copy of *The Indian Tipi*, which I consider a very valuable book
in my collection . . . When I wrote before I was in the Air Force,
so I did not have a lot of time to work on the tipi. Finally my carrying rack was completed, and then I got lucky. I got a permit right
away to cut my poles. Anyway, for the first time I finally put up
my tipi. I must tell you it was simply beautiful! I can truthfully
say that the time, money, and work I spent on it were very well
worth it, and I want to thank you again for making it all possible
with your book.

I do have one problem with the cover on my tipi with which
you might be able to advise me. With the tipi *completely* pitched,
my cover has some bad wrinkles or folds on the North side (with
the door facing East). The wrinkles are horizontal to the ground
and are one to three feet in length. They are at a point half way

between the bottom of the tipi and the smoke flaps. Half way up the cover, in other words.

At first, I thought that a simple matter of raising the crossing of the tripod poles would solve it, but it didn't. Also, I tried raising the location where the cover is tied to the lifting pole, but it still didn't pull out the wrinkles or folds. Then I thought my poles on the North side might be swayed inward a bit, so I twisted the poles around, but it didn't help. I tried pushing the poles out against the cover as tight as possible, but that only increased the wrinkles and raised the bottom of the cover much too high off the ground. In short, I've tried everything! Do you have any suggestions? Your tipi looks so tight and perfectly neat.

In writing this letter I also wanted to let you know the results of my tipi in addition to the other things I mentioned. But I think, most of all, I wanted to write for the sake of contact with others who love and appreciate the "old ways" of Indian life as much as I do.

Answer—We are happy to hear that you were able to get such a nice set of poles and finally set your tipi up.

Wrinkles such as you describe are usually caused by the tripod being *tied too high*. If too low, the canvas will easily pull to the ground, no wrinkles, but it would be slack on the ground and you couldn't peg it down properly. Spacing the tripod poles is also important. If they are spread too far the canvas won't fit, or if not spread enough you get the same effect as if tied too high, only in this case the canvas won't fit the poles and probably won't even reach the ground. *The tripod must be tied within an inch or two of being perfect.* A few inches above or below will mean either wrinkles, or the opposite, being too slack all around (which means the canvas is loose between the poles).

In our tipi book we mention that occasionally one ties the door pole too high. This is easily and quickly discovered and we've seen Indians make the same mistake. Usually, instead of taking the tipi down and doing the job all over again, they either bury the butt of the pole, or chop it off!

New Yorkers excited about making tipi—I have just finished reading your book and mostly I wanted to write to let you know how much I appreciated it. A friend of mine and I are planning to build a tipi on our land in up-state New York and we found your book was just perfect for our needs. It's clear, precise, and detailed and a whole lot of fun to read. I'm sure you must know how valuable it is—this is just to let you know that we think so too.

I do have a couple of questions that I want to ask you. Because we live in the East, most of the kinds of wood that you mentioned to use for poles are not available to us. We have tamarac, but most of the trees here are too small. We have maple, ash, walnut, willow, and various poplars and aspens, and we don't really know which kind to use.

Also, we can't really afford canvas, and were wondering about using parachutes. Are they desirable? How can they be made to fit your pattern? Are there any less expensive materials we can use?

We are getting really excited about making the tipi and living in it and using most of your recommendations for furniture, etc., and we would appreciate any advice that we can get. One last thing—I would like to see a tipi done in Indian style. Are there any around that can be viewed by the public?

Thank you for everything and more power to you in your attempt to bring things Indian back to Americans.

Answer—Thank you for your letter and for your nice compliments. Years ago we did some camping in the tipi in the East—Indiana, Connecticut, Vermont and Maine. Tamarac was not available in some of these places, so we used anything that was straight— mostly maple, which, of course, is very heavy, as are ash and hickory. The worst of these hard woods is that it takes a long time to dry or season them properly, and unless they are seasoned they warp. I would not use poplar or aspen. Even if you can find straight ones (which is doubtful) they are brittle and brashy, without much "spine," or stiffness. We used some gray birch, but again straight ones are hard to find and it also has no spine. No matter how long it is dried, it never withstands the weight of the canvas very well. We know many people who have used tamarac poles and like them very much. They are heavier than pine but not as heavy as maple or ash. The smaller around, the better, if you can get them long enough.

We have no personal experience with parachutes, but according to those who have used them, the cloth is waterproof and tough, but you must have your poles well peeled and *smooth* because it is so light in weight. Also, it would not last as long in hard winds. As a parachute comes, it will make about a 12 foot tipi, which is quite small. To make a large tipi, using two or three "chutes," might require some manipulation.

Sears and Wards used to carry a good grade of canvas and also unbleached muslin, but it must be waterproofed. You might also try Army and Navy surplus stores. We made a good tipi one time of unbleached muslin. Camp outfitters usually carry chemical waterproofings that can be applied with a brush. One friend used a solution, as mentioned in the text of the tipi book, in the bath tub and dipped his cloth in it. The muslin is much cheaper than canvas, but of course is not nearly as durable.

I don't know if the Blackfeet tipi that used to be in the American Museum of Natural History in New York is still on display or not. The only other real Indian tipi we know of in the East is an Arapaho tipi in the National Museum in Washington.

Colorado Mountain Camping—I have read your book and am about to set up my tipi. Knowing that winter is approaching I am interested in what things I should do to "winterize" my home.

I would appreciate some comments from you or hints of how to prepare my tipi for an onslaught of a Colorado winter at 8500 feet elevation.

Answer—There is more about winter camping in this new edition of *The Indian Tipi*. We have done considerable winter camping in the tipi but never at such altitudes as you mention. It is 6500 feet here in Jackson's Hole—2000 feet lower than yours and yet most people think we are high! We wonder if Indians ever did camp at such an altitude in winter. We know they never stayed here all year around. Your country was home to the Arapaho but they would have moved to a lower elevation in winter and found a nice place in some river bottom, sheltered from the wind and with plenty of firewood, grass and cottonwood bark for their horses.

However, if one is to camp at such an altitude in winter we are sure the tipi will do a first rate job. We have kept comfortable here at 27 below zero and we are sure one could be comfortable for the ordinary short spells of even colder weather. But it takes lots of good, dry wood. The tipi will never be like a steam-heated apartment but ours has been warm enough to do craft work and we found it a delightful experience.

Michigan Boy Needs Help—I am 15 years old and you have never met me, but that's not important. The important thing is that I need help and advice. I am what you might call an Indian enthusiast. But I am more than that, I love the American Indian as nobody ever has.

My biggest wish was to experience what the Indian felt, how he lived, hunted, and camped. I still wish I could speak with real Indians, full bloods — or experts like you and get a lesson in how to live like an Indian.

Last summer I tried to build a tipi, using a semi-waterproof fabric that stunk whenever it was wet. I followed directions as far as I could, being just a one-man team. My biggest failures were the poles. I had to resort to box elder, birch and other crooked trees. At first I tried to get pine or red cedar, but that was impossible. Tying the poles was another problem. When the mess was complete, I felt so ashamed, when I saw the ugliest tipi in the world. Dirty brown, no dew cloth, painting, waterproofing, straight, snug-fitting poles, and no smoke flaps. This took five weeks to construct and I kept saying it will look better when it is complete. But I was wrong. I was ready to give up. I thought, all those things I hoped for were only dreams, like a little kid.

When I read your book it was like a miracle. I saw how you actually lived in tipis on Indian reservations. I thought that nobody had ever done that before. You proved it to me though. I envy that boy that stayed with you in your tipi a whole summer.

Do the Indians really still perform ceremonies and rituals? Do they still sometimes camp in tipis? So please, Mr. and Mrs. Laubin, give me some advice as to how I can fulfill my wishes. What should I do? I've searched for organizations to join but I haven't found any. You were a dream made real. I hope that some day I'll meet you and you'll be proud of me. But I am alone in my efforts and I think I need a shove to get started.

Answer — We are glad to hear of your interest in Indians and are happy to know you enjoyed our tipi book so much.

Your trials and tribulations with the tipi reminded me of some of my boyhood experiences. I made my first tipi when I was about ten years old and it wasn't very good either. I had no one to show me about Indian things for a long time but just kept trying. At least there are many books available now which weren't in existence when I was a boy.

When we first went to live with the Indians there was no one else doing that either. We thought there wasn't much left when we were there but at least old people were still alive who had actually lived in the Buffalo Days, and they taught us the old ways and how to make old-style Indian things. But now many boys go to visit Indians each year, although there is less remaining on the reservations today, and the old folk, who taught us, are gone. There are still some Indian "doings" that you might find interesting. Write to the Information Office, Bureau of Indian Affairs, Washington, D.C., for places and dates. *A Guide to America's Indians* by Arnold Marquis is also a good source of information.

In the meantime, the best thing to do is keep on studying. The University of Oklahoma Press has printed many good books on Indians from all over the country. Your library should have these. *National Geographic* and *American Heritage* societies have also published books on Indians. *A Pictorial History of the American Indian*, by Oliver LaFarge, is also very interesting. If you go to college perhaps you should take a course in anthropology which can give you the real scientific approach to the study, not only of Indians, but of all sorts of people all over the world—for it is the study of mankind.

You live in good Indian country—at least it once was—and not too long ago. There are still Chippewa and Ottawa Indians not very far away. They were once a great people and a few of them still know how to make and do some fine Indian things.

Rawhide for Moccasin Soles—Do you have any ideas on the processing of rawhide, the typical translucent, dark brown item as procured from the heartless local tanneries? (Chicago.)

I would like to make Sioux type moccasins. The Indian soles I have examined are rather flexible and not like the iron-hard rawhide from these tanneries.

What processing did the tribes use to get the so-desired flexible results?

Is there any way to get the white or cream color of the rawhide besides the hammering or axing technique as described in your book on the tipi?

Answer—I have not had much luck in trying to convert commercially produced rawhide into Indian rawhide. The best substitute would be an alum-tanned leather. Of the many tanneries in the Chicago area perhaps you can find one which produces this alum tan.

The next best thing would be to use a thin saddle leather or a chrome tan. I have even used oak tan for moccasin soles. It is the same thing as is used for shoe soles. You can select some thin enough for moccasin soles. In some ways these leather soles are better than rawhide, for even Indian rawhide can be slippery on wet grass or on forest leaves and pine needles, whereas the leather does not get quite as slick.

If you handle a steer hide the way we describe in the tipi book I am sure you will produce a real Indian-type rawhide, but the pounding does no good on the commercial variety. They do something to it that really ruins it for any Indian project.

Smoke in Colorado—We have the tipi set up at an altitude of 10,000 feet and everything is fine except the smoke will not go out the hole. As of today we have spent only one night in the tipi and that time we couldn't breathe because of the smoke. We have tried everything you mention in your book and quite a few more things. Yesterday we even built us a hood and stove pipe contraption, but that didn't even work.

I will try and give you a description of our camp and maybe you can point out what we are doing wrong. We are surrounded for the most part by tall pine trees, but we still get a good breeze. The tipi is facing southeast and is on bare ground with approximately four feet of snow surrounding it—but maybe two feet away from the tipi. Our tipi is sealed, in that we have snow against the edges. The lining is also in place. Please reply as soon as possible.

Answer—It sounds as if you are really in high country and we are sorry to hear that you are having such trouble with your fire.

Of course a little tipi is always harder to keep free of smoke than a larger one but we used a 12-footer for many years and enjoyed it very much. Actually we had very little trouble with it.

In the first place, the fact that you are camped in heavy timber and at such a high altitude, where the air is so thin, could make a difference, but we don't think that is the real answer. We are sure that you are not doing something that should be done. It seems to us to be in the fact that you have the snow sealed all around the bottom of the tipi. In the book we mention our unhappy experience in that way. *You must have some air coming in from under the cover some place.* It's usually best on the windward side, es-

pecially if there isn't much wind. All you need is a few inches—
scrape the snow away a few inches, so the air goes up behind the
dew cloth. If your dew cloth has a flap that will cover the door, pull
it across and leave the door itself open. This added ventilation
may result in some loss of heat but it's a lot better than smoke!

If your tipi is facing southeast, then it should draw all right
from all other directions. Of course you cannot make it draw with
a southeast wind right down the hole. But even such a wind can be
successfully handled, provided it does not keep continually shifting,
by quartering one smoke flap over the hole and dropping the other
one almost completely down. This shifting is the problem we have
here in Jackson's Hole, but this is the only place we've ever had
so much of a problem with it. Wind blows all day from the south
or west but at night it shifts back and forth from north to east and
sometimes we have to change flaps about every five minutes, which
can become rather monotonous.

We think we'd try everything else before trying a stove, especially in such a small tipi, but if you want to know about a stove
we've included some information in this edition of the tipi book,
as well as more on winter camping generally. If you can still drive
pegs into the ground (you can use heavy spikes) it might help to
set the bottom of your lining a bit farther in from the outside
cover. The more air space you have between the lining and the
cover, the better.

Inquiry from Maine about Children—We know you through your
book, *The Indian Tipi,* and on the basis of that are seeking information, which you might have, to help us. We are about to have
a little one, in April, and are suddenly discovering the imprac-
ticality of modern child care. The thought occurred to us that perhaps you would have some knowledge of methods used by Indians.

We live fairly simply, will still be on our own land, without
electricity, plumbing, etc., and are looking for ways to manage,
without plastic cribs, carriers, and such. Any information you might
be able to give us would really be appreciated. Thanks.

Answer—Congratulations on a new papoose coming to your tipi!
We are glad to hear of your interest in raising your little one in
Indian fashion.

Because there is so much interest in the way Indians brought
up their children and in tipi life we decided to include an extra

section pertaining to these subjects in this edition, and trust you will find the information of some value to you.

Lady Makes Tipi Models—The purpose of this letter is to compliment you on the adequate instructions I acquired upon reading your book on tipis. I got it not only for information purposes but for enjoyment as well.

I recently made to scale two models of tipis for center pieces for an Indian celebration. I made a Cheyenne and a Crow tipi. Your drawings for placement of poles, smoke flaps, etc., were so clear that I, who knew nothing of the construction of a tipi (I've never even *seen* a real tipi), was able to make the models quite realistically accurate.

You may be interested in knowing that I used 3/16" doweling for the 3-poles in the Cheyenne and the 4-poles in the Crow and 1/8" for all the other poles. String was used for rope and canvas pocketing for the covers. As you said in your book—it took me five or six tries to pitch them—even at that scale! Straight pins closed the front and pegs were 1/8" doweling. I faced the top and even put tiny pockets for the smoke poles on the Cheyenne and made small holes with buttonholes on the sewing machine for the smoke poles to go through on the Crow. I wrote an explanation of the construction of them with the credit to your book clearly stated.

Please accept my thanks for the information *you* so clearly stated. Your book has opened a complete new interest for me. Please tell me if you have written other books on the American Indian. Thank you again.

Answer—It was nice of you to write and tell us about making your Cheyenne and Crow tipi models and we appreciate your giving us credit.

We realize not everyone is in a position to make a full-sized tipi and it is good to know you found our diagrams and instructions so easy to follow. We find it interesting that grown-ups also like to make models.

An English instructor in a junior high school wrote that when she was a youngster she made a model of our tipi, with all the inner furnishings in miniature—decorated dew cloth, backrests, pillows, rawhide boxes, etc. She showed her model, still intact, to her classes and found them so interested that she also introduced them to the tipi book.

We found both boys and girls at summer camps had lots of fun making tipi models. Each one with a different design, together they made quite an attractive village.

By contrast, one adult was really carried away with his plans for a tipi and made one of 30 feet diameter. This must have been quite a project for one with no previous tipi experience. After he had it all made up he found that poles for it had to be so long and heavy that he used a derrick to put them up!

We are glad to hear that the tipi book opened up a new interest for you and we hope that our new book on *Indian Dances of North America* will enable you to continue your interest in our native Americans.

Indian Needs Help Painting Robes—I just received your tipi book as a gift. I will always cherish it.

If I may, I wish to ask for your expert advice on choosing attractive colors to apply to four buffalo robes. I plan to paint a design on the skin side of each and present these robes to my mother, my mother-in-law, my wife, and my only son.

I have a few designs copied from books but I am at a loss to know what colors to use, nor have I been able to ascertain the meaning of these designs. I am inclosing rough sketches of these designs. Any assistance you can supply will be very much appreciated.

Answer—You have quite a project cut out for yourself in the painting of four buffalo robes. In our experience there is no modern paint nor modern method of painting that will do the job satisfactorily. The only way is the old Indian way. In this book you will find something about making bone paint brushes. They can't be beat.

You can still get powdered paints from a good paint or art supply store. All the old robes we have ever seen used just primary colors—red, blue, yellow, plus green and black. When seen in black and white illustrations it is sometimes hard to tell which color is which. Recent black and white photos give good color definition but old photographs are all off. For instance, red, brown, black, all come out about the same value. Yellow shows not quite as dark, but blue comes out light or even white.

The robe pictured in the tipi book, with us and Julia and Chief Wades-in-the-Water, we painted years ago, using hide glue for sizing, which is hard to get these days. You can make your own from hide scrapings, or you could use liquid glue, or even mucilage.

As far as the meanings of colors go, we don't think it is possible to give just one meaning for each color, such as blue for sky, yellow for rock, red for sun, green for grass or earth, black for intense devotion, white for purity, although there are times when this particular symbolism does apply. From what we have been able to find out, color symbolism is sometimes different in different ceremonies, perhaps depending upon the man in charge.

As to meanings of the designs themselves, a visitor to our tipi, not knowing we had painted the robe, asked an Indian what the design on it meant. He replied, "You'll have to ask the man that painted the robe." That's about the size of it. The same design sometimes has different meanings to different people who use it. Some designs are so old that if they ever had a particular meaning it has been lost, and they just go by the names that have been applied to them and have been handed down for a long time.

Help! My Tipi is Round instead of Egg-shaped—I am really ashamed that I have not gotten in touch with you sooner. Two years ago I would never have thought that my interest in Indians and *The Indian Tipi* would have led into the many wonderful things that I am doing today. I am in the process of making my own rawhide. I was able to get a hide from a friend who was having a cow butchered and was able to get it without any salt. I made a frame of 1 x 6 inch boards so that I could stretch it without worrying about it moulding while staked to the ground. Anyway, it worked out real well, so hopefully I'll have a fresh supply of some "Indian" rawhide to make many new items for my tipi.

I just realized that my 18-foot tipi is cut wrong. The slope down the front should be more graduated. I spent a lot of time putting the tipi up and taking it down, etc., to try to get it to look right. I found the interior is much more round than egg-shaped. So I finally took the canvas down and measured it, as you explain in your book. It is the same length down the front as it is down the back. The canvas is wearing fine but it is the cut of the material that is disturbing to me. Could you help me rectify it? I must say thanks for all your help.

Answer—We are glad you are enjoying making Indian rawhide and furnishings for your tipi, but sorry to hear that the tipi doesn't look right—round instead of egg-shaped.

In your case it looks as if you used an 18-foot radius set at a point within the tie flap, which would lay your tipi out in a true half circle, which of course it should not be.

The simplest solution would be to set the tipi up the way you want it to look and cut off six, eight or even more inches at the rear. In other words, keep your door pole tied where it now is, but tie the two rear tripod poles at least six inches lower, or even more, than you have been doing. Spread the poles tight against the cover; then cut off the bottom where it lays on the ground. This is easier than laying it all out flat and scribing a new arc. You can use some of the peg loops where they already are but of course you will have to re-tie some of them to correspond with the new position of the tipi. This will make your tipi a little smaller, but you wouldn't notice much difference because it would give you more head room in the rear, and it would be all the better for winter camping—less area to heat.

The only other thing you could do would be to insert a piece of canvas above the door (ripping out the strips from there to the ground) and add pieces to the other strips to fill out the arc of a 19-foot 3-inch radius. If you added a piece below the door it would make the doorway longer and much too high.

Or it could be your tipi was cut right originally but shrank if it was not properly waterproofed. In all the years we have had tipis, we have had just one shrink down the front—the greatest length of the canvas. The other strips, being progressively shorter, would not shrink as much and would not be as noticeable. Anyway, here are several suggestions, and we hope one works for you to correct your problem.

Muzzle-Loaders are Tipi Lovers—We have a sixteen-foot Sioux tipi we built from the instructions in your book. We have been camping in it for a year now and love it, even our two year old loves it. We mostly camp at muzzle-loading events, where we wear buckskin outfits that go along with the tipi. Reading your book, I thought you were lucky to be camping with so many people that knew the old ways. I greatly love the old Indian ways.

We went to a muzzle-loading event last year and there were at least fifty tipis. It was beautiful! I want to thank you for writing your book. It is one of the few that really tells everything and definitely the best of those. We've told several people it's a must for tipi building.

Answer—We appreciate your enthusiastic letter and good words about our tipi book. You have found, as have so many others, that one of the nicest things about the tipi is that the whole family can enjoy it. We are glad that the tipi helps to make the muzzle-loading events more enjoyable. We've received many invitations to attend these black powder round-ups, all telling us that we opened to them a way of life they otherwise would not have known and that will not soon pass. We look forward to the time we can pitch our red-topped tipi at the end of one of these camp circles. Until then may all of you find nice places to camp, with good grass, good water, and plenty of dry wood.

BIBLIOGRAPHY

Benavides, Alonso de. *The Memorial of Fray Alonso de Benavides,* 1630. Translated by Mrs. Edward E. Ayer, annotated by Frederick Webb Hodge and Charles Fletcher Lummis. Chicago, private printing [R. R. Donnelly and Sons], 1916.

Bolton, Herbert Eugene. *Coronado, Knight of Pueblos and Plains.* Albuquerque, University of New Mexico Press, 1949.

———, ed. *Spanish Exploration in the Southwest, 1542 to 1706 (Original Narratives of Early American History).* New York, C. Scribner's Sons, 1916.

Bradley, James H. *"Characteristics, Habits, and Customs of the Blackfoot Indians."* Montana Historical Society *Contributions,* Vol. IX, 1923.

Brown, Joseph Epes. *The Sacred Pipe.* Norman, University of Oklahoma Press, 1953.

Cadzow, Donald A. *Indian Notes,* published quarterly in the interest of the American Museum of Natural History, Vol. III. New York, Heye Foundation, 1926.

Campbell, Walter Stanley. "The Cheyenne Tipi," *American Anthropologist* (N. S.), Vol. XVII, No. 4 (October-December, 1915).

———. "The Tipis of the Crow Indians," *American Anthropologist* (N. S.), Vol. XXIX, No. 1 (January-March, 1927).

Carleton, Lieutenant J. Henry. *The Prairie Logbooks, Dragoon Campaigns to the Pawnee Villages in 1844, and to the Rocky Mountains in 1845.* Edited with an Introduction by Louis Pelzer. Chicago, The Caxton Club, 1943.

Catlin, George. *Letters and Notes on the Manners, Customs and Conditions of the North American Indians, Written During Eight Years Travel, 1832–39.* 2 vols. New York, Wiley and Putnam, 1841.

Clark, W. P. *The Indian Sign Language with Brief Explanatory Notes. . . .* Philadelphia, L. R. Hamersly, 1885.

Curtis, Edward S. *The North American Indian. Being a series of volumes picturing and describing the Indians of the United States and Alaska, written, illustrated, and published by Edward S. Curtis;* edited by Frederick Webb Hodge, foreword by Theodore Roosevelt; field research conducted under the patronage of J. Pierpont Morgan. 20 vols., Seattle, E. S. Curtis; Cambridge, The University Press, 1907–30.

Denig, Edwin T. *Indian Tribes of the Upper Missouri.* Bureau of American Ethnology, 46th Annual Report, 1928–29.

Densmore, Frances. "Teton Sioux Music," Smithsonian Institution, Bureau of American Ethnology, *Bulletin 61.* Washington, Government Printing Office, 1918.

Dorsey, James Owen. "Omaha Sociology," Smithsonian Institution, Bureau of American Ethnology, *Third Annual Report,* 1881–82. Washington, Government Printing Office, 1884.

Driggs, Howard R. *The Old West Speaks.* Water Color Paintings by William Henry Jackson. Englewood Cliffs, New Jersey, Prentice Hall, 1956.

Ewers, John C. "The Horse in Blackfoot Indian Culture, with Comparative Material from Other Western Tribes," Smithsonian Institution, Bureau of American Ethnology, *Bulletin 159.* Washington, Government Printing Office, 1955.

———. "The Blackfoot War Lodge; Its Construction and Use," *American Anthropologist,* Vol. XLVI, No. 2 (April–June, 1944).

———. *Plains Indian Painting.* Palo Alto, Stanford University Press, 1939.

Flannery, Regina. *The Gros Ventres of Montana: Part I Social Life* (The Catholic University of America Anthropological Series No. 15). Washington, The Catholic University of America Press, 1953.

Fletcher, Alice. "The Omaha Tribe," Smithsonian Institution, Bureau of American Ethnology, *Twenty-seventh Annual Report,* 1905–1906. Washington, Government Printing Office, 1911.

Grinnell, George Bird. *The Cheyenne Indians, Their History and Ways of Life.* 2 vols. New Haven and London, Yale University Press, 1923.

———. "The Cheyenne Medicine Lodge," *American Anthropologist,* Vol. XVI, No. 2 (April–June, 1914).

———. *Pawnee Hero Stories and Folk-Tales, with notes on the Origin, Customs and Character of the Pawnee People.* New York, Forest and Stream, 1889.

Hassrick, Royal B. *The Sioux: Life and Customs of a Warrior Society.* Norman, University of Oklahoma Press, 1964.

Hilger, Sister M. Inez. "Arapaho Child Life and Its Cultural Background," Smithsonian Institution, Bureau of American Ethnology, *Bulletin 148*. Washington, Government Printing Office, 1952.

Hoffman, J. Jacob. *Comments on the Use and Distribution of Tipi Rings in Montana, North Dakota, South Dakota, and Wyoming.* (Anthropology and Sociology Papers, Number 14.) Missoula, Montana State University, 1953.

Hosmer, James K., ed. *History of the Expedition of Captains Lewis and Clark, 1804–5–6.* Chicago, A. C. McClury & Co., 1903.

Jochelson, Waldemar. *Peoples of Asiatic Russia.* Chapter II, "The Americanoids of Siberia"; Chapter IX, "Mode of Life." New York, American Museum of Natural History, 1928.

——. *The Yukaghir and the Yukaghirized Tungus (Publications of the Jesup North Pacific Expedition.* Vol. IX, Part III). Leiden, E. J. Brill, New York, G. E. Stechert, 1926.

Jones, J. A. "The Sun Dance of the Northern Ute," Smithsonian Institution, Bureau of American Ethnology, *Bulletin 157, Anthropological Papers No. 47.* Washington, Government Printing Office, 1955.

Kephart, Horace. *Camping & Woodcraft.* New York, Macmillan, 1948.

Kroeber, Alfred Lewis. "The Arapaho," *Bulletin of the American Museum of Natural History,* Vol. XVIII (1902). (For tipi decorations, see pp. 70–77.)

——. "Ethnology of the Gros Ventre," *Anthropological Papers of the American Museum of Natural History,* Vol. I, Part IV 1908).

Kurz, Rudolph Friederich. "Journal of Rudolph Friedrich Kurz," Smithsonian Institution, Bureau of American Ethnology, *Bulletin 115.* Translated by Myrtis Jarrell, edited by J. N. B. Hewitt. Washington, Government Printing Office, 1937.

Laubin, Reginald and Gladys. *Indian Dances of North America, Their Importance to Indian Life.* Norman, University of Oklahoma Press, 1977.

Long, Stephen H. *Report of an Expedition from Pittsburgh to the Rocky Mountains performed in the years 1819 and '20 by order of the Hon. J. C. Calhoun, Sec'y of War; under the command of Major Stephen H. Long, From the Notes of Major Long, Mr. T. Say and other gentlemen of the exploring party, compiled by Edwin James Botanist and Geologist for the Expedition in Two Vols. with an Atlas.* Philadelphia, 1823.

Lowie, Robert Harry. "The Assiniboine," *Anthropological Papers of the American Museum of Natural History*, Vol. IV, Part I (1910).

———. *The Crow Indians.* New York, Farrar and Rinehart, 1935.

———. "The Material Culture of the Crow Indians," *Anthropological Papers of the American Museum of Natural History*, Vol. XXI, Part III (1922).

———. "Notes on Shoshonean Ethnography," *Anthropological Papers of the American Museum of Natural History*, Vol. XX, Part III (1924).

Malouf, Carling. *Anthropology and Sociology Papers*, Montana State University, 1950–54. Nos. 1 to 16.

Marquis, Arnold. *A Guide to America's Indians: Ceremonials, Reservations, and Museums.* Norman, University of Oklahoma Press, 1974.

Maximilian, Prince of Wied. *Travels in the Interior of North America, 1833–1834*, vol. XXV (Atlas) in *Early Western Travels*, ed. by Reuben Gold Thwaites. 32 vols., Cleveland, Arthur H. Clark, 1904–1907.

McClintock, Walter. *The Blackfoot Tipi.* Los Angeles, Southwest Museum, 1936.

———. *The Old North Trail of Life, Legends and Religion of the Blackfeet Indians.* London, Macmillan, 1910.

Miller, Alfred Jacob. *The West of Alfred Jacob Miller* (1837). From the Notes and Watercolors in the Walters Art Gallery, with an Account of the artist by Marvin C. Ross. Norman, University of Oklahoma Press, 1951.

Mulloy, William. *Archaeological Investigations in the Shoshone Basin of Wyoming. University of Wyoming Publications*, Vol. XVIII, No. 1 (July 15, 1954).

———. "The Northern Plains," in *Archaeology of Eastern United States*, ed. by James B. Griffin. Chicago, University of Chicago Press, 1952.

Neihardt, John. *Black Elk Speaks.* New York, W. Morrow, 1932.

The Plains Indian Tipi. Leaflet No. 19, Department of Indian Art, Denver Art Museum, Colorado.

Renaud, Etienne B. *Indian Stone Enclosures of Colorado and New Mexico.* (Archaeological Series, Second Paper.) University of Denver, Department of Anthropology, January, 1942.

———. *Archaeology of the High Western Plains: Seventeen Years of Archaeological Research.* Denver, The University of Denver, Department of Anthropology, May, 1947.

Seton, Ernest Thompson. *Two Little Savages.* New York, W. W. Norton and Co., 1902.

──────. *The Book of Woodcraft.* Garden City, Doubleday, Page and Co., 1920.

Skinner, Alanson. "Notes on the Plains Cree," *American Anthropologist* (N. S.), Vol. XVI, No. 1 (January-March, 1914).

Starr, Jean and Frane. "North with Finland's Lapps," *National Geographic Magazine,* Vol. CVI, No. 2 (August, 1954).

Wallace, Ernest, and Hoebel, E. Adamson. *The Comanches: Lords of the South Plains.* Norman, University of Oklahoma Press, 1952.

Wedel, Waldo R. "Prehistory and the Missouri Valley Development Program: Summary Report on the Missouri River Basin Archaeological Survey in 1947" (with eight plates), *Smithsonian Miscellaneous Collections,* Vol. III, No. 2. Washington, Smithsonian Institution, November 23, 1948.

Weygold, Friederich. *"Das indianische Lederzelt im Königlichen Museum für Völkerkunde zu Berlin,"* in *Globus; illustrierte Zeitschrift für Länder und Völkerkunde* (Braunschweig, F. Vieweg und Sohn. Gl.G57), Vol. LXXXIII (January 1, 1903), 1–7. *Note:* The large color plate and drawings with text describe a Sioux painted hide tipi only eight feet in diameter collected in the mid-nineteenth century. The pictures on the tent were chiefly of religious character and were painted on the inside of the tent and not, as in the illustration, on the outside, as is proved by the position of the pockets on the smoke flaps. Weygold, after publication, realized and admitted this error. As religious architecture has been notably conservative, the small size of this tipi may suggest the size of common tents before horses were acquired by the northern tribes or among Indians who possessed only a few dogs.

Will, George F. "Archaeology of the Missouri Valley," *Anthropological Papers of the American Museum of Natural History,* Vol. XXII, Part VI (1924).

Wilson, George Livingstone. *The Hidatsa Indians.* Washington, Bureau of American Ethnology, 1924.

──────. "The Horse and Dog in Hidatsa Culture," *Anthropological Papers of the American Museum of Natural History,* Vol. XV,

Part II (1924).

Winship, George Parker. "The Coronado Expedition, 1540–1542," Bureau of American Ethnology, *Fourteenth Annual Report*, Part I, pp. 329–613 (Washington, 1892–93).

Wissler, Clark. "The Influence of the Horse in the Development of Plains Culture," *American Anthropologist* (N. S.), Vol. XVI, No. 1 (January-March, 1914).

———. "Material Culture of the Blackfoot Indians," *Anthropological Papers of the American Museum of Natural History*, Vol. V, Part I (1910).

———. *North American Indians of the Plains* (Handbook Series, No. 1). New York, American Museum of Natural History, 1912.

———. "Societies and Dance Associations of the Blackfoot Indians," *Anthropological Papers of the American Museum of Natural History*, Vol. XI, Part 4 (1913).

INDEX

337

The Civilization of the American Indian Series

was inaugurated in 1932 by the University of Oklahoma Press, and has as its purpose the reconstruction of American Indian civilization by presenting aboriginal, historical, and contemporary Indian life. The following list is complete as of the date of publication of this volume.

1. *Forgotten Frontiers:* A Study of the Spanish Indian Policy of Don Juan Bautista de Anza, Governor of New Mexico 1777–1787. Translated and edited by Alfred Barnaby Thomas.
2. Grant Foreman. *Indian Removal:* The Emigration of the Five Civilized Tribes of Indians.
3. John Joseph Mathews. *Wah´ Kon-Tah:* The Osage and the White Man's Road.
4. Grant Foreman. *Advancing the Frontier, 1830–1860.*
5. John H. Seger. *Early Days Among the Cheyenne and Arapahoe Indians.* Edited by Stanley Vestal. Out of print.
6. Angie Debo. *The Rise and Fall of the Choctaw Republic.*
7. Stanley Vestal. *New Sources of Indian History, 1850–1891:* A Miscellany. Out of print.
8. Grant Foreman. *The Five Civilized Tribes.*
9. *After Coronado:* Spanish Exploration Northeast of New Mexico, 1696–1727. Translated and edited by Alfred Barnaby Thomas.
10. Frank G. Speck. *Naskapi:* The Savage Hunters of the Labrador Peninsula.
11. Elaine Goodale Eastman. *Pratt:* The Red Man's Moses. Out of print.
12. Althea Bass. *Cherokee Messenger:* A Life of Samuel Austin Worcester.
13. Thomas Wildcat Alford. *Civilization,* As told to Florence Drake. Out of print.
14. Grant Foreman. *Indians and Pioneers:* The Story of the American Southwest Before 1830.
15. George E. Hyde. *Red Cloud's Folk:* A History of the Oglala Sioux Indians.

344

16. Grant Foreman. *Sequoyah.*
17. Morris L. Wardell. *A Political History of the Cherokee Nation, 1838–1907.*
18. John Walton Caughey. *McGillivray of the Creeks.* Out of print.
19. Edward Everett Dale and Gaston Litton. *Cherokee Cavaliers:* Forty Years of Cherokee History as Told in the Correspondence of the Ridge-Watie-Boudinot Family.
20. Ralph Henry Gabriel. *Elias Boudinot, Cherokee, and His America.* Out of print.
21. Karl N. Llewellyn and E. Adamson Hoebel. *The Cheyenne Way:* Conflict and Case Law in Primitive Jurisprudence.
22. Angie Debo. *The Road to Disappearance.* Out of print.
23. Oliver La Farge and others. *The Changing Indian.* Out of print.
24. Carolyn Thomas Foreman. *Indians Abroad.* Out of print.
25. John Adair. *The Navajo and Pueblo Silversmiths.*
26. Alice Marriott. *The Ten Grandmothers.*
27. Alice Marriott. *Maria:* The Potter of San Ildefonso.
28. Edward Everett Dale. *The Indians of the Southwest:* A Century of Development Under the United States.
29. *Popol Vuh:* The Sacred Book of the Ancient Quiché Maya. English version by Delia Goetz and Sylvanus G. Morley from the translation of Adrián Recinos.
30. Walter Collins O'Kane. *Sun in the Sky.*
31. Stanley A. Stubbs. *Bird's-Eye View of the Pueblos.* Out of print.
32. Katharine C. Turner. *Red Men Calling on the Great White Father.*
33. Muriel H. Wright. *A Guide to the Indian Tribes of Oklahoma.*
34. Ernest Wallace and E. Adamson Hoebel. *The Comanches:* Lords of the South Plains.
35. Walter Collins O'Kane. *The Hopis:* Portrait of a Desert People.
36. *The Sacred Pipe:* Black Elk's Account of the Seven Rites of the Oglala Sioux. Edited by Joseph Epes Brown.
37. *The Annals of the Cakchiquels*, translated from the Cakchiquel Maya by Adrián Recinos and Delia Goetz with *Title of the Lords of Totonicapán*, translated from the Quiché text into Spanish by Dionisio José Chonay, English version by Delia Goetz.
38. R. S. Cotterill. *The Southern Indians:* The Story of the Civilized Tribes Before Removal.
39. J. Eric S. Thompson. *The Rise and Fall of Maya Civilization.* (Revised Edition).
40. Robert Emmitt. *The Last War Trail:* The Utes and the Settlement of Colorado.

41. Frank Gilbert Roe. *The Indian and the Horse.*
42. Francis Haines. *The Nez Percés:* Tribesmen of the Columbia Plateau.
43. Ruth M. Underhill. *The Navajos.*
44. George Bird Grinnell. *The Fighting Cheyennes.*
45. George E. Hyde. *A Sioux Chronicle.* Out of print.
46. Stanley Vestal. *Sitting Bull, Champion of the Sioux:* A Biography.
47. Edwin C. McReynolds. *The Seminoles.*
48. William T. Hagan. *The Sac and Fox Indians.* Out of print.
49. John C. Ewers. *The Blackfeet:* Raiders on the Northwestern Plains.
50. Alfonso Caso. *The Aztecs:* People of the Sun. Translated by Lowell Dunham.
51. C. L. Sonnichsen. *The Mescalero Apaches.*
52. Keith A. Murray. *The Modocs and Their War.*
53. *The Incas of Pedro de Cieza de León.* Edited by Victor Wolfgang von Hagen and translated by Harriet de Onis.
54. George E. Hyde. *Indians of the High Plains:* From the Prehistoric Period to the Coming of Europeans.
55. *George Catlin:* Episodes from "Life Among the Indians" and "Last Rambles." Edited by Marvin C. Ross. Out of print.
56. J. Eric S. Thompson. *Maya Hieroglyphic Writing:* An Introduction.
57. George E. Hyde. *Spotted Tail's Folk:* A History of the Brulé Sioux.
58. James Larpenteur Long. *The Assiniboines:* From the Accounts of the Old Ones Told to First Boy (James Larpenteur Long). Edited and with an introduction by Michael Stephen Kennedy. Out of print.
59. Edwin Thompson Denig. *Five Indian Tribes of the Upper Missouri:* Sioux, Arickaras, Assiniboines, Crees, Crows. Edited and with an introduction by John C. Ewers.
60. John Joseph Mathews. *The Osages:* Children of the Middle Waters.
61. Mary Elizabeth Young. *Redskins, Ruffleshirts, and Rednecks:* Indian Allotments in Alabama and Mississippi, 1830–1860.
62. J. Eric S. Thompson. *A Catalog of Maya Hieroglyphs.*
63. Mildred P. Mayhall. *The Kiowas.*
64. George E. Hyde. *Indians of the Woodlands:* From Prehistoric Times to 1725.
65. Grace Steele Woodward. *The Cherokees.*
66. Donald J. Berthrong. *The Southern Cheyennes.*